IT'S A DIFFERENT WORLD!

The Challenge for Today's Pastor

Lyle E. Schaller

ABINGDON PRESS
Nashville

IT'S A DIFFERENT WORLD!

The Challenge for Today's Pastor

Copyright © 1987 by Abingdon Press

Fourth Printing 1988

This book is printed on acid-free paper.

Library of Congress Cataloging-in-Publication Data

SCHALLER, LYLE E.
It's a different world!
1. Clergy—Office. 2. United States—Church history—20th century.
3. United States—Social life and customs—1971-   I. Title.
BV660.2.S33   1987   253   86-26533

ISBN 0-687-19729-5
(alk. paper)

MANUFACTURED BY THE PARTHENON PRESS AT
NASHVILLE, TENNESSEE, UNITED STATES OF AMERICA

To
Carla Lovesy
George Brown
Melvin Kupke
Joan Uebele
James W. Macgregor

TABLE OF CONTENTS

INTRODUCTION

On a sunny afternoon in May twenty retired ministers were drinking coffee and reminiscing about the "good old days." "I can remember when we were the dominant religious group here in the colonies," recalled a 348-year-old Congregational minister. "Back in 1700 there were only about four hundred congregations in the colonies and 146 of them were Congregational churches. Those were the days! Back then people showed the clergy the respect we had earned. It was a lot easier being a minister back in those days when we were the number-one religious group in the land. It's a lot harder being a pastor today. Even with our merger with the Evangelical and Reformed Church thirty years ago we now account for less than 2 percent of the congregations in the United States. I have a great-great-great-great-great-great-great-great-great granddaughter who is a UCC minister in Texas, and half of the time people think she's part of the Church of Christ."

"You're right, it was a lot better back in the old days," agreed a 317-year-old Episcopal priest. "For one thing, when someone referred to the minister everyone knew it was a man. Now, sometimes you can't even tell the gender when you see the name. The parish I served back in Virginia many years ago now has a rector named Terry Brown. I called him on the phone the other day. It turned out that Terry Brown is a woman. You can't even tell by the names anymore!

"I must confess that sometimes I do long for those good old days," continued the elderly priest. "I can remember back to 1700 when more than a fourth of the churches in the colonies were Anglican parishes and we were *the* church. It sure is different today! Now the United Methodists and the Southern Baptists each have about five times as many congregations as we have in the Episcopal Church."

"It certainly was different back then," agreed a Congregational minister who had celebrated his two-hundred-thirty-fifth birthday the previous week. "I graduated from Yale in 1773. My class included sixteen men who entered the ministry in the Congregational Church. Ten served only one church in their whole life, and five others served only two pastorates. That was typical of the graduates from Yale in the eighteenth century. Very, very few served more than two congregations in their entire career. When you got a call, everyone assumed you would be with that congregation for the rest of your life. Now everybody expects a minister to move after a few years in one pastorate. It sure was easier back when a minister settled in and stayed in one place for the rest of his life! Close to half of the Congregational ministers of the eighteenth century served at least thirty years in one pastorate."[1]

"I can't agree with you on that one," argued a 237-year-old Methodist minister. "I think today's preachers have it a lot easier. They can marry and raise a family and a growing number even own their own home. Out of the first 672 Methodist preachers in America two-thirds died before they had preached twelve years. By 1844 half of our departed brethren had died before their thirty-third birthday. I was a preacher in Virginia, and in 1809 out of the eighty-four preachers in our conference only three were married. I remember that when Bishop Coke went back to

England and married, Bishop Asbury commented, 'Marriage is honorable in all, but to me it is a ceremony awful as death. . . . We have lost the traveling labors of two hundred [of our preachers] by marriage and consequence location.' It was assumed back then that if you married, you planned to leave the ministry. Close to half of our preachers chose that option in the early days.

"Life was a lot tougher for a preacher two hundred years ago than it is now," continued this ancient Methodist preacher. "I recall that in 1800 the General Conference raised our stipend to $80 a year, it had been $64 before that, but we had to buy our horse and clothing out of that. A good saddle horse cost anywhere from $25 to $100 in those days. You also had to keep a strict account of every penny you spent, and if you had anything left over at the end of the year, you had to hand it back to the Annual Conference."[2]

"There's no question about it, you old-timers had a hard life," agreed a relatively young 97-year-old Methodist minister, "but in some ways it was easier than it is today because you only had one thing to do. That was to preach and save souls. I've always considered myself to be a liberal on social, economic, and political issues, and it's hard to know what is the liberal position. For example, back in 1948, after the United States Senate had approved a bill introduced by Senator Robert A. Taft providing federal aid to public education, a number of us liberals got together and blocked that legislation in the House of Representatives. Three of my close friends, Bishop G. Bromley Oxnam, who was one of the great Methodist liberals of the twentieth century, John A. MacKay, then president of Princeton Theological Seminary, and Dr. Louie D. Newton, who was president of the Southern Baptist Convention at the time, were among the leaders of that successful effort to block federal aid to the public schools. Now all of today's liberals want more federal aid to public education. It's harder today to define the liberal position. In the 1960s the liberals opposed the idea of racially segregated schools and now the liberals are busy raising money to keep the black colleges open."

"There's a big difference," interrupted the 348-year-old Congregational minister. "We started a lot of schools for the freed men after the Civil War, but we've opposed the forced segregation of public schools. The liberal position is that blacks should have an all-black private college. That's why we're still supporting black colleges. Freedom of choice the the key to understanding the liberal position today."

"If freedom of choice is the liberal position," demanded the fiery old Methodist preacher, "how come so many liberal Catholic bishops and cardinals as well as Protestant ministers are opposed to giving pregnant women the freedom of choice in regard to abortion? How come today's liberals insist on quotas? How come today's liberals oppose private clubs if freedom of choice is the liberal position?

"I can remember," continued this belligerent Methodist minister, "when all of us liberals opposed Al Smith for the presidency of the United States in 1928 because he was Catholic, but thirty-two years later a lot of my liberal colleagues supported another Catholic, John F. Kennedy, when he ran for president. I can remember back in the 1940s when liberal ministers opposed the use of tobacco; then in the 1960s it seemed to be okay for ministers to smoke and now the liberals want to ban smoking in airplanes, restaurants, schools, and even in the office. I recall in the 1970s we liberals all favored the application of the antitrust laws to break up the telephone company and today the liberal position is that was a mistake.[3] Back in the 1870s northern Methodists created, staffed, and supported private Christian schools for the freed slaves, but now we oppose the idea of private Christian elementary schools for black children. It sure is a lot harder to define the liberal position today than it was forty or a hundred years ago!"

"In my opinion, the number-one reason it's harder to be a pastor today than it used to be," reflected a 109-year-old Lutheran minister, "is television. I retired in 1946, just before television began to replace books. I had four advantages over today's pastors. First, I had time to read. Instead of watching television, I read. Second, my people read a lot and that made it easier for me to prepare a sermon they could understand. Third, the only comparison base my people had was some other dull preacher in another church across the street or down the road. Today, while they eat breakfast, the people watch those flashy television preachers in living color. Then they come to church to a dull black-and-white service that looks pretty bad compared to what they saw on television an hour or two earlier. Fourth, when I was a pastor we scheduled church council meetings on Monday evening, but you can't do that anymore because of Monday night baseball and football. It also didn't upset anyone much if we ran over a few minutes at that eleven o'clock service. Now everyone wants to be out before noon in order to watch the football games. Television is dictating the schedule to the churches today!"

"Back when I graduated from seminary in 1883 everyone knew where they belonged and stayed in their place," reminisced a 132-year-old Lutheran pastor. "My first parish was in the old Joint Synod of Ohio. We knew who we were and, even more clearly, we knew who we weren't. While it's true there were a lot of pastors who were sheep stealers, all a pastor really had to do was to take care of his own flock and the people were satisfied. Most pastors recognized parish boundaries and didn't stray beyond their own turf. Now, with all the mergers most of the people don't know which synod they belong to as they drift from parish to parish. I have a great grandson in Minnesota who serves a parish that overlaps the boundaries of a dozen other Lutheran churches. Instead of witnessing to Jesus Christ and saving souls, those pastors have to spend most of their time competing with all of the other Lutheran parishes for new members.[4] I'm sure glad I was able to retire when I did! It's a lot harder to be a pastor today than it was eighty years ago."

"For me the big difference is whether you're part of a growing denomination or a shrinking one," declared a 125-year-old Presbyterian minister. "I graduated from the Seminary at Princeton a little over a hundred years ago and began serving churches in the former Presbyterian Church, U.S.A. In the eighty years between 1870 and 1950 our denomination more *13* ▪

than quintupled in size, from 450,000 members in 1870 to over 2.3 million in 1950. By 1960, after our merger with the United Presbyterian Church of North America in 1958, we had nearly three and a quarter million members. While we had some bitter fights over theology and social action and a lot of people were called heretics, we were able to survive and grow. In fact, our fastest growth came when we had some of our bitterest battles over doctrine and theology. A growing organization usually is more tolerant of the maverick personality and of extreme points of view than is the shrinking organization. When a few people did pull out to form the Orthodox Presbyterian Church and the Bible Presbyterian Church in the mid-1930s, we continued to grow and by 1960 we had a hundred times as many members as those two splinter groups combined. I think history shows the Christian churches have the greatest vitality and growth when there is a lot of dissidence.

"Now, after thirty years of concentrating on mergers and unity and after our reunion with the Southern church, we're back up to about three million members and we're still a shrinking denomination. Our two denominations have shrunk by over a million members since we began to push unity back in 1960. It's a lot harder to be a part of a shrinking denomination! The tolerance of diversity is less, morale is lower, and we worry more about survival and means-to-an-end issues than about ministry and mission. I'm convinced my colleagues of today have a harder time of it than I did when I was a pastor in a growing denomination."

"You're right, it's harder to be a pastor today than it used to be," agreed a 191-year-old retired Lutheran pastor. "I graduated from the Theological Seminary of the General Synod at Gettysburg back in 1836, just ten years after it had been founded by Samuel Simon Schmucker, who also was a Princeton Seminary graduate. Back in those days Lutherans were splitting off from one another to go their separate ways. The Ministerium of Pennsylvania withdrew from the General Synod in 1823 and the seminary was seen as a way to build unity and cohesion into the denomination. Now, instead of building unity, the seminaries create division. 'Steam Boat,' as the students called

Dr. Schmucker, saw the seminary as a way of promoting unanimity of views and harmony of feelings.[5] Now we have so many seminaries they end up promoting disharmony and a lack of unity."

"I agree that it really is more comfortable being part of a growing group," chimed in a 137-year-old Unitarian minister. "We almost doubled the number of our congregations between the Civil War and 1900. We claimed 455 congregations in 1900 and the Universalists had 800. Today, three decades after our merger, we have fewer than a thousand churches and we're still having some divisive debates over our identity and role as well as over theology."

"Listen to my story if you want to know what it is to be part of a shrinking denomination," offered a 148-year-old Disciples minister. "Between 1860, when I preached my first sermon, and 1900, when we began to recognize our more conservative brethren wanted to form their own fellowship, our Brotherhood grew from 2,100 congregations to over 10,000! Now we're down to fewer than 5,000 churches that claim to be part of our Brotherhood. We've talked about union with the United Church of Christ, but they don't seem to want to merge with us. It sure was a lot easier to be a preacher back when we were helping win the West to Jesus Christ."

"Well, at least you still have a denominational body to be a part of. That's more than I can say," lamented a 205-year-old Evangelical minister in a sorrowful voice. "As a German–speaking boy I was converted under the preaching of Jacob Albright and I became a preacher in the old Evangelical Association. We split in 1891, reunited in 1922, merged with the United Brethren in 1946, and in 1968 were swallowed up by the Methodists. So, here I am in retirement and the denomination to which I devoted a hundred and fifty years of my life no longer exists."

"Back when I was a pastor, at least you could get a good night's sleep," recalled a 118-year-old minister. "When I began my ministry in 1890, hardly anyone had a telephone and when I retired in 1940, less than a third of my parishioners had a *15* •

telephone. Now everybody's got a telephone and people call at six o'clock in the morning and at eleven o'clock at night. I've always been a baseball fan and I've lived most of my life in Georgia. In the old days you could get all the day's baseball scores by suppertime, or by eight o'clock in the evening at the latest. Now, with night baseball and teams out on the West Coast, it often is two o'clock in the morning before I can find out how my Braves did when they're playing the Giants or Dodgers or Padres out in California. I don't know how these young preachers can stay up that late and be any good the next day."

"I can remember when our churches did our own thing," recalled a 107-year-old minister. "We had our own colleges, our own publishing houses, our own missionaries, our own denominational magazine, our own seminaries, our own youth programs, our own Sunday school materials, and our own radio programs. Now we job most of that out to others."

"I'm not sure I know what you're talking about," said a 88-year-old pastor. "What do you mean, we job it out?"

"Today between a third and a half of our theological students are in seminaries not related to our denomination," replied the 107-year-old dourly. "Most of our kids go to public universities or community colleges rather than to our denominational colleges. Our members send money to a variety of parachurch organizations so they can recruit and service our youth. Our people send money to all those radio and television preachers rather than buy the time to put our own preachers on radio and television. Very few of the books written by our ministers and laypeople are published by our own publishing house. A lot of our members contribute to the support of independent missionaries. Our churches buy their church school materials from independent supply houses and subscribe to nondenominational magazines. I think it was easier to be a pastor back when our denomination took care of all of our needs and every nickel we sent away reinforced our ties to our denomination."

"I can remember," declared a 103-year-old, 257-pound Baptist minister with a porcine appearance, "when being female and being a minister were seen as mutually exclusive terms. I think it was a lot easier to be a pastor back when men ran the churches the way God intended His churches to be run."

"Perhaps, but was it as much fun as it is now?" challenged a 79-year-old Unitarian minister.

"This may be the first time I've ever found myself in agreement with a Baptist," declared a 139-year-old Roman Catholic priest with just a trace of a smile, "but you're right. It was easier back when women knew their place and stayed in it. In the good old days if a woman did get an abortion, she knew she had sinned. Now women brag about it. They're even running ads in the *New York Times* now. I can remember when the Baptists or the Methodists might publicly attack the Pope, but never a Catholic. Now we're in a world where the Pope and the Protestant fundamentalists are on one side of the abortion issue and a lot of the young Catholics and the liberal Protestants are on the other side.

"Let me tell you something else," continued the priest. "It was a lot easier running a parochial school back when all the pupils came from your own parish and there were plenty of sisters to staff the school. Now most of the schools have to hire lay teachers and pay them a big salary and in a lot of the inner city schools, I understand, close to half of the students are Protestants.

"It also was better back in the old days when Catholics married their own. If a Catholic did marry outside the faith, it was clearly understood that the couple would promise to bring their children up Catholic," concluded the priest. "Now we lose more people by marriage than we gain."

"I have to agree with my Lutheran brother over here who pointed out a few minutes ago how television has changed the world," reflected an 83-year-old Reformed minister. "Television has taught kids to be passive, to believe that sex is what life is all about, that marriage is like a car, you trade in the old model for a new one every few years, and that adults are objects to be laughed at."[6]

"Yes, in addition, television has taught everyone, regardless of their age, that their main obligation is to be a consumer," *17* ▪

agreed a 131-year-old minister who had spent his entire life below the Mason-Dixon line. "Everybody is supposed to have three or four credit cards, to be in debt over their heads, and to talk like a Yankee. I don't know which is worse, seeing all of those Yankees moving down and taking over the South or to hear your grandchildren go around talking like Yankees. I've got a great, great granddaughter who claims she can't understand me."

These comments from this mythical gathering reflect the dual thesis of this book. It is a different world today, and it is far more difficult to be a pastor in today's world than it was as recently as the 1950s.

The first chapter lifts up more than a score of changes that have enhanced the complexity of parish life and increased the difficulties facing the average congregational leader, either lay or clergy, in today's world. In more precise terms, it is more difficult today for a minister with an average level of skill and competence to be a happy and effective parish pastor than it was in the 1950s. The second chapter offers a brief look at the sunny side of the street to suggest that while it is a different world, it also is a far better world in many respects.

The third chapter is an attempt to offer a many-faceted explanation for the numerical decline of the "mainline" Protestant denominations in recent decades and to suggest some of the implications and consequences of that change in the religious scene.

While not everyone agrees with this diagnosis, the statistics suggest the theologically conservative denominations and independent congregations have been experiencing numerical growth while some, but not all, of the liberal congregations have been declining in numbers. This really oversimplifies a far more complex subject. One aspect of that complex subject, defining the "liberal" or the "conservative" position, is far more complex than it was thirty or forty years ago. That is the theme of the fourth chapter and that thesis reappears in subsequent chapters.

The most highly visible change of the past forty-five years has been the shift of women from their history as a minority of the

American population to the new majority. That change, plus a review of some of the implications and consequences, is the subject of the fifth chapter.

For many people the most alarming change of the past quarter century has been the sharp increase in the number of women who are both unmarried mothers and grandmothers before their thirtieth birthday. This subject is the focus of chapter 6.

Two major changes have been taking place within the ranks of several vocations. One is the transformation from vocation to profession and the second is the entrance of a huge number of paraprofessionals. Several of the implications of this trend for the parish ministry are described in chapter 7.

Another influential change has been occurring in retail trade, and the implications for those interested in direct mail evangelism are discussed in chapter 8.

Finally, today's world is filled with an abundance of choices for an increasing number of people, and the number of people who expect the churches to offer choices also is increasing. That is one of the big reasons why the average minister in the average parish is finding it more difficult to be responsive to the needs and wants of parishioners. That is the theme of the last chapter.

The reader is asked to keep four cautions in mind. First, in many respects today is not only a different world than the 1950s, it also in many respects is a better world. The increased complexity that often accompanies change frequently is the price of a better world. The decrease in discrimination and the increase in the range of choices are but two of the marks of a better world, but both have price tags.

Second, this book is intended to be diagnostic and descriptive, not prescriptive. It is based on the assumption that the individual who holds a reasonably accurate view of the nature of contemporary reality will be able to design the appropriate course of action. The widely sought prescription, which is impossible to write, is how to do yesterday over again, only better. One of the purposes of this book is to explain why many of the favorite prescriptions from yesterday have become obsolete. They may *19* •

have worked in the old world, but it's a different world out there today.

Third, it is easy to slip into the mind-set of the eighty-three-year-old who is convinced the good old days have been replaced by the bad new days. I hope this book will not encourage the reader to do that. Different often is better.[7]

Fourth, this is not intended to be an exhaustive account of all the changes that have occurred during the past four decades. The effort here simply is to lift up a small number of the changes that have radically transformed congregational life and the role of the pastor in contemporary American Protestantism.

For the benefit of readers interested in sources several dozen notes are included, but the numer-one source has been that indispensable collection of statistics, the *Statistical Abstract of the United States*, published annually for more than a century by the Bureau of the Census. Other publications from the Bureau of the Census in the P Series constitute the second most useful source for this book.

NOTES

1. The references to the tenure of Congregational ministers is Donald M. Scott, *From Office to Profession* (Philadelphia: University of Pennsylvania Press, 1978), pp. 3-4.

2. The statistical references are drawn from Charles W. Ferguson, *Organizing to Beat the Devil* (New York: Doubleday & Co., 1971), pp. 95-117.

3. For a critique of the divestiture of the American Telephone and Telegraph Company by a liberal writer in a liberal magazine see Gregg Easterbrook, "Off the Hook: How the Breakup Is Helping AT & T—at Your Expense," *The New Republic*, January 28, 1985. For the perspective of a famous management consultant see Peter F. Drucker, "Beyond the Bell Breakup," *Public Interest*, Fall, 1984, pp. 3-27.

4. For a revealing account of the "sales" role of the contemporary pastor see Steven L. McKinley, "Pastor or Peddlers?" *Lutheran Partners*, March/April, 1986, p. 31.

5. A brief, but lucid introduction to the founding of Gettysburg Seminary can be found in E. Theodore Bachmann, "Samuel Simon Schmucker," in *Sons of the Prophets*, ed. Hugh T. Kerr (Princeton, N.J.: Princeton University Press, 1963), pp. 39-68.

6. For a brilliant analysis of the impact of television in society see Joshua Meyrowitz, *No Sense of Place: The Impact of the Electronic Media on Social Behavior* (New York: Oxford University Press, 1985).

7. Those with a special interest in early childhood development and the contrast between the world of the 1950s and the world of the 1980s may be interested in James Traub, "Goodbye, Dr. Spock," *Harper's*, March, 1986, pp. 57-64.

IT IS HARDER TODAY!

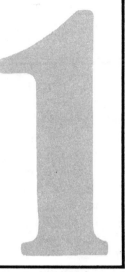

"The day after I graduated from seminary in 1949 Helen and I were married, and two weeks later we were living in the parsonage of the first church I ever served," recalled the Reverend Herbert Swanson. "At one time we thought we had it kind of hard, but now I realize we really had it fairly easy. In those days it didn't cost much to go to seminary. I had a part-time job and my folks picked up the rest of the tab. An uncle of mine gave me $500 as a birthday present and I used it to buy a secondhand car. I drove that car nearly 50,000 miles before we traded it in a couple of years later. Helen had saved some money in the two years she had worked after graduating from college in 1947. We didn't owe anybody a dime and we had a car and some money in the bank when we moved into that parsonage. Now I hear about today's seminary graduates who, when they go out to serve their first church may have a family and $10,000 or $15,000 in debts they piled up while going to school. It sure was a lot easier back when Helen and I went out to serve our first church."

"I graduated from seminary a year after you did," commented Sam Rizzo, "and I have to agree it was easier back then. I was twenty-five years old and green as grass, but the people put up with me in a very loving and supportive way. One reason, of course, is that to them, I guess, I appeared to be a good preacher. Everyone told me my predecessor, while he was a very dedicated Christian, was a disaster in the pulpit. Compared to him I guess I looked good. Today a lot of people watch one or two of those television preachers before they come to church and that's their comparison base. It's a lot harder today when the people walk into a small church on Sunday morning to see a tiny choir that may be off-key and hear a green preacher after they've spent an hour watching one of those television preachers with a big choir and everything in living color."

"You're right," agreed Jack Miller. "Back in 1950 when I began, what the seminaries taught me about preaching was compatible with what the people expected. Today I think there's a huge gap between the standards or criteria the seminaries use in teaching excellence in preaching and the style and approach followed by the preacher in today's huge churches. The models taught in seminary don't match what really sells out there in the marketplace."

"I agree with your conclusion," interrupted Harold Appleton, "but I think you're being unfair in your criticism of the seminaries. They're staffed today by scholars, not by former pastors, so they should not be expected to produce preachers. Their focus today is scholarship, not pleasing the people in the pews."

"I agree it's a lot harder being a pastor today than it was back in the 1950s," declared Chuck Rogers as he sought to move the discussion away from second-guessing the seminaries, "and I place part, but not all of the blame on television. My first call was to be the associate minister in a big church in a small town in Minnesota and my major responsibility was youth work. I tried to do three things, in addition to being a good friend to the kids and creating some happy memories of church for them to look back on later. I tried to teach them as much as I could about the faith and the Bible. I tried to help them develop a Christian value system that would stick with them for the rest of their lives and I tried to develop their competence as leaders.

"In doing this," continued Chuck, "I had the support of the public school system which still taught values. I had the support of the home since about nine out of ten of our kids lived with a mother and father, both of whom were in their first marriage. I could go to the movies with the kids and usually we could find a movie that reinforced what I was trying to teach. Most of the kids were in Scouting or a 4-H Club or Future Farmers of America or some extracurricular activity in the high school that also reinforced my efforts at helping the kids develop their abilities as leaders. Today the schools are afraid to teach any value system; half of the high school juniors and seniors have part-time jobs rather than being in Scouting or 4-H or FFA and most of them don't participate in extracurricular school activities; the radio and television preachers teach a version of the faith I cannot support; the movies tell us that sex is for everyone past fourteen years of age; television teaches passivity; and the whole world in which we live teaches serial polygamy. I would hate to have to be a youth minister today! I'm convinced the reason we have so few young leaders in the churches today is because when television came along our whole society stopped teaching leadership."

"You're right," agreed Margaret Hudson. "I didn't go to seminary until after my husband died and my children were through high school. I was forty–eight the month before I graduated in 1973. When I got into my first pastorate, I found that the world for children today is different from what it was when my husband and I were rearing a family. Today the children dress and talk like adults in three-piece suits and designer dresses while the adults of my generation wear T-shirts, jogging suits, and what we used to call tennis shoes. All those things that adults didn't talk about before children are now presented to children on television. The libraries used to have a shelf of books that were for adults only, but television doesn't keep anything from anyone today. Back when I was a Sunday school teacher and our kids were little, we were taught that children *23* •

should, and do, develop by stages. Television gives everything to them all at once."

These six ministers agree that the task of being a parish pastor today is more difficult than it was in 1950 or 1955, and they are right in at least one respect. Television has changed the comparison base. It has changed people's expectations and it has created a new setting for children,[1] but that is only one of many changes that has transformed the role and responsibilities of the parish pastor. Another reflects the erosion of both denominational *and congregational* loyalties.

The Mobile Member

"This is my church; this is where I've been a member since 1948 and regardless of who the minister is, I don't plan to leave," declared a sixty-three-year-old member of First Church. "I've been a member of this denomination all my life and I'm too old to change. This is where all my friends are and even though I'm not happy with our current pastor, I'm staying! I've outlived two other ministers here that I didn't like and I expect to outlast this one!"

"Well, I must admit I admire your tenacity," replied his thirty-four-year-old longtime friend and fellow member, "but my wife and I are leaving. For the past few months we've been attending the Sunday evening services out at that new church on the north side of town and on six of the past eight Sunday mornings we've gone out there for church. The other night we decided to join. That minister is a superb preacher and the church has a magnificent choir that must include at least seventy or eighty people. Both of our kids prefer the Sunday school classes out there, and we're looking forward to the day when our eleven-year-old will be in the youth group. We do hate to leave here, but all four of us have decided to make the change."

"I'm really surprised and I must add I'm sorry to hear this," responded the first man. "Your mother has been a member here all her life, your dad was buried from this church a couple of years ago, you and your wife were married here, your wife's parents are both active members here, and your kids have grown up here. How can you walk out on all of that?"

"It's not easy," replied the younger man, "but we decided that since we're not being fed spiritually anymore, we have no choice but to go where we know we'll be fed. I guess my wife still has mixed feelings about leaving here, but I've become convinced this is God's will for us."

"Well, I wish I could persuade you to change your mind, but you appear to be determined to leave," observed the older man. "Back about 1950, right after our first daughter was born, we were stuck with a terrible preacher here for a couple of years, and my wife and I talked about leaving. But we stayed. When the preacher left, we got the best pastor we've ever known, so I'm glad we didn't leave. Maybe you ought to think about hanging in for a while. Sooner or later this minister is certain to leave."

In the 1950s the loyalty expressed by people to institutions in general and to denominations and congregations in particular was a powerful cohesive force in parish life.

As recently as 1965 eight out of ten Methodist church members said they had always been Methodists, 85 percent of all Baptist church members declared they had always been Baptists, three out of four Lutherans said they always had been Lutherans, nine out of ten Catholics reported they always had been Catholics, two out of three Presbyterians said they always had been Presbyterians of one kind or another, and three out of five Episcopalians reported they always had been Episcopalians. (Source: Gallup Poll)

In the 1950s it was relatively easy for the pastor of a Lutheran or Methodist or Presbyterian congregation to "push the denominational loyalty" button as the primary motivational factor in raising money for denominational causes or enlisting volunteers to help launch a new congregation or to motivate members to attend a denominational meeting. That still is true, but to a lesser extent, for Lutherans in Minnesota or Missouri or Montana and for Southern Baptists in Mississippi, but not for Lutherans in Kentucky or Methodists in Illinois or Presbyterians in Arizona.

From a broad national perspective six factors can be identified *25* •

that are behind this decrease in institutional or brand loyalties. They are: (1) the coming of age of a new generation of consumers; (2) the introduction of new products and new brands into the marketplace; (3) the increased competition around quality, price, and service; (4) the general decline in the trust level accorded by the American people to the institutions of society (political parties, corporations, public schools, Congress, the churches, the military, business); (5) the rash of corporate mergers and the change in corporate names which has made it difficult to maintain a loyalty to a particular institution or product; and (6) the entrance of many new firms, including some from overseas, into the American marketplace. All six factors are not irrelevant to the changes that have occurred on the church scene.

At least a score of factors can be identified that appear to have facilitated the erosion of denominational loyalty. These include: (1) the sharp increase in interdenominational and interfaith marriages since 1945; (2) the rise of the ecumenical movement which tended to make denominational loyalties appear to be archaic; (3) the increase in the upward social and economic mobility of the American people since 1945, and upward mobility often results in the termination of old loyalties in favor of new ties; (4) the decision by national denominational leaders and agencies to make public pronouncements that have alienated members of those denominations; (5) the remarkably large number of denominational mergers since 1950—denominational mergers almost invariably weaken old loyalties without replacing them with new cohesive forces; (6) the rise of the huge array of nondenominational parachurch organizations and Bible study movements that catch the allegiance of members of denominational churches who may not offer anything equally appealing; (7) the emergence in the late 1960s of the Charismatic Renewal Movement, by far the most appealing expression of ecumenicity in this century; (8) the emergence of the house church movement in the 1950s; (9) the large number of ministers who were not trained in the seminaries of the denomination in which they are now serving and thus were not socialized into that denomination while in seminary; (10) the high visibility of hundreds of relatively new and often very large independent or nondenominational congregations with an attractive program concurrently with the declining interest in new church development by many "mainline" denominations; (11) the decision by millions of persons reared in a Roman Catholic home to leave the Catholic Church and seek a Protestant church home, but with no allegiance to any particular denomination; (12) the decision by leaders of several denominations to minimize the emphasis on denominational loyalties in order to encourage intercongregational and interdenominational cooperation; (13) the national climate that has nurtured anticentralization and antiheadquarters sentiments; (14) the emergence of that new generation of younger adults who do not display a strong brand loyalty; (15) the reluctance of many denominationally affiliated congregations to advertise and the very aggressive public relations efforts of the independent or nondenominational churches; (16) the relative decline in the emphasis given by many denominations to missions, to summer camping experiences for both youth and adults and to the women's organizations, each of which in the past was a strong cohesive force; (17) the sharp decline in the proportion of children of church members who go to colleges affiliated with their denomination; (18) in many denominations, the decline in the proportion of members who subscribe to the magazine of that denomination; (19) the Americanization of the younger members of several denominations in which language and nationality identity were strong cohesive forces as recently as 1960; and (20) the decision in several denominations to merge theological seminaries as part of an effort to create schools with a larger enrollment and a broader curriculum as well as to emphasize that concept of the 1950s that a theological seminary should be urban, ecumenical, and university-related with the trade-off being a decline in denominational loyalty.

One result of this erosion of institutional loyalties is the increased freedom of choice felt and expressed by a new generation of churchgoers (see chapter 9). A second result is that many congregations today have to work harder and more *27* ▪

systematically at assimilating new members and at creating a redundant network of cohesive forces to reinforce the allegiance of members. A third is that being a parish pastor is a more complex and a more difficult responsibility than it was in 1950.

Other Changes

In addition to the factors already mentioned a score of other changes can be identified that make the vocation of parish pastor a more demanding and more difficult role.

Some would place at the top of that list the changes in family life and the decline in the stability of the family (see chapters 5 and 6). The percentage of adults who are currently divorced has quadrupled since 1950. The number of couples living together, but not married, increased at least tenfold between 1970 and 1985. The number of children living with a stepparent more than tripled between 1970 and 1985. The number of children living with only one parent doubled between 1970 and 1985 while the number of two-parent households (with at least one child under age 18) actually declined by over a half million.[2]

The "family-centered" congregation was far more compatible with the realities of 1959 than with the realities of 1987.

A second change is that back in the 1950s denominational loyalties caused many newcomers to the community to seek out and join the congregation of their denomination that was close to where they lived. This provided that congregation with at least a modest supply of replacement members, even though it may have had a mediocre minister. In addition, in many communities where this was the only congregation of a denomination in town, strong loyalty to the denomination kept many discontended members from leaving. There was no place to go.

Third, children today are less likely to follow in the footsteps of their parents than was the pattern thirty years ago. Inherited loyalties were a stronger motivating force in 1955 than they are today.

Fourth, today a far greater emphasis is placed on the competence, personality, and performance of the minister. In the 1950s many members were satisfied if their minister was a committed Christian, an obedient servant of God, and obviously sincere in the faith.

Fifth, the 1950s marked an era in American history when the social pressures were the strongest in regard to church attendance. Every respectable and upwardly mobile citizen was expected to be in church on Sunday morning and the children were expected to be in Sunday school. Today the social pressures are less, the expectations are lower, and the competition for people's time on Sunday morning is far greater.

Sixth, the increasing affirmation of diversity and pluralism in our culture has reduced the degree of homogeneity in the typical congregation. This makes it much more difficult for one minister to please everyone. That also is one reason why large churches with a multiple staff are growing. Almost everyone can find a compatible minister on that large staff if it is intentionally diverse.

Seventh, the almost unbelievable increase in the expectations people have for the minister to be able to serve as an effective pastoral counselor means the acquisition of one more area of competence to be a good pastor.

An eighth change, and one that many pastors contend is one of the most influential, is the shift in several of the mainline Protestant denominations from an era of growth to an era of numerical decline (see chapter 3 for a more detailed discussion of this point). Numerical growth is easier to achieve in those congregations affiliated with a numerically growing denomination. It also is more fun to be part of an instituion with expanding opportunities and an increasing bundle of resources and opportunities.

For those pastors interested in changing the world and improving our society, it was easier to be a parish pastor in the 1950s and early 1960s when the churches saw the federal government as an ally, and the federal government repeatedly turned to the churches for the managerial capability necessary for rebuilding the cities, for constructing housing for the elderly, and for helping the underprivileged. Some of these pastors *29* ▪

would place this at the top of this list of influential changes since the late 1950s.

A tenth factor that has made it harder to be a parish pastor is that today it is far more difficult to identify the "liberal" or the "conservative" stance in issues of public policy (see chapter 4 for a more extended discussion of this point).

From a larger context, an eleventh change is that in the 1950–68 era the churches were serving in a society marked by rapidly expanding resources. The pie was growing in size every year and thus it was relatively easy not only to give everyone a larger slice every year, but also to share a piece of that economic pie with newcomers. From 1969 to 1987 the national economic pie has remained about the same size, after allowing for the impact of inflation, and that has made it more difficult to allocate resources among competing and expanding demands.

A twelfth and overlapping change is felt most deeply by the pastor who is ready to move, but cannot find a call. Back in the days when there was a shortage of pastors and a surplus of vacancies, it was far easier to find an attractive parish when the time came to move.

Perhaps the easiest-to-measure change is the one faced by the pastor of a congregation who wants to build and has to borrow money to complete the building program. Back in the 1950s national policy declared that savers should subsidize borrowers. When that policy was reversed in the late 1970s, it became far more difficult to finance a building program (see chapter 4).

A fourteenth, and one of the most highly visible changes, is that back in the 1950s the typical Protestant minister was a man married to a woman who was not employed outside the home. A fair number of mediocre pastors "got by" on the fact that while members of the congregation were not very happy with *his* level of performance, they were delighted with *her* contributions to the life, program, ministry, and outreach of that congregation. The members were willing to put up with him in order to avoid losing her. But today, a far larger proportion of pastors are unmarried; and the majority of the spouses of those who are married are employed outside the home, or in school or otherwise occupied.

Perhaps the least widely noted change, and one that some rank near the top rather than fifteenth on this list of reasons why it is more difficult to be a parish pastor today, is that back in the 1950s many people saw uniting with a church as a destination in a religious pilgrimage. It was for life, unless one moved too far away to continue that relationship. It was the end of the journey. Today, for many adults, uniting with a congregation is a way station on a religious pilgrimage. After two or three or five years at that way station, some church members conclude they have "graduated" and are ready to move on to what they see as the next stop in their religious pilgrimage. Relationships do not have the degree of permanence they had in the 1950s.

A sixteenth factor can be summarized in one word—competition. The competition is greater today. This is the era of *(a)* the very large congregation with a huge program and an extensive professional staff, and *(b)* the church shopper who may visit a half dozen or more congregations from three or four denominations plus an independent church or two before choosing a new church home. This means the pastor with an average level of competence in the average-sized congregation with an average quality of programming may not provide a highly attractive appearance to the comparison shopper.

This may be accentuated by the fact that many of these relatively new and very large congregations with the big staffs and huge programs also gather in new buildings designed to meet contemporary standards for places of public assemblage including an enormous off-street parking lot. The congregation meeting in the "new" building constructed in 1952 on a two-acre parcel of land has moved from being in a highly advantageous position, compared to most other congregations of that day, to seeing itself as limited by space, design, stairs, and inadequate parking.

Another change is that back in the 1950s our society displayed widespread agreement on a huge variety of questions about values. These ranged from the frequency of Holy Communion to the central organizing principles for the youth program to abortion to patriotism to the work ethic to divorce to the value of a college degree to the importance of saving to dress codes for those attending worship on Sunday morning. Today few basic values win universal support among the members.

While some will debate whether this is good or bad, an eighteenth change that affects parish life is the replacement of loyalty by performance in how people evaluate resources. The obvious example is that the slogan "Buy American" no longer influences most people when they go out to purchase an automobile, a television set, shoes, a sewing machine, clothes, or a 35mm camera.

The parallel is that denominational loyalties no longer are as influential as they once were in the process of selecting a new hymnal, choosing the curriculum resources for the Sunday school, deciding on where to participate in a continuing education event or in the choice of a summer camp for a child. What once was a source of reinforcement of unity and cohesion may now be a devisive issue that produces winners and losers. The return of the marketplace as the means of evaluation has had far-reaching consequence for the churches!

While this is a very subjective issue and one that produces highly emotional discussions, many ministers will insist that a central factor behind the increasingly difficult role of the parish pastor is the growing separation between the perspective and value system of the people in the pews and the official leadership of the denomination. The evidence suggests this gap is far greater than it was in the 1950s.[3]

Finally, the post-1960s era has been marked by a general rising of the level of expectations in all institutions. Far more is expected of the public schools, of the federal government, of private business, of the military, of the legal system, as well as of the churches, than people expected in the years following the end of World War II. *Excellence, equality*, and *choice* have replaced survival as the key words in the evaluation of the institutions of our society. The affluent society has made the depression ethic obsolete, and the old choices of "take it or leave it" no longer are adequate. Today the reward system places a premium on excellence, performance, personality, and a range of choices.

Back in the 1950s faithfulness, obedience, tenacity, and simply "hanging in there" ranked higher on the reward scale.

While this is far from an exhaustive review of all the changes affecting the role of the parish pastor, these do support the thesis that it is far more difficult to be a pastor in the rapidly changing world of today than it was back in the 1950s.

In order to adequately understand this new era it is necessary to review the numerical decline of the old mainline Protestant denominations and to examine the growth of other streams of American Protestantism.

Before doing that, however, it may be refreshing to take a brief walk on the sunny side of the street to note that, while it is a different world, in many respects it also is a better world than it was back in the 1950s.

NOTES

1. For an excellent book on how television has produced a different world for the rearing of children see Joshua Meyrowitz, *No Sense of Place: The Impact of the Electronic Media on Social Behavior* (New York: Oxford University Press, 1985), pp. 226-67.

2. An excellent analysis, from an economist's perspective, of the changes in American life is Victor R. Fuchs, *How We Live* (Cambridge, Mass.: Harvard University Press, 1983).

3. For an extensively documented, but brief and lucid discussion, see A. James Reichley, *Religion in American Public Life* (Washington, D.C.: The Brookings Institution, 1985), pp. 243-339.

The Sunny Side of the Street

"In 1974 the United States government . . . announces it will no longer send food to India, Egypt and some other countries which it considers beyond hope." These were the opening words in a "cheerful scenario" first published in 1968 about a coming world famine. That best of three suggested scenarios for the future projected food rationing in the United States in 1974, predicted the Pope would approve abortion and all forms of contraception, that famine would cause the toppling of the central governments of China and India while most of Africa and South America would "slide backward into famine and local warfare." This "optimistic" scenario anticipated the death of one-fifth of the planet's population by starvation by 1985.[1]

What happened?

By 1985 China was exporting 5 million tons of corn annually, India had increased its wheat production to the point it had

surpluses, and Bangladesh could feed its own people. America's exports of food, which had totaled 162 million tons in 1981, had dropped to 120 million tons in 1985. Farmers in the breadbasket of the United States were facing an economic crisis because they had overextended themselves to produce food for export and now were being priced out of the world market. The United States Congress had concluded that the surplus of dairy products on the world market was so severe that legislation was adopted to pay farmers to slaughter 600,000 dairy cows. Food production among the world's underdeveloped countries had increased by 33 percent since 1970. Several countries in Eastern Europe publicly were expressing fears about a decline in their population and were adopting policies to encourge childbearing.[2] Instead of food shortages and famine dominating the planet by the 1980s, it turned out that life expectancy in the poor countries of the world actually had increased by an average of over fifteen years between 1945 and 1985. The increases in the standard of living of densely populated places such as Hong Kong, South Korea, Taiwan, Boston, New York City, and Rio de Janeiro have not coincided with the projections of the 1960s.

History is filled with the dire predictions of the prophets of gloom and doom. In the seventeenth century it was expected the shortage of wood in England would become so severe that people would not be able to heat their homes. A law as passed that for every barrel, crate, or piece of wood exported an equivalent amount must be imported. Two hundred years later, after coal had replaced wood as a source of fuel, one of the great economists of the era, William S. Jevons, argued that the industrial development of England would come to a halt because of a shortage of coal and the coming scarcity of coal would price it out of the market. A hundred years later the real price of coal was the same as in 1860.[3]

Famine does exist in the world today. It will not be easy to eradicate. The heart of the problem, however, is not a surplus of people and a shortage of food, but largely political and economic considerations that make it difficult, and sometimes impossible, as in Ethiopia, to bring the resources together with the needy people.

It is a different world today than was anticipated by those who *35* ▪

in the 1950s and 1960s were predicting world famine by 1985. That is only one of the cheerful bits of news for those who prefer to walk on the sunny side of the street. The theme of this chapter is that it not only is a different world than it was in the 1950s but also is a better world. For those who remember the Russian blockade of Berlin, the Cold War, and the constant fear of another great war, a cause of celebration came on a day in May of the year that also was the title of a famous book.

In 1949 one of the best selling novels of this century was published. George Orwell's *Nineteen Eighty-Four* was both an allegory that came out near the peak of the Cold War and a fascinating novel. The novel portrayed the England of 1984 as a totalitarian society engaged in war with one of the two other great powers of the world. It is ironic, yet reassuring that 1984 now stands out in history as symbolizing peace, not war.

May 15, 1984

The worldwide concern, ever since 1945, over the possibility of a devastating nuclear war meant that few people even noticed, much less celebrated one of the landmark dates of modern history. For nearly two thousand years following the end of the Pax Romana the Western world has not known any extended periods of general peace. Over a period of seventeen centuries the longest era without a major war involving two or more of the "great powers" of that era, lasted for thirty-eight years, nine months, and five days. That was from the day of Napoleon's defeat at Waterloo on June 22, 1815, to the beginning of the Crimean War on March 27, 1854. That record was broken on May 15, 1984.[4] While that new record was not widely noted, much less celebrated, on May 16, 1984, we began to live in the longest era in western history without a major war. For many, including the millions who were not killed in that great war that in the 1950s was feared to be part of the immediate future, May 15, rather than Orwell's novel, is the realistic symbol of 1984. That is the best news to be found on the sunny side of the street.

Where There Is Hope

In 1975 the son of Israeli immigrant parents enrolled at Yale University. He was surprised to hear the rumors of earlier discrimination against Jews at Yale, but found he did not experience any anti-Semitic discrimination. This conflict between his own experiences in the late 1970s and the rumors of earlier bigotry caused him to investigate the situation at Yale. He found the rumors did reflect the past, but the past was in the past. Back in the 1920s Yale had devised an informal quota that had limited Jewish enrollment to approximately 10 percent for nearly forty years. That policy was phased out in the 1960s under the leadership of Yale President A. Griswold.[5] In 1965 the first Jew was elected to the board of the Yale Corporation that sets policy for the University. By 1985 Jews accounted for approximately 30 percent of the enrollment at Yale, compared to perhaps 3 percent of the American population.

While there is considerable dispute among social scientists whether the 12 percent of the Jews in New York City who marry outside the faith is the current norm, or whether it is closer to the Boston rate of 20 percent or the 45 percent of Milwaukee or the 20 percent in Chicago or the 40 percent in Los Angeles, is a debate that cannot be resolved here. Likewise this is not the place to decide whether interfaith marriages should be defined as good or bad. What is clear, however, is that the proportion of marriages that are Jewish-Christian or Catholic-Protestant has at least doubled since 1955. Likewise the number of interracial marriages has at least tripled since 1960. The freedom to choose one's spouse has been greatly expanded in the space of one generation. Some would argue that is bad, but many would contend that the expansion of freedom of choice is good. Currently, of course, the big debate over whether freedom of choice is good or bad is over a pregnant woman's right to abortion. The polls suggest the American people are on one side of that issue and the United States Supreme Court is on the other side.

After six years of research Charles E. Silberman concluded, *37* •

with one major exception, that anti-Semitism declined at a remarkable pace in the 1960–84 era. The exception is among younger and better educated blacks.[6] In most of his carefully documented book, however, Silberman argues that equality no longer is a dream for Jews, it is a fact. The discrimination against Jews that had been so widespread in 1955 had practically disappeared thirty years later.

Many other groups that had been the victims of discrimination for generations find it is a different world. For some the dramatic case study is Miami. The city that had been experiencing a significant decline in the 1960s welcomed the Cuban refugees who fled from Fidel Castro. The Cubans have rebuilt the city and greatly expanded the economy.

The Asian immigrants to the United States have been able, after more than a century of discrimination, to move into the front ranks of academic, technical, medical, and professional circles in the United Staes in recent years.

In 1928 Alfred Smith was not able to overcome the handicap of being a Catholic in his candidacy for the presidency. In 1960 John F. Kennedy was elected as the first Catholic to hold that office. In 1965 no big American city had a black mayor. Twenty years later twenty of the largest cities in the nation were governed by a black mayor.

The Gallup Poll reported in 1956 that only 38 percent of the electorate would vote for a black presidential candidate. By 1971 that figure had climbed to 70 percent and in 1983 it was 77 percent. Those figures compare with the 71 percent in 1960 who said they would vote for a well-qualified candidate even if that candidate were Catholic.

The less positive side of this account of the decline in discrimination appears to be the failure of American society to integrate millions of blacks into the social and economic progress that has been accomplished since 1955.

That statement, however, may oversimplify what appears to be a more complex issue. The evidence suggests that people filled with hope have been able to move ahead in American society at a remarkable pace in the space of only one generation. That list includes Cuban refugees, millions of American-born blacks, Jews, black immigrants from other countries including the Caribbean, immigrants from Japan, Korea, Hong Kong, China, India, and a remarkably large portion of the second-generation Vietnamese and Hmong as well as many other newcomers to America. Three-quarters of the 4,369 applicants for a license to drive a taxi in New York City in 1985 were immigrants. More new drivers came from Haiti than from New York City. A total of 133 applicants came from the Soviet Union compared to one from Kansas. More than one-half of the applicants stated that English was not their native language. [7]

The groups that have not shared in the rising economic tide of the past four decades appear to share one common characteristic. They display little hope that tomorrow will be better than today. Among the more highly visible clusters are the young blacks in the inner city who have dropped out of school and the labor market (see chapter 6 for a discussion of one facet of that issue), Native Americans living on Indian reservations, whites and blacks in the chronically depressed rural areas of the South and perhaps a fourth of the 1.3 million residents in nursing homes.

It is not irrelevant to note that from the days of the New Testament churches to today, orthodox Christianity has experienced great difficulty in reaching and including in worshiping congregations people who have no hope for tomorrow.

Despite this significant reservation, however, the progress in reducing discrimination in American society stands out as a remarkable achievement of the past three decades.

We Are Living Longer

Close to 3 million Americans are alive today who, if the advances in the medical sciences made since 1970 had not been accomplished, would be dead. If the rate of deaths from traffic accidents that prevailed in 1965 had continued for the next twenty years, at least a half million additional people would have *39* ▪

been killed in automobile accidents. This is another 500,000 people who today are looking at life from the sunny side of the street, rather than resting in a grave. One of the most remarkable, and perhaps the easiest, ways to measure changes of the past few decades has been the ability to prolong life. Five sets of statistics can be offered to illustrate this point.

As recently as 1950 twenty-nine babies out of every thousand live births died within a year. By 1983 that rate had dropped to eleven infant deaths per one thousand live births.

The death rate from motor vehicle accidents dropped from 30.0 per 100,000 population in 1941 to 22.9 in 1980, despite a fivefold increase in the number of miles driven. To be more precise, the number of traffic deaths per 100 million vehicle miles driven (which is a better yardstick than population) dropped from 18.2 deaths per 100 million vehicle miles in 1925 to 11.6 in 1941, to 7.6 in 1950, to 5.3 in 1965, and to 3.45 in 1975. After rising slightly between 1975 and 1980, when the speed limit was reduced, that rate was down to 2.4 in 1986. A continuation of the traffic death rate of 1950 would have resulted in approximately 130,000 traffic deaths in 1985 alone rather than the 46,000 actually reported. A continuation of the rate of 1941 would have resulted in over 200,000 traffic deaths in 1985. The big factors, of course, behind this remarkable decrease in the death rate from motor vehicle accidents have been the improvements in the design of the nation's highways, redundant safety factors built into automobiles and, more recently, the raising of the drinking age to twenty-one in many states.

Those who argue that the automobile has produced more social disruption than good, as well as having been the cause of 1.7 million deaths since the end of the World War II, and who lament the hundreds of thousands of cars abandoned on city streets every month may need to be reminded that abandoned cars are less of a health hazard than dead horses, and automobile emissions are less of a nuisance than horse manure.

A third illustration is the reduction in the number of deaths from pneumonia and influenza. The combined death rate for those two once-common causes of death peaked in 1918 at 588 per 100,000 population, dropped to 104 in 1935, to 52 in 1945, to 27 in 1955, and stood at 24 in 1980. The recent ability of the medical profession to help people recover from pneumonia, which was once called "the old man's friend," has been an influential factor in both the increase in the number of residents of nursing homes and the fact that Medicare has turned out to be a far more expensive program than was predicted when the original legislation was adopted by Congress.

Far more dramatic has been the decrease in deaths from tuberculosis from 113 per 100,000 population in 1920 to 46 in 1940 to 6 in 1960 to 0.9 in 1980. The breakthrough, of course, came with streptomycin in 1945. For the past three decades local governments have been closing and converting to other uses the sanitariums that had been constructed when "consumption" or the "white plague" was the leading cause of death. As recently as the early 1940s twice as many people died from tuberculosis as were killed in traffic accidents.

Finally, a fifth illustration of the fact we are living longer runs counter to the conventional wisdom about the "epidemic of teenage deaths." In recent years the popular press has publicized enough sensational incidents of teenage suicides, of young people being killed by drunken drivers, and of the teenage use of drugs to support the impression of an epidemic. The facts run counter to the conventional wisdom. The death rate for persons aged 15-24 was 106 per 100,000 in 1960. It peaked at 129 in 1969 and dropped to 96 in 1983. The facts reinforce the view from the sunny side of the street that life really is better today than it was in 1955.

For those who prefer to walk on the gloomy side of the street it must be admitted that these decreases in the causes of death have resulted in a rise in Social Security taxes, an increase in the divorce rate (as recently as 1964 three marriages were terminated by death for every two that ended in divorce), a sharp increase in the number of people who die of cancer, a rise in the demand for more nursing home beds, and increase in Medicare costs, a population boom in Florida and Arizona, and the emergence of an influential lobbying group on behalf of the elderly.

Not all the advantages have accrued to adults, however. As was pointed out earlier, the infant mortality rate today has dropped by nearly two-thirds since 1950. For every six children with a case of the measles in 1980, as recently as 1960 245 caught the measles. The mumps were fourteen times more common in 1970 than in 1980, and whopping cough, which killed nearly 5,000 people as recently as 1937, is now almost nonexistent. Likewise, diphtheria which killed 5,000 to 15,000 annually in the 1920s has been practically eliminated.

The Air Is Cleaner

For those with respiratory problems one of the most dramatic changes that can be seen from the sunny side of the street is the air. The quantity of soot, lead, carbon monoxide, ozone, sulfur dioxide, and dirt in the air has decreased substantially since 1975 when scientific measurements first became widespread. The legislation adopted by Congress in 1985–86 to reduce soil erosion undoubtedly will reduce the amount of dirt in the air in 1999.

Mainstreaming Can Work!

While it is far from an unqualified success story, one of the most remarkable advances of the past thirty years has been the improvements on behalf of the handicapped.

Children with severe disabilities are learning and growing in educational settings from which they were barred before the passage of Public Law 94-142. Handicapped adults are riding buses, trains, and airplanes and driving automobiles in a way that simply was not perceived as possible in 1955.

Churches have improved their acoustics and sound systems, installed elevators and constructed ramps for the benefit of a segment of society previously excluded. Hundreds of churches now offer special programs, classes, parties, and activities on a regular schedule for both the physically handicapped and the developmentally disabled.

Perhaps the biggest gain, next to better health care, has been the employment opportunities for handicapped adults. While much remains to be accomplished,[8] the progress of the past two or three decades stands out as a significant accomplishment for those who look at life from the sunny side of the street.

Elderly No Longer Means Poor

"The primary reason for such a low level of giving in our congregation is that our membership includes so many elderly members who are living on Social Security and a fixed income." This statement stands out as one of the most frequently cited reasons to explain why a particular congregation cannot undertake a proposed new ministry or pay its fair share of the denomination's benevolent causes or increase the pastor's salary or expand the staff. That excuse made a lot of sense in 1950 when the average monthly Social Security check for a retired worker was $44 or even as recently as 1970 when the average Social Security check was $139 and relatively few retirees had the benefit of a company or government pension. By 1985, however, the average monthly Social Security check for a couple was $776 and $449 for an individual.

Thanks to a shift in the national policies the elderly have become the major beneficiaries of "transfer payments." For much of American political history the concept of the government's responsibility to take money from one group of citizens and transfer that money to a different segment of the nation's population was based on the ancient premise of taking from the rich to help the poor. More recently that was changed to take from one generation to benefit another generation, typically to take from the older generation to help a younger generation, especially in the form of a free education. Older people paid taxes to provide a free education for a younger generation.

The introduction of Old-Age, Survivors, and Disability Insurance (Social Security) changed that system to tax the working population on behalf of the elderly and the disabled. The rapid growth in the proportion of all voters who are recipients of Social Security payments encouraged the Congress to increase the benefits for the elderly and the disabled and also to increase the taxes on the younger working population. This was *43* ∎

accompanied by a national tax policy that encouraged the growth of private pension systems, home ownership, individual retirement accounts, investments in the stock market, and the purchase of life insurance.

One result is that by 1986 Social Security beneficiaries totaled over 37 million and was projected to reach 58 million in thirty years. In 1959 more than a third of the elderly were classified as living in poverty. If all benefits are included in calculating income, only 3 percent of the elderly were living in poverty in 1983. While they constitute only 12 percent of the population, nearly 30 percent of the 1985 federal budget was allocated for benefits for the elderly, up from 21 percent in 1971.

Another result is the growing number of men in their fifties who are choosing early retirement. In some cases union policies or employer decisions have made retirement economically more attractive than working. In 1950 13 percent of all men in the 55-64 age bracket were not in the labor force. By 1985 that had climbed to 31 percent. The proportion of men aged 45-54 not working more than doubled from 4.2 percent in 1950 to over 9 percent in 1985. Some churches see those people as a big new source of volunteers.

Another result of the change in national policies is that seven out of eight elderly couples own their own home. The after-tax per capita income of the elderly is 13 percent *greater* than the after-tax income of the average American.[9] Several studies suggest that today the majority of mature Americans in the United States can maintain in retirement the same standard of living they reached in their middle-age working years.[10] One of the reasons it is more difficult to be a pastor today than it was in 1955 is old stereotypes fade away very slowly!

The good news for ministers in mainline Protestant congregations is that as they see their congregations grow older, today that means an increase in congregational financial resources, not a diminishing of resources of the financial base as once was true.

Old and poor are no longer synonyms. The bad news is that "child" and "single parent mother" have become the new synonyms for poor, but those are the subjects of subsequent chapters.

That Remarkable Job Machine!

A number of economists maintain that the best news of the past three decades is the unprecedented expansion of the economy and the creation of tens of millions of new jobs.

During the six-year period of 1920–25 nearly 18 million babies were born in the United States. That was the only time in American history before the 1940s in which more than 16 million babies were born in a six-year period. Any future-oriented person of the 1920s could predict that would create an oversupply of job seekers when those babies entered the labor force in the late 1930s and early 1940s. By contrast, only 14.3 million babies were born in the birth dearth of 1931–36.

The coming of World War II, however, meant that the nation had a labor shortage in the 1940s, not a surplus. The birth dearth of the 1930s meant that the anticipated post-World War II depression did not materialize because there were relatively few new entrants into the labor force in the late 1940s. The Korean conflict came along just in time to help absorb the increase in the labor force resulting from the increase in the birth rate of the late 1930s. This same approach led some observers to predict an unemployment problem in the mid and late 1970s when the babies born in the 1956-61 era would be ready to enter the labor force. [11]

A different way of looking at the same issue is to count jobs rather than the number of babies born eighteen years earlier.

During the 1930s, for example, the number of employed people in the American labor force fluctuated sharply. The high was 47.6 million jobs in 1930. That figure dropped to 38.8 million jobs in 1933 and climbed back to the 1930 level by the end of the decade. Agricultural employment dropped by nearly a million during the 1930s so that meant a net increase of only 900,000 in civilian non-agricultural jobs. (The statistics are not completely comparable and an argument can be made that 45 •

civilian non-agricultural jobs increased by over 2 million during the 1930s.)

Between 1940 and 1950 the number of agricultural jobs dropped by 2 million, but the number of non-agricultural jobs jumped by 14.5 million jobs for a net gain of over 12 million jobs. That was a big surprise to those who had predicted a depression after World War II.

The 1950s brought a decrease of 1.7 million in the number of agricultural jobs and an increase of nearly 9 million in the number of jobs outside agriculture. That net gain of over 7 million jobs in a decade was seen by contemporary observers as commendable and the unemployment rate ranged between 4 and 5 percent. One reason for the comparatively low unemployment rate was, as was pointed out earlier, that the 1950s were the years when the "birth dearth" babies of the 1930s came into the labor force.

The 1960s brought a record-setting era in job creation and for most years the unemployment rate dropped below 4 percent. The number of agricultural jobs dropped by another 2 million to a total of 3.5 million in 1970. Offsetting this was the unprecedented increase of 15 million jobs outside agriculture. This was widely regarded as at least a middle-sized miracle but by 1970 the unemployment rate had climbed to 5 percent. This was due, of course, to the entrance of that early wave of post-World War II babies entering the labor market. Of that net increase of 13 million jobs during the 1960s, 5 million went to men and 8 million to women.

The coming of the 1970s, however, meant a huge strain on the job market. The record number of babies born in the 1950s would be coming into the labor force, plus an unexpectedly large number of women, 4 million immigrants, and the farm-to-city migration.

What happened?

Between 1970 and 1980 the American economy produced a net increase of over 20 million jobs. That was nearly triple the number of jobs created during the 1950s and a 50 percent increase over the 1960s. This increase stands out as a more remarkable accomplishment when it is noted that *(a)* the companies listed as the "Fortune 500" reduced their combined employment by approximately 5 million jobs between 1964 and 1984, *(b)* the proportion of mothers employed outside the home who also have young children went from one in five in 1970 to one in two in 1985, *(c)* government employment in 1985 was lower than in 1975, and *(d)* the widely publicized "high tech" industry accounted for only one in seven of the new jobs created between 1965 and 1985.[12]

Sixty percent of that net increase in jobs went to women and 40 percent to men. Between 1960 and 1980 the economy was able to absorb a doubling in the number of women in the labor force and still produce a record number of new jobs for men. By contrast, the number of jobs in western Europe actually decreased between 1970 and 1985 by at least 3 million jobs. Employment in Japan increased at approximately one-half the rate it increased in the United States. Those figures look like remarkably good news for those who walk on the sunny side of the street!

These examples of what could be seen from the sunny side of the street in recent years represent only a tiny sample of a wealth of good news. Other examples include the fact that in the 1980s Americans waste only one-sixth of their food compared to nearly one-third in the early 1940s[13]; tooth decay has dropped dramatically for those with access to fluoridated water; the number of air-conditioned homes has increased eightfold between 1960 and 1985; the reserves of natural gas are many times what was believed to be true in 1977; the Oakland A's won the World Series three years in a row; societal permission has been granted for mature women to wear slacks to church; people in their twenties are only half as likely to drink coffee today as was true of the 20-29 age group of 1962; the gasoline mileage of the average new car has nearly doubled since 1970; the introduction of computers and video cassette recorders into Soviet Russia has threatened that government's monopoly on information that influences public opinion; Americans have dropped their consumption of potatoes by one-third since 1964; four times as many Americans in 1985 were served by a public sewage disposal system which treats the waste water than was the case in 1960; per capita cigarette smoking has been dropping ever since the peak in 1963; the number of people earning a college degree in 1985 was triple the number in 1950; per capita personal income in constant dollars (after allowing for inflation) nearly doubled between 1955 and 1985; and the number of blacks enrolled in college increased tenfold between 1950 and 1985. The list of good news and progress could go on for hundreds of pages.[14] Why do people prefer the bad news?

Why Is Good News Neglected?

Many reasons can be offered to explain why people prefer to look at the world from the gloomy side of the street. Among the reasons is the fact that bad news is more effective than good news for raising money or peddling newspapers or recruiting a following or winning an election or creating a new denomination or winning viewers for the evening television news program or unifying a community or getting a manuscript published or gaining a widely publicized hearing before a congressional committee or building a movement or mobilizing an army or selling a book.

At times, however, the good news is balanced by some bad news. For example, worship attendance in American Protestant churches, if measured by the number of people present on the average Sunday, has been setting new records year after year for more than a decade. The bad news for some is that most of that increase has been occurring in churches outside the mainline Protestant denominations. The reasons for that are complex and need to be set in a historical perspective. That means a new chapter.

NOTES

1. Paul R. Ehrlich, *The Population Bomb* (San Francisco: Sierra Club Books, 1969), pp. 67-69. For a less emotional and historically grounded counterview to the population crisis see Julian Simon, *The Ultimate Resource* (Princeton, N.J.: Princeton University Press, 1982). See also *Population Today*, vol. 14, March, 1986, pp. 3-8.

2. Michael S. Teitelbaum and Jay M. Winter, *The Fear of Population Decline* (San Diego: Academic Press/Harcourt Brace Jovanovich, 1985).

3. Charles Maurice and Charles W. Smithson, *The Doomsday Myth: Ten Thousand Years of Economic Crises* (Stanford, Calif.: Hoover Institution Press, 1984).

4. Paul Schroeder, "Does Murphy's Law Apply to History?" *The Wilson Quarterly*, vol. IX, 1985, pp. 84-93.

5. Dan A. Oren, *Joining the Club: A History of Jews and Yale* (New Haven: Yale University Press, 1986).

6. Charles E. Silberman, *A Certain People* (New York: Summit Books, 1985), pp. 339-41. A number of black intellectuals, as well as Jewish leaders, are increasingly pessimistic about restoring black-Jewish relationships to the cooperation that marked the 1960s. For one example of that view see Glenn C. Loury, "Behind the Black-Jewish Split," *Commentary*, January, 1986, pp. 23-27.

7. Maureen Dowd, "New Breed Drives New York's Cabs," *New York Times*, January 23, 1986.

8. See Robert Bogdan, " 'Does Mainstreaming Work?' Is a Silly Question," for a balanced view of what has happened in public schools, *Phi Delta Kappan*, February, 1983, pp. 427-28.

9. Cheryl Russell, "Let's Bust This Myth," *American Demographics*, August, 1985, p. 9.

10. John L. Palmer and Stephanie G. Gould, "The Economic Consequences of an Aging Society," *Daedalus*, Winter, 1986, pp. 295-323.

11. Lyle E. Schaller, "Joblessness: The Coming Challenge," *The Christian Century*, February 6, 1963, pp. 171-73.

12. Peter F. Drucker, *Innovation and Entrepreneurship* (New York: Harper & Row, 1985), pp. 1-17.

13. William Rathje, "Why We Throw Food Away," *The Atlantic Monthly*, April, 1986, pp. 14-16.

14. A revealing book with a wonderful title is Ben J. Wattenberg, *The Good News Is the Bad News Is Wrong* (New York: Simon & Schuster, 1984).

FROM MAINLINE TO NONDENOMINA-TIONAL

3

"When my wife and I were married, back in 1946, there were five big churches in this city," recalled John Elson, a longtime member of a midwestern congregation. "The biggest, of course, was St. Mary's Catholic. The other four were First Methodist, First Presbyterian, St. Paul's Lutheran, a German parish, and Augustana, which was a Swedish Lutheran church. Today only two of those, St. Mary's and St. Paul's Lutheran, are among the five largest churches in the city. The other three are Calvary Temple, an Assemblies of God congregation, the Evangelical Free Church that just moved into a new building, and that independent Baptist church that has that huge building out on the west edge of the city. I understand both Calvary Temple and that independent Baptist church have bigger crowds on Sunday morning than St. Mary's."

"I grew up in Texas," reflected a fifty-six-year-old woman who had married into this congregation thirty-two years earlier, "and there the big churches are Southern Baptist or Methodist or

Presbyterian with an occasional big Disciples of Christ congregation. The big three in most communities, however, are Baptist, Methodist, and Presbyterian."

"My memory isn't as good as it used to be," admitted a third person in the group, "and you may be right, John, but I thought that right after the war first Congregational and the Episcopal Cathedral also were big congregations and ranked right up there with First Methodist and First Presbyterian in size."

"They may have reported as many members," conceded John Elson, "but I don't think either one drew as many people on Sunday morning as the five I mentioned. Back then we lived two blocks east of the First Congregational Church and I don't recall seeing big crowds there except on Easter and a couple of other Sundays. Let's assume you're right, however, and there really were seven big churches in town forty years ago. That simply reinforces the basic point I was trying to make. In my adult life I've witnessed a big shift from back when the Catholics and the mainline Protestants dominated the church scene to today when only a few of the big churches are related to the old-line Protestant denominations. It's a different world than it was forty years ago!"

For many of the readers of this book John Elson has identified a very significant change, but it is not without precedent. The change John described can be traced back to the early years of this century. In 1925, for example, three-fourths of all Protestant church members belonged to congregations affiliated with what often are described as the "mainline denominations."[1] Today fewer than one-half of all Protestant church members are members of churches that identify themselves as a part of mainline Protestantism. Before looking at the implications of that change it may help to review the historical perspective.

The Eighteenth-Century Scene

For most of the four hundred years since the first English settlers came to America the religious scene has been dominated by a handful of Protestant denominations. In 1700, for example, two out of every three organized congregations in the colonies were either Congregational or Anglican.* The Baptists, who ranked third in the number of churches, accounted for only 9 percent of all colonial congregations.[2]

Eighty years later, by the time of the American Revolution, the Presbyterians had moved up to second place behind the Congregationalists in the number of churches. Four denominations accounted for most of the organized religious congregations in what was soon to be called the United States of America. The Congregationalists had quintupled the number of congregations in eighty years and retained their lead with 748 churches; the Presbyterians had grown to nearly 500 congregations; the Baptists continued in third place with approximately 460 churches; and while the Anglicans had nearly quadrupled the number of parishes to slightly over 400, that left them in fourth place. Two latecomers from Germany, the Lutherans with 242 parishes and the German Reformed with slightly over 200 congregations, accounted for most of the remaining congregations in 1780.[3]

By 1800 the Quakers, with perhaps 200 meeting houses and an estimated 50,000 members, were a part of this second tier of Christian bodies.[4] The Roman Catholics also grew rapidly in the years after the Revolution, with an estimated 50,000 adherents in 1800, double the 1785 total.

The religious scene in what became the United States of America was dominated by these eight religious groups during the eighteenth century, but the nineteenth century brought radical changes.

The Circuit Rider and the Farmer Preacher

As the frontier moved west the Episcopalians waited for the railroads to be built and the Congregationalists concentrated on

---

*The references here are to the thirteen colonies on the eastern seaboard. By 1630 the Franciscans reported twenty-five Roman Catholic missions in what is now New Mexico with 35,000 Christian Indians, and a permanent Catholic mission had been established in St. Augustine long before the white settlers came to Virginia.

founding schools, while the Methodist circuit rider and the Baptist farmer preacher moved on west. In 1860, when Abraham Lincoln was elected president of the United States, the United States had a population of slightly more than 31 million residents and included an estimated 54,000 organized religious congregations. Nearly four out of ten (19,883) carried a Methodist affiliation and nearly a fourth (12,150) was Baptist. A distant third in the number of congregations was the Presbyterians with 6,406 churches, who, thanks to the Plan of Union, had been able to move ahead of the Congregationalists in size. One out of twenty Christian congregations was a Roman Catholic parish, but the Catholics were about to experience huge numerical growth with the immigration from southern Europe that marked the post-Civil War era as their numbers quadrupled from 3 to 12 million souls while the Methodists tripled from 2 to nearly 6 million members between 1860 and 1900. During these same forty years the Presbyterians tripled their membership from 5 million to 1.5 million, and the Congregationalists doubled from a quarter million members in 1860 to a half million in 1900. Only the Baptists and the Lutherans, among the larger denominations, kept pace with the numerical growth of the Roman Catholics. Both also quadrupled in membership in the four decades following the Civil War. The Baptists grew from one to four million members while the Lutherans grew from approximately 400,000 members to over 1.5 million.[5]

One of the remarkable statistics of that era is that the average week during the nineteenth century saw the organization of sixteen new Methodist and at least a dozen new Baptist congregations. That happened, on the average, fifty-two weeks a year for more than two decades!

In summary, while the Congregationalists, Anglicans, Presbyterians, and Baptists dominated the religious scene in America during the eighteenth century, only the Baptists continued as a leader in organizing new congregations in the nineteenth century. They were joined by the Methodists, the Lutherans, and the Catholics in planting new churches and winning millions of new members during the 1800–1900 era. *53* ∎

The twentieth century brought a new trend. In 1890 the membership of the Northern Baptist Convention was equivalent to 1.27 percent of the American population, the Disciples of Christ listed 1.1 percent of the population as members, and the six predecessor denominations of what is now The United Methodist Church reported 6.23 percent of all Americans as members. By 1984 those proportions had dropped by approximately one-half to 0.48, 0.69, and 3.8 percent respectively. In 1890 the Congregational Church's membership was equal to 0.81 percent of the population. Two mergers later in 1984 the membership of The United Church of Christ was equal to 0.72 percent of the population.

By contrast, the Southern Baptist Convention claimed 2.03 percent of the American population as members in 1890, 3.0 percent in 1926 and 6.1 percent in 1985. The proportion of Americans belonging to the Seventh-Day Adventist Church jumped from 0.07 percent in 1906 to 0.18 percent in 1961 to 0.27 percent in 1984. The Church of Jesus Christ of the Latter-Day Saints (Mormons) claimed 0.23 percent of the American population as members in 1890, 0.88 percent in 1961 and 1.55 percent in 1923. The membership of the Roman Catholic Church in 1890 was equal to 11.6 percent of the population. By 1984 that proportion had nearly doubled to 22.1 percent.

Broadening the Base

When the twentieth century began, the mainline Protestants and the Roman Catholics still dominated the church scene. The religious census conducted by the United States Government in 1906 reported that thirty-one religious bodies claimed as many as 100,000 members. Seven of these thirty-one were Lutheran, six were Methodist, four were Baptist, and four were Presbyterian. Eighty years later at least seventy-four religious bodies reported more than 100,000 of which fourteen were Baptist, five were Lutheran, four were Methodist, and two were Presbyterian.

In 1906 only eight religious families reported more than

700,000 members. The Roman Catholic Church led with 12 million members followed by the Methodists (5.8 million members), the Baptists (5.7 million members), the Presbyterians (1.8 million members), the Lutherans (2.1 million members), the Disciples of Christ (1.1 million members), the Episcopalians (0.9 million members), and the Congregationalists (0.7 million members). The total Protestant church membership was reported to be slightly under 21 million in 1906. The next eight decades brought the changes referred to by John Elson in the opening paragraphs of this chapter.

By 1986 the religious landscape had been enlarged to include a rapidly growing number of churches that do not identify themselves with these historic denominations. Some are congregations who have withdrawn from these denominations, many are relatively new independent churches and most are affiliated with fellowships and denominations formed in recent decades.

These changes can be illustrated by a few comparisons. In 1700, 257 or 68 percent of the 373 organized congregations in the original colonies were affiliated with either the Congregationalists or the Anglicans. Today those two denominations include nearly 14,000 congregations, but that is less than 4 percent of the estimated 375,000 religious congregations in the United States. *

Currently only five religious bodies report more than 9,000 local organizations or congregations in the United States.[6] Two

---

*One of the most elusive figures to document is the number of religious congregations in the United States. The United States *Census of Religious Bodies of 1936*, with an admitted undercount which may have been as high as 20 percent or more, reported 199,302 "local organizations," down from the 232,154 reported in the 1926 *Census of Religious Bodies*. The population of the United States in 1926 was 117 million compared to 245 million in 1986. One survey covering 111 denominations reported these denominations accounted for 231,708 congregations that included 112.5 million "adherents" (basically that is the equivalent of baptized members and children not yet baptized). Bernard Quinn, et al., *Churches and Church Membership in the United States 1980* (Atlanta: Glenmary Research Center, 1982). This survey missed at least a hundred thousand congregations including those in the denominations that did not participate in the survey, house churches, independent congregations, and a huge number of Black, Asian, and Hispanic churches. A conservative estimate is that at least 375,000 organized religious congregations exist in the United States today and that total may be closer to 450,000.

of these, the Churches of Christ and the Assemblies of God, are relatively new. Since 1906, when 2,549 congregations banded together to form their own fellowship, the Churches of Christ have grown to approximately 13,000 congregations with nearly 1.5 million active members.

The Assemblies of God, the largest and fastest growing predominantly Anglo Pentecostal body, traces its origin back to April 1914 and now has over 2 million members in ten thousand congregations.

The Southern Baptist Convention, which was organized in 1845, now reports 15 million members in 37,000 congregations, but usually is not included as a part of the mainline Protestant category.

The Roman Catholic Church with 53 million baptized souls in nearly 25,000 parishes, now reports nearly twice as many members as the combined baptized membership of the nine largest mainline Protestant denominations.

The United Methodist Church, with 9.2 million confirmed members in 37,988 congregations, is the only one of these five that is widely accepted as a part of the mainline Protestant family.

In recent years the biggest change has been the emergence of literally hundreds of large and rapidly growing congregations that do not claim an affiliation with any denomination, the rapid growth of the Seventh-Day Adventists, the Mormons (The Church of Jesus Christ of Latter-Day Saints), and the Charismatic Renewal Movement.

In 1986 at least sixty identifiable denominations each reported a total membership of fewer than 5,000 persons. By contrast, at least one hundred independent congregations reported a membership exceeding 5,000.

The Seventh-Day Adventists have grown from approximately 60,000 members in 1903, when they moved their headquarters from Battle Creek, Michigan, to Washington, D.C., to over 600,000 members in approximately 4,000 congregations in the United States. The vast majority of their members, however, do not live in the United States, a tribute to their emphasis on world missions.

The Church of Jesus Christ of Latter-Day Saints (Mormons) also has displayed a remarkable rate of growth and now includes nearly 4 million members in 8,000 local organizations.

In recent years the fastest growing religious movement in America has been the increase in the number of self-identified Charismatic Christians. Unlike the Pentecostal Movement, which drew heavily from the working class and experienced a phenomenal rate of growth in the 1915–40 era, the new Charismatic Renewal Movement has drawn millions of adherents from the middle and upper socioeconomic classes of contemporary society. The majority of the "new charismatics" continue their membership in the Catholic, Presbyterian, Methodist, and other Protestant congregations of which they have been members for years or, in some cases, for generations. Many worship in their "home church" on Sunday morning, and on Sunday evening, or perhaps on an evening during the week, attend a "prayer and praise" service.

While no one has been able to produce an exact count, the combined total of self-identified Pentecostal and Charismatic Christians in the United States certainly exceeds 5 million and may be closer to 20 million, depending on the definition used.

One result of the rapid increase in the membership of the independent churches, and the sects and the growth of the Charismatic Renewal Movement, is that today it is far more difficult than it was thirty years ago to devise a simple and widely acceptable set of categories for classifying the religious affiliation of the American population. In 1955 few quarreled with the threefold system of Protestant, Catholic, and Jew.[7] By 1984 Americans who classified themselves as "other" when asked their religious affiliation outnumbered, by a two-to-one margin, those who responded "Jewish." The Gallup organization reported, on the basis of 29,216 in-person interviews, that in 1984 57 percent of the adult American population classified themselves as Protestant, 28 percent Catholic, 2 percent Jewish, 4 percent "other," and 9 percent "none." In 1952 those ratios were 67 percent Protestant, 25 percent Catholic, 4 percent Jewish, 1 percent other, and 2 percent none.[8]

In thirty-two years the self-identified Protestants had shrunk by 10 percentage points while "none" had grown by 7 percentage points and "other" had quadrupled from one to 4 percentage points.

While not everyone will agree who belongs under that umbrella, the nine large cooperative Protestant denominations usually identified as mainline Protestant* claimed a combined total of approximately 32 million members, including children, in 1986. A variety of public opinion surveys suggests at least 40 million people, age eighteen and over, claim membership in a congregation affiliated with one of these nine denominations. That 32-million-member figure compares with 53 million Americans who are Roman Catholics and an estimated 45 to 50 million Americans who claim membership in a Protestant church affiliated with some other denomination or with one of the growing number of independent or nondenominational churches. While precise figures, or even good estimates of the membership of these independent churches are not available, a reasonable guess is they include 5 million adherents including children and adults who are not carried as members.

The Methodists, Presbyterians, Lutherans, Disciples of Christ, Episcopalians, and Congregationalists accounted for almost exactly 60 percent of all Protestant church members in 1906. Eighty years later these six groups, despite the growth through mergers of the Methodists and Congregationalists, accounted for approximately one-third of the members of all Protestant churches in the nation. (The Gallup polls for 1984 suggest this proportion may be closer to 35 or 36 percent.)

---

*These nine were the American Baptist Churches, The American Lutheran Church, the Christian Church (Disciples of Christ), The Episcopal Church, the Lutheran Church in America, The Lutheran Church—Missouri Synod, the Presbyterian Church (U.S.A.), the United Church of Christ, and The United Methodist Church.

Another dozen or so smaller denominations, such as the Church of the Brethren, the Reformed Church in America, the Cumberland Presbyterian Church, the Moravian Church, and the Unitarian Universalist Association often are included under that umbrella term mainline Protestant, but not everyone is comfortable with those additions, particularly some of the members of those churches.

What Are the Implications?

Perhaps the most significant implication of the change, and certainly the most subtle for the typical pastor or member of a congregation affiliated with a mainline Protestant denomination is the change from majority to minority status. As recently as 1950 the Methodists, Lutherans, Presbyterians, Congregationalists, American Baptists, The Evangelical and Reformed Church, The Christian Church (Disciples of Christ), and the Episcopalians together accounted for a majority of the Protestant churches in the vast majority of counties in the United States.

In the early 1950s these denominations launched most of the new congregations that were being organized in suburbia, their pastors were the ones who had their sermons quoted or reviewed in the Monday morning newspapers, their representatives controlled the local ministerial associations and the councils of churches, and their influence was felt throughout the community. These were the churches people talked about when the subject of religion came up at a Saturday evening social affair or a Tuesday luncheon. Service clubs, municipal officials, governors, and congregational leaders offered public deference to the clergy from these mainline Protestant denominations.

It matters little whether it is a religious organization, a public school, a private corporation, a bank, or a municipality, it is easier and more comfortable to be part of an organization that is growing than one that is shrinking. Superintendents of schools found it was easier to plan for the locating, building, and staffing of new schools in the 1950s than it was to close schools and reduce staffs in the 1980s. Similarly, church leaders are more comfortable planning for growth than for decline.

The growing organization usually finds it easier than does the shrinking organization to mobilize resources, to encourage and support creativity, to offer promotions and other rewards to employees, to tolerate the maverick personality, to take risks and venture forth on uncharted waters, to ignore the pressures of seniority, to create new positions that mean the first person to fill that office is free from the precedents and traditions left by a

59 •

predecessor, to attract venturesome people, and to reach and serve a new generation of people.

For many people it simply is more fun to be a member of an organization that is growing in size and numbers and frequently is commended by outsiders for its vigor, vitality, enthusiasm, growth, and impact. From a ministerial perspective it is more comfortable to be a member of a denomination that is growing in numbers than to be part of a denomination that is shrinking in size.

A second consequence of the comparative decline of the mainline Protestant denominations has been the emergence of a huge array of parachurch organizations and groups. Thirty-five or forty years ago ministers and congregations naturally turned to denominational headquarters for bulletin covers, Sunday school literature, workshops on youth ministries, advice and/or counsel in fund raising, continuing education experiences for either lay leaders or pastors, periodicals, films, and helps in evangelism or Christian education or record keeping of stewardship or worship or music. Today a growing number of nondenominational agencies are supplying needs once filled by denominational agencies.

It probably is not an unrelated coincidence that the boom in new church development in the decade following World War II was sparked by the mainline Protestant denominations, but the church growth movement of the 1970s not only came out of nondenominational and parachurch sources, but also was vehemently opposed by scores of leaders within those mainline Protestant denominations.

A third consequence can be seen in theological education. In 1956 the ten accredited seminaries with the largest enrollment were Southern, Southwestern, Concordia, Union of New York, Garrett, Yale, Luther, Princeton, New Orleans, and Candler. Thirty years later the top ten in terms of enrollment were Southwestern, Fuller, Southern, New Orleans, Southeastern, San Francisco, Trinity (Deerfield), Golden Gate, Princeton, and Luther Northwestern followed by Candler, Asbury, and Talbot.

One reason for the growth in the enrollment of the evangelical seminaries is that a growing proportion of seminarians (with Southern Baptists and Lutherans the two big exceptions) are choosing to attend theological seminaries that are not affiliated with any one denomination.

While it is impossible to prove a cause and effect relationship, organizations that are experiencing numerical and/or financial decline frequently look to a merger as a means of strengthening their position in society. One form of this in the 1950s was the annexation of outlying tracts of land by central cities that otherwise would have been experiencing a population decrease. Another expression of the same phenomenon in the 1980s, following the failure by many oil companies to find new reserves to replace supplies that were being used up, was for one oil company to "take over" or merge with another company that had substantial reserves. The legal battle between Pennzoil and Texaco in the mid-1980s for the reserves owned by Getty was the most widely publicized example, but this struggle to expand resources and to gain new markets was behind scores of other corporate mergers in the 1980s.

Another expression of this response to numerical decline and/or strained resources can be seen in the merger of several mainline denominations in the past quarter century and the proposals for new mergers, such as the Christian Church (Disciples of Christ) and United Church of Christ courtship, which came to an end in 1985 or the reunion of Northern and Southern Presbyterians or the decision to create the new Evangelical Lutheran Church in America.

Where Are the Men?

From the perspective of the people in the pews the most alarming consequence of this change has been the aging and the feminization of the membership. In 1952 the adult attenders on Sunday morning in the typical Methodist, Presbyterian, Episcopal, Lutheran, Disciples, or Congregational worship service were approximately 53 percent female and 47 percent male, almost exactly the same as the distribution of the adult population. By 1986, with the exception of the Lutheran Church—Missouri Synod, these ratios were closer to 60 percent female and 40 percent male with many congregations reporting a 63-37 or 65-35 ratio. The female-male ratio in the adult population had changed only from 52-48 in 1952 to 53-47 in 1986.

The decision by the United Methodist Church in 1984, the recommendation by the Commission for a New Lutheran Church in 1985, or the proposed mission design for the new Presbyterian Church (U.S.A.) to place a legal ceiling on male participation may not turn out to be an effective means for reversing this trend.

From this writer's perspective in parish consultations, it appears men are showing up in substantial numbers in churches that display at least eight or ten of these characteristics: (1) the pastor is willing and able to accept a strong role as an initiating leader; (2) the membership is largely or entirely Anglo or Asian; (3) the congregation is on the conservative half of the theological spectrum; (4) men are challenged to express their commitment with their hands rather than entirely through verbal skills; (5) the pastor came into the ministry as a second career; (6) there is a strong emphasis on visual, right-brained communication in the preaching and teaching ministries; (7) at least one or two all-male classes or organizations (such as a Men's Fellowship or usher corps or adult Sunday school class or a male chorus or an early Tuesday morning men's Bible study group) are part of the ongoing life of that congregation; (8) no legal ceiling exists that limits male participation; (9) Sunday morning attendance at worship exceeds two hundred; (10) the congregation is not subsidized by the denomination; (11) clearly defined and demanding expectations are placed on the members in terms of attendance at worship, financial support, and missionary outreach; (12) a very strong emphasis is placed on the study of the Scriptures and this may include one or more all-male classes and/or expository preaching; (13) storytelling and/or expository preaching constitute the most frequent approaches to sermon preparation and delivery; (14) the pastor is a mature female; (15) the congregation is now constructing a new building with most of the work being done by volunteers; (16) the congregation sponsors one or two mission work trips for adults once every year or two; (17) the Sunday school is staffed largely by men; or (18) the median age of the members, age fourteen and over, is under forty.

While these characteristics are not offered as a recipe for attracting more males, there may be a cause-and-effect relationship. It also can be argued that the critical variable is how long the congregation has been meeting in this building at this location. While again it is impossible to prove a cause-and-effect relationship, new congregations that are still in the area when they are building their meeting place tend to have a larger proportion of men at worship on Sunday morning.

Influences in the Political Arena

For some the most interesting evidence that the religious scene has changed since the 1950s is in the cast of characters who are seeking to influence partisan policies. The general interest in this change is reflected in the fact that *Time* ran a seven-page article on the subject in its September 2, 1985, issue. In the 1950s and 1960s liberals from both the mainline Protestant churches and Catholic parishes united in their efforts to influence national policy on such issues as race, poverty, housing, public education, urban renewal, and the war in Vietnam.

By the mid-1980s the conservatives, evangelicals, and fundamentalists had become the social and political activists and were vigorously attempting to shape national and local governmental policy on public prayer in the schools, abortion, restrictions on homosexuals, women's rights, the United States' relationships with Israel, aid to nonpublic schools, apartheid, and pornography. Many politicians are convinced the religious right can be more influential than the old-line liberals in municipal, state, and national elections as well as in attracting male supporters.

Where Are My Children?

For generations the dominant pattern on the American religious scene was that children, as they reached adulthood, *63* ▪

tended to be more liberal on questions of biblical interpretation and doctrine than were their parents. While there have been a few exceptions to that broad generalization, such as the 1740s, the 1820s, and the 1920s, that has been the dominant trend in American religious history. It is a different world today.

Fourth-generation Methodist, fifth-generation Presbyterian, and third-generation Lutheran parents repeatedly are reporting, sometimes with obvious embarrassment, that "one of our children is now a very active member of an Assemblies of God church, another is in a new independent fundamentalist congregation, and a third is a leader in an evangelical church related to one of the smaller, but rapidly growing denominations" (such as the Evangelical Free Church). These statements sometimes are accompanied by the comment, "I don't know what we did or didn't do when they were growing up, but now they aren't interested in a church of our denomination."

When asked why they have left the denomination in which they were reared, these children born back in the 1940-65 era may reply with such comments as, "I wasn't being fed spiritually there," or "I didn't know worship could be as exciting as it is here," or "The people here really love and care for one another!" or "The Holy Spirit directed me to come here."

A clearer understanding of what happened can be gained by looking at a new religious subculture which has attracted a remarkably large number of adults, born after 1950, who grew up in mainline Protestant churches.

The Southern California Subculture

"We sing, preach, and pray," explains the pastor of an Assemblies of God congregation in Southern California that has grown from 12 members in 1969, when it was a sixteen-year-old church, to over 3,000 by early 1986.

As he speaks he repeatedly affirms that those are the top priorities in that rapidly growing congregation, which today • *64* includes several hundred members reared in mainline Protestant congregations. This pastor also emphasizes that he deliberately listed those three activities in that order of importance.

Later a Lutheran layman in Ohio explained, "This parish is like a three-legged stool. One leg is the word and the sacraments, a second is pastoral care, and the third is Christian education. Our next pastor must be someone who believes in the importance of all three legs. Our last pastor, who just left, understood the importance of the first and third but neglected his pastoral care responsibilities."

These two comments illustrate an important emerging development in society's religious subculture.

This new phenomenon can be seen most clearly on the West Coast. But it also has spread from the West to the East and is increasingly common in the Midwest and, to a lesser degree, the Northeast.

At last four characteristics of this new phenomenon should be of special interest to those who wonder why their children have migrated from mainline Protestantism to a different religious subculture.

The clearest deviation from traditional mainline Protestant teachings is that one's personal religious experiences, rather than the promises of God, constitute the central validation of one's faith.

A second characteristic, as stated clearly by the Assemblies preacher, is that the centrality of word and sacrament has been supplanted by word *and music.*

Third, a theology of glory overshadows the theology of the cross.

Fourth, a far greater emphasis is placed on the immanence of God, rather than on the transcendence of God.

From a theological perspective these are charateristics that separate this subculture from traditional mainline Protestant teachings, but that is not the whole picture.

From an institutional perspective the congregations that reflect this subculture frequently display several characteristics that distinguish them from congregations affiliated with mainline Protestantism.

Typically, these churches either do not carry a denominational label, or if they do have a denominational affiliation, it is subdued and may not be reflected in the parish name. "Faith Community Church," "Calvary Temple," "The Church of the Open Door," "Calvary Chapel," and "The Church of the Holy Spirit" illustrate the absence of a denominational affiliation. Some of these congregations are supportive of a denomination, but many are independent or "nondenominational" churches.

Frequently, such churches are built around the attractiveness of a magnetic preacher who possesses a strong personality. Long pastorates are the rule. Members often declare their basic local loyalty is to the pastor, rather than to that parish or denomination.

Another characteristic is that a remarkably large proportion of parishioners in these churches apparently see uniting with a congregation as a way station for the individual on a religious pilgrimage, not as a destination. In part, this reflects the lack of a strong emphasis on building congregational loyalty and in part the central role of the pastor; it is also a reflection of the individuals who are attracted by this religious subculture. Many of them declare they are on a pilgrimage. One result is these congregations often embrace persons from the entire ecumenical spectrum. Former Catholics, Lutherans, Methodists, Baptists, and Presbyterians are present in substantial numbers. Another result is a high turnover. One study of recent new members of some of these churches referred to "the rotation of the saints."[9]

Another common characteristic of these churches is a strong emphasis on Bible teaching. It is not uncommon for the sermon to resemble a lecture on a particular Scripture passage with a homily hooked onto the end.

In most, but not all of these churches, the pace of worship is much faster than in the typical mainline Protestant church and thus is more comfortable for people reared in the era of electronic media.

As was pointed out earlier, one of the most distinctive characteristics in this subculture is the music. Not only does music play a greater role in the corporate worship experience, but it is also frequently substantially different from the traditional music one hears in the typical mainline Protestant parish. Gospel songs are more numerous than the classical hymns. Frequently the songs one hears were composed within the past five years, and some may be the creation of the music director. The congregation participates more actively, with more enthusiasm than one encounters in the typical Protestant parish. Frequently a song leader directs congregational singing. In most mainline Protestant churches those who have the greatest competence in vocal music are segregated into a separate section and have a director. (The less competent are expected to sing without the assistance of a director.) The chancel choir in these congregations often is very large, has great visibility, and frequently is applauded after an anthem. The music is one of the factors in that faster pace.

Finally, such a church tends to be highly vulnerable when the long-term pastor leaves, especially if the departure was an unhappy experience for both parties.

Interviews with members of these churches, and especially with new members, suggest the people attracted by this subculture differ substantially from the members one encounters in the typical Lutheran, Methodist, or Presbyterian congregation in the Midwest or Northeast.

While some married into the congregation where they are now members, few of today's adults were born into these congregations. This is not an inherited religion, but rather a matter of choice. Typically, the members do not display a high level of denominational loyalty. Of those churches that do carry denominational labels, only a tiny proportion of new members were reared in that denominational family. In addition to reflecting the attractiveness of this subculture, it also reflects the result of the recent erosion of denominational loyalty all across the United States.

Many of the adult new members comment very openly that they are far more conservative theologically than their parents. A few express obvious concern about what they expect will happen to their parents when they die.

In the 1950s a great many parents chose a church on the basis of what it offered their children. Parents of today attracted by this religious subculture often pick a church because it appears to meet their own needs, rather than for what it offers their children.

For thousands of worried parents the most important characteristic of this subculture is that it has helped a son or daughter once addicted to hard drugs know and accept Jesus Christ as Lord and Savior. These parents explain that is the reason they are now among the most loyal members of this congregation. They are filled with gratitude for something they may not fully comprehend, but for which they are deeply grateful.

A remarkably large proportion of the people in these churches were born after World War II and grew up in a home where the parents were faithful members of a Methodist, Lutheran, Presbyterian, Roman Catholic congregation, or some other long-established denominational family. In their late teens or early twenties they dropped out of church. Some of them "found the Lord" back in the late 1960s or early 1970s in the movement often referred to as "The Jesus People," which attracted tens of thousands of sixteen- to twenty-one-year-olds. With others their return to the church came later in life when a friend insisted, "Come to church with me next Sunday." They were attracted by a religious phenomenon that contrasts sharply with "the church I grew up in back home" and made the denominational switch without hesitation.

One reason for the high member turnover is the relative youthfulness. Adults under forty are more likely to change their residence than are adults past age fifty. Another is that many of these people are on a religious search that carries them from one church to another. A third is that after several years some members conclude, "This really isn't the church for me" and move on. A fourth is that a change of pastors often produces a substantial exodus. Loyalty to the pastor and the meeting of one's own religious needs are far more important to many of these members than parish loyalties or denominational allegiance.

Two other characteristics can be illustrated by the comments of mature parents who are active members of a denominational church and have an adult son or daughter who belongs to a congregation reflecting this religious culture.

"The world I grew up in taught me that faith was a private matter. You just didn't talk about sex or religion. I must confess I never learned to share my faith with others. My daughter (or son) is different. The church she goes to teaches her how to talk about her faith. She doesn't have any hesitation about talking about Jesus and in sharing her faith with others. Sometimes I wish I were able to do that." This religious subculture places a great emphasis on teaching members how to share the faith.

"My wife and I have always been very active in the church, and we brought up our kids that way. Our daughter, however, married a man with absolutely no church background, and, except for the day they were married, he simply refused to go to church. It's not surprising, I guess, that before long our daughter stopped going. I never did learn exactly what happened, but after they had been married for about twelve years, they started to go to church where they're now members. You never saw such a change in a man! Now our son-in-law is in church three times a week and seems to be a lot more religious than our daughter. Both of their kids, of course, are very active in that church. While we don't like the theology, we're glad to see the whole family in church now." This religious subculture does attract men. As was pointed out earlier, in the typical Methodist, Presbyterian, or Lutheran church, 60 percent of the adults at worship are women. In the churches that reflect this religious subculture that ratio often is closer to 50 percent women and 50 percent men. (Fifty-three percent of all American adults are women and 47 percent are men.)

The emergence of this new religious subculture has many implications for leaders in the mainline Protestant churches. First of all, it is difficult to say it is all bad or all good. Life is rarely a simple either/or proposition. An awareness of this subculture does help explain the growing number of adults reared in Lutheran or Methodist or Presbyterian families who today are not in churches related to those denominations.

One result is that some parish leaders see this word-and- *69* ∎

music recipe as an automatic formula for numerical growth. In some congregations the emergence of this religious subculture has become a source of conflict between the pastor and a few parishioners. "Pastor, why can't we change our style of worship and become more like that new church out on the west side of town that is attracting all the young people?" A fair number of highly traditional pastors display little support for such suggestions.

Others urge, "Pastor, why don't we place less emphasis on being a confessional church and place more importance on experiential religion?" Should we be a "confessional" church or try to copy success?

Those mainline Protestant congregations that display a few of the characteristics of this subculture frequently are the recipients of severe criticism from other pastors in the community, and that can undercut interchurch harmony.

While there are many exceptions, a remarkably large proportion of the churches reflecting this religious subculture (a) average over five hundred at Sunday morning worship, (b) draw many of their paid program staff out of the membership rather than from theological schools, and (c) place most of their lay volunteers in positions of ministry rather than on administrative committees.

This religious subculture appears to flourish most easily in a highly congregational form of church government in which little importance is attached to denominational ties or traditions. This not only reduces the sense of interdependence among the churches within a denominational family, but it also encourages church shopping across denominational lines.

Finally, the eastward movement of this religious subculture causes one to ask, "How many mainline Protestant congregations now reflect this new subculture? Is that number growing? What is the impact on denominational loyalty? Can you see expressions of this religious subculture in your community? In your congregation?"

Why the Decline?

The appeal of what has been described here as the Southern California religious subculture explains part of the numerical decline among the mainline Protestant denominations, but that is only a partial explanation. As recently as 1850 the Methodists, the Congregationalists, the Presbyterians, the Lutherans, the German and Dutch Reformed Churches, the Episcopalians, and the Disciples of Christ dominated the total religious scene in America. By the turn of the century their combined numbers had shrunk to approximately two-thirds of the Protestant total. Today these denominations, and their successors as the result of mergers, account for only slightly over a third of all Protestant church members and for less than a third of the Protestant church attenders on a typical Sunday morning.

During the 1970s eight of the largest mainline denomina-tions* reported a combined net loss of slightly over 3 million members. During that same decade the Assemblies of God reported a 70 percent increase in numbers, the Jehovah's Witnesses grew by 45 percent, Seventh-Day Adventists experi-enced an increase of 36 percent, the Southern Baptist Convention reported a 16 percent increase in baptized members, and the Mormons became the seventh largest denomination in the United States with an increase of 36 percent. Thanks to the huge influx of Hispanics from Latin America—and perhaps to a loose system of reporting membership figures—the Roman Catholic Church reported a growth of 5 percent during the 1970s.

One reason for this numerical decline among the mainline Protestant denominations has been the migration of millions of Methodists, Presbyterians, Lutherans, Epicopalians, Disciples, and members of the United Church of Christ to theologically more conservative churches. The most widely accepted explanation for this probably is the one offered by a United Methodist minister, Dean M. Kelley. In his book, *Why Conservative Churches Are Growing*, Kelley argued that the churches affiliated with mainline denominations have not, in

---

*The American Lutheran Church, the Christian Church (Disciples of Christ), The Episcopal Church, the Lutheran Church in America, The Presbyterian Church in the U.S., the United Church of Christ, The United Methodist Church, and the United Presbyterian Church in the U.S.A.

recent years, been responding to the primary reason why people come to church. [10] Kelley argued, in what many called the most influential book to be published during the 1970s, that people look to the churches, not for a social action agenda, but for meaning in life. [11] The theologically more conservative churches concentrated their messages on helping other people understand what God is saying to them and their life in today's world.

Others have argued the decline is a result of population shifts from the northeastern and north central states to the South and West. [12] That migration, however, raises the question of what happened in those regional judicatories in the states that received the migration. A substantial number of both the laity and clergy argue that the primary reason for the decline is that the paid staff members and elected leaders of the mainline denomination are far too liberal and are "out of touch" with the people in the news. While that gap has widened in recent years and has been documented repeatedly, [13] it is overly simplistic to suggest that explains three decades of comparative decline. This gap on social, economic, and theological issues between the people in the pews and denominational leaders may be more influential in explaining why people born after 1945 have not been joining churches affiliated with the mainline denominations than it is in explaining why longtime members have left.

From this writer's perspective the number-one reason for the numerical decline of the mainline denominations can be summarized in one word: death. During the 1960–80 period the eight mainline denominations identified earlier in this section lost nearly 6 million members by death. Far more members were lost by death than by leaving in anger over the increasingly liberal agenda of the national leaders.

A more comprehensive statement would be that the number-one factor in the numerical decline has been the inability of these denominations to attract replacements for those 6 million members lost by death.

Back in the 1950s and the early 1960s it was reasonable to expect that births and deaths would result in a net growth pattern. The husband-wife couple with three or four or five children were producing more future members than was necessary to replace them. As these children became members through the initiatory rites of confirmation or believer's baptism, the result was net growth. As these denominations aged, as the size of families shrank, and as the number of children decreased, the result was decline. In 1958 the United Presbyterian Church, for example, received nineteen new members by profession of faith, reaffirmation of faith, and restoration for every four communicant members lost by death. Twenty-four years later, in 1982, only seven new members were received by these same initiatory rites for every four United Presbyterians who died. In 1960 Methodist churches received fourteen members by profession of faith for every four lost by death. Twenty years later that ratio had dropped to seven new members by profession for every four lost by death. A similar, but less dramatic pattern occurred in the Lutheran Church in America. In 1963 LCA parishes received sixteen new members by the basic initiatory rites (adult baptisms, confirmation, restoration) for every four confirmed members who died. Twenty years later that ratio had dropped to ten confirmations, restorations, and adult baptisms for every four deaths.

In 1960 three denominations came together to form The American Lutheran Church (ALC). In that first year the combined statistics revealed that nineteen adult members were received by the initiatory rites (exclusive of transfers) for every four adults lost by death. In 1984 thirteen new adult members were received by initiatory rites for every four confirmed members lost by death.

Searchers, Pilgrims, and Converts

A second reason for this numerical decline, as was pointed out earlier, is the "game of musical chairs," in which all denominations participate. The mainline denominations have been losing more members to churches of other denominations and to independent congregations than they have gained from other churches. For years, for example, the four biggest sources of new members for the churches in the Southern Baptist Convention have been children of members, marriage, *73* ▪

Methodists, and Presbyterians. As recently as the 1950s the mainline Protestant churches gained as many people as they lost because these denominations still dominated the Anglo church scene including new church development. When a Methodist or Presbyterian left for a new church home, the statistical odds were either that person would transfer to another congregation of that same denomination or join a church affiliated with one of the other mainline denominations. That pattern continued into the 1950s, but changed radically in the past quarter century.

During the typical year in the 1950s, for example, 450,000 members were received by Methodist churches via a letter of transfer from another Methodist congregation. That was an average of 1,200 intradenominational transfers per day. During recent years, however, the number of new members received by United Methodist churches by a letter of transfer from other United Methodist congregations dropped to an average of 175,000 annually in the later 1970s and to an average of 160,000 in the early 1980s or an average of fewer than 500 per day. New members being received by United Methodist congregations from *all* sources (profession of faith, restoration, intradenominational transfers, and interdenominational transfers) averaged only 1,300 per day in the early 1980s compared to nearly 2,100 a day back in the 1950s. In the Lutheran Church in America the number of new members received from all sources dropped from an average of 510 a day in 1963 to 375 per day twenty years later. A similar pattern prevailed in the United Presbyterian Church as the number of new members received from all sources dropped from an average of 785 per day in 1958 to 444 in 1982.

This decline in the turnover rate illustrates a basic principle of church growth. Those churches and denominations that experience significant net growth also can be expected to experience a high turnover in the membership. Every year many people leave, but even more join. By contrast, those denominations with a high degree of stability tend to be numerically declining denominations.

Likewise the typical long-established congregation with a hundred or two hundred members that reports a loss of 3 to 5 percent of its members in a given year usually will be on a plateau in size or experiencing numerical decline. The large congregations that are reporting significant growth in membership and attendance usually bid farewell to 8 to 12 percent of the members every year while welcoming a number equal to 10 to 15 percent of the membership at the end of the previous year.

This is another reason why it is more difficult to be a pastor today. The conventional wisdom insists that in order to grow "we must retain our youth" or "close that back door" or "reactivate our inactive members." To argue that these should be no higher than second- or third-level priorities is not the way to win a popularity contest in most congregations today.

Some of the clearest evidence on the growth of the nondenominational and independent churches comes from a report analyzing the migration of the churchgoers. The basic thrust of one section of the report is summarized in one sentence, "No religion with high stability gained more converts than it lost, and all net gainers were religious groups with low stability."[14] That statement also describes the data reported for The United Methodist Church and the United Presbyterian Church in the previous paragraphs.

This study reports that only 28 percent of the members of the churches categorized as "Internondenominational" were reared in that same faith compared to 60 percent of Presbyterian members, 72 percent of Methodists, 76 percent of Lutherans, 54 percent of Episcopalians, and 90 percent of all Catholic members.

These interdenominational and independent churches, however, gained twenty-seven converts from other churches for every ten lost by disaffiliation.

By contrast, in this game of musical chairs which excludes losses by death, Episcopalians gained thirteen for every thirteen who left while Catholics and Methodists claimed six converts for every ten who disaffiliated, the fundamentalists won fifteen converts for every ten who left while both the Lutherans and the Presbyterians welcomed eight converts for every ten who left for a church of a different denomination.[15]

While part of this decrease in the number of intradenomina-   *75* •

tional transfers among Methodists and Presbyterians referred to earlier can be explained by the aging of the membership (people past age forty are far less likely to change their place of residence in any given year than are persons in the 17-35 age group), this decrease also appears to be a major factor in the aging of these and other mainline denominations. A great many of those children who were baptized and confirmed in the 1950s and early 1960s either have dropped out of church altogether or have transferred to a congregation that does not accept new members by letter of transfer from a mainline Protestant congregation.

It is impossible to single out any one factor as the sole cause for the numerical losses resulting from "ecclesiastical migration," but five do stand out. These are: (a) the huge increase in the number of new independent and evangelical congregations while most mainline Protestant denominations were cutting back on new church development after 1963 (as a general rule new congregations focus on enlisting new members while long-established churches often tend to focus on taking care of the longtime members); (b) the decision to attempt to perpetuate the definition of the geographical parish when that concept was being undercut by several forces including the widespread use of the private automobile, the separation of familiar places from experiences by the electronic media,[16] and the new freedom of the American people; (c) the shift to a liberal point on the theological spectrum by the clergy when many of the people born after 1940 were seeking a theologically more conservative congregation; (d) the move up the social class ladder of several denominations just as many working class adults began attending church (in the 1920s two-thirds of the working class never went to church); and (e) in a few denominations, an actual reduction in the number of congregations.*

---

*The United Presbyterian Church decreased from 9,383 congregations in 1960 to 8,770 in 1980; The Methodist Church of 1952 included 39,906 congregations and the Evangelical and United Brethren Church reported 4,248 congregations in 1953 while The United Methodist Church reported only 37,988 churches at the end of 1984—a net loss of 6,300 despite the organization of nearly 3,000 new congregations since 1952; the number of congregations in the Lutheran Church in America dropped to 5,815 in 1984 compared to over 5,852 in 1968.

The dream of some social activists of the 1960s that a greater emphasis on issues-centered ministries would attract a new generation turned out to be a dream, not a representation of reality. The reality appears to be reflected in the statement, "The historic evidence suggests . . . that activism can work as a substitute for faith for no more than one or two generations."[17]

By the mid-1980s these and other factors meant that the person leaving a mainline Protestant congregation was more likely to end up in a church not related to one of those nine denominations than to stay within the mainline segment of American Protestantism.

The Decreasing Proportion of Anglos

Another influential factor, and one that has not received the attention it deserves, can be found by examining three sets of numbers.

POPULATION CHANGES IN THE UNITED STATES
In Millions

Year	White	Black	Spanish	Asian	Amer. Indian	Others
1900	56.7	8.8	?	0.1	0.3	?
1980	188.3	26.5	14.6	3.2	1.4	7.0

Between 1900 and 1980 the proportion of whites in the population of the United States dropped from 85 percent to 78 percent. As the Anglo proportion shrank, who was most effective in reaching and serving blacks and the new immigrants?

While this minimizes the influence of theological, doctrinal, and liturgical differences, it is now possible to compare the results of two strategies. One can be summarized by the word "inclusion," the other by the word "evangelization." The first was followed by Lutherans, Presbyterians, and Methodists and emphasized the use of quotas to guarantee Blacks, Asians, Native

77 ·

Americans, and Hispanics (and women) positions in regional and national denominational offices so their views could influence policy formulation and the allocation of funds. This approach also encouraged the integration of ethnic minority groups into existing congregations composed largely or entirely of Anglos. Some articulate Black, Hispanic, and Asian leaders protested this melting pot approach on the grounds that it really meant a dilution of their power and the forsaking of their cultural heritage. They argued the salad bowl would be a better metaphor than the melting pot. This strategy contrasts with the self-controlled, self-financed, and self-propagating strategy used to reach the immigrants from Europe in the nineteenth century.* While the concept of America as a melting pot can explain the strategies of the 1960s, it is difficult to understand why that concept continued to be so influential in the 1970s and 1980s after it had been abandoned by some of its early advocates[18] and was being rejected by many Asians, Blacks, and Hispanic leaders.

While the Presbyterians talked about reunion, while the Lutherans planned for the creation of a new denomination, and while the United Methodists made the ethnic minority churches a missional priority in raising money, the Assemblies of God and the Southern Baptist Convention followed the second strategy of evangelization. Instead of making sure that blacks, women, and the new immigrants were fully represented in the decision-making processes of the denomination, these two evangelistic groups concentrated their efforts on starting new congregations. By the end of 1985 the Southern Baptist Convention included more than 2,000 Hispanic congregations, the Assemblies of God had 1,125 Hispanic churches, the United Methodists had approxi-

---

*In 1906, for example, twenty-four separate Lutheran denominations existed in the United States, seven of which had over 100,000 members. By 1963 fifteen of these twenty-four had combined to create two large denominations. As recently as 1924, to cite another example of separate non-geographical judicatories for each ethnic or language or nationality group, the Methodist Episcopal Church included ten German, six Swedish, and two Norwegian Danish annual conferences. The United Methodist Church still includes three non-geographical conferences but thus far has refused to create new ones.

mately 250, the three Lutheran bodies and the Presbyterian Church (U.S.A.) had fewer than a hundred each. The Southern Baptist Convention, which is now the most inclusive Protestant denomination in the nation, also included at the end of 1985 600,000 black members in nearly 1,000 congregations, 466 Native American congregations reaching people from 97 tribes, 151 Chinese congregations, 85 Laotian congregations, and 77 Vietnamese churches as well as congregations representing 60 language, nationality, and ethnic groups.

The results suggest that if the primary goal is to reach and serve people through worshiping congregations, the strategy followed by the Assemblies of God and the Southern Baptist Convention has been more effective than the strategies followed by Lutherans, Presbyterians, and United Methodists. One variable, of course, is the strategy chosen. It also will influence the definition of criteria for ordination. The greater the emphasis on integration, the greater the pressures to expect Black, Spanish, Asian, and Native American candidates for the ministry to meet the same requirements as those set by Anglos for Anglos. If the primary focus is on organizing new congregations, gifts and performance may be given more weight than diplomas and degrees.

Perhaps the biggest barrier, however, has been the expectation by several predominantly Anglo denominations that the large financial subsidy granted the typical upper-middle class new mission must also be granted every new Black, Hispanic, or Asian congregation. This emphasis on egalitarianism overlooked the fact that the vast majority of new Black, Hispanic, or Asian congregations started in a typical year do not receive a financial subsidy from anyone. Subsidies in America are largely for upper-middle and upper-class Anglos. Subsidies also tend to create a dependency relationship that eventually often evolves into an adversary relationship. Large financial subsidies simply have not been an effective means of starting new churches, especially those designed to reach blacks or the new immi-

79 ∎

grants.[19] Subsidies, however, have proved to be an attractive issue for those interested in ecclesiastical patronage.

Who Is Organizing New Congregations?

Another facet of this subject can be seen by looking at the statistics in new church development. Five of the many reasons for organizing new congregations are relevant to this discussion. First, new churches represent the best approach for reaching and assimilating people not actively involved in any worshiping community. They provide the "drop-out" with a fresh start. Second, as the Assemblies of God and the Southern Baptist Convention have demonstrated so clearly in recent years, new congregations constitute the most effective means of reaching the new immigrants to America. That is the strategy followed in the nineteenth century with amazing results by Roman Catholics, Lutherans, the Reformed churches, and Methodists. Third, if a denomination has several congregations representing different religious subcultures in a community, the disaffected member leaving one congregation may find a new church home without leaving the denomination. Fourth, as was mentioned earlier, new churches tend to focus on outreach while most long-established congregations tend to focus on "inreach," the care of their own members. Fifth, as a general rule, congregations that have competition from another church of their own denomination tend to be more vital, more open to ideas, more likely to launch new ministries in response to the needs of people, and more eager to allow new members to become policy-makers than are the congregations that have a denominational monopoly in that community. (*Caution:* Ministerial leadership is a far more influential factor than competition in all of the characteristics that enhance congregational health and vitality!)

Three sets of figures can be used to place recent trends in an historical perspective. Nearly 70,000 new Protestant congregations were organized in the 1870–1889 era. Almost exactly one-third of these were organized by the denominations now represented in The United Methodist Church, the United

Church of Christ, the Presbyterian Church (U.S.A.), and the Christian Church (Disciples of Christ). These four denominations accounted for fewer than 4 percent of all new congregations organized in the 1970s, and they will account for no more than 8 percent of all new churches organized during the 1980s.

Second, in 1960 the former Presbyterian Church in the U.S., the United Presbyterians, the Methodists, and the United Church of Christ organized a combined total of 320 new congregations. In 1975 the combined total had dropped to approximately 55 new missions.

Third, the original proposal for the new Evangelical Lutheran Church in America was to plan for 70 new missions annually in the late 1980s. Subsequently the new denomination was challenged to more than double that goal. By contrast, in the 1880–1906 era an average of three hundred new Lutheran churches were organized annually.

The gap was filled by new churches organized by the Church of the Nazarene, the Seventh-Day Adventists, the Assemblies of God, the Southern Baptists, the Wisconsin Evangelical Lutheran Synod, the Evangelical Free Church, the Evangelical Covenant Church, the Christian and Missionary Alliance, the Church of God (Cleveland, Tennessee), the Churches of Christ, the Church of God in Christ (which grew from 4,500 congregations in 1965 to nearly 10,000 in 1982), the General Association of Regular Baptist Churches, the Jehovah's Witnesses, the Grace Brethren, the Church of Jesus Christ of Latter-Day Saints (the Mormons grew from 2 million members in 4,828 congregations in 1970 to 3.6 million in 8,017 congregations in 1983), and a hundred other denominations and fellowships. More significant, however, were the hundreds of new congregations organized each year that do not carry a denominational label and do not identify with any particular fellowship of churches. The concept of new churches to reach new people was increasingly being implemented outside the mainline denominations and that has been a powerful factor in the lack of numerical growth.   *81* •

The Growing Number of "Nones"

Perhaps the most widely ignored factor behind the numerical decline of the mainline denominations is the increasing number of Americans who, when asked their religious affiliation, reply, "None." The special census on religion conducted in 1957 reported that only 2.7 percent of all adults questioned about their religious affiliation replied, "None." The surveys conducted by the National Opinion Research Center found that proportion had increased to 6.7 percent by 1980.[20] The polls taken by the Gallup organization indicate the proportion replying "none" has climbed from 3 percent in 1957 (the same as reported by the 1957 census of religion) to 6 percent in 1976 to 9 percent in 1984. Perhaps the most significant changes are in the figures by generations. When asked their religious affiliation, slightly over 3 percent of those born before 1924 replied, "None." By contrast, 10.8 percent of those born in the 1941–57 era and 13.0 percent of those born in the 1957–65 period answered, "None." For each birth cohort approximately 5 times as many reply "none" as name some religion other than Protestant, Catholic, or Jewish. For every 10 adults who leave the "no religious affiliation" category to join a church, 33 leave a church behind as they move into this "none" category.

Where do these people come from who respond "none" to questions about religious affiliation? First of all, they come in disproportionately large numbers from among men born in the 1930–60 era who have had at least some college education.

A reasonable guess is that a significant proportion of those 15 million Americans, age eighteen and over, who reply "none" when asked their religious affiliation, were among the millions of children baptized and confirmed in mainline Protestant churches back in the 1950s.

One study reports that by a two-to-one margin the "Nones" tend to be male, and they tend to have had at least some college training, but income does not appear to be a factor. In disproportionately large numbers they reside in the West or the Northeast. The higher the father's occupation, status, education, and income, the more likely the children, when they reach the 18-35 age bracket, will answer "none" to that question.[21]

More significant to this dicussion, however, are the church backgrounds of those who have abandoned their childhood religious affiliation. Children growing up in a Protestant congregation at the "liberal" or "moderate" points of the theological spectrum are twice as likely as those reared in a conservative church to abandon their religious ties by the time they reach the 18-25 age bracket.[22] This defection of young adults from the liberal and moderate churches obviously is one reason behind the aging of the membership of several mainline Protestant denominations as well as their numerical decline.

This inability of the mainline Protestant churches to attract and retain white males born after 1950 is a widely known fact of life to anyone who visits a couple of dozen of these churches on Sunday morning every year. What is not as widely discussed is the inability of the seminaries affiliated with these denominations to attract white male students in the 21-24 age bracket in anything approaching the numbers that were enrolled in the 1950s. It should be added that the twenty-three-year-old white male of 1984 was born in 1961 while the twenty-three-year-old white male of 1955 was born in 1932. The number of white male babies born in 1961 was 1.8 million compared to slightly over 1 million in 1932. The inability of these seminaries to attract even the same number, much less the same proportion of young white males, has been overshadowed by the tremendous increase in the enrollment of women, of second-career students, both male and female, and of Blacks and Asians.

In a somewhat parallel trend the inability of congregations related to the mainline denominations to retain their own children has been partially offset by a new trend which has complicated the social life of many young pastors and their families.

Growing Old Together

John F. Kennedy was the first of five presidents of the United States to have been born during the first two decades of the   *83* ▪

twentieth century. Jimmy Carter was the first, and perhaps, depending on what happens in 1988, the only president to have been born during the 1920s. As the decades roll by, the generation that once provided the leadership is replaced by a new generation of leaders.

During the "religious boom" of the 1950s the mainline Protestant denominations drew their leaders largely from among those persons born just before or soon after the turn of the century. The members came in large numbers from members of the "baby boom" of the World War I era. (The number of live births in the United States reached 3 million for the first time in American history in 1921 and ranged between 2.9 and 3.0 million for every other year but two from 1914 through 1925. The next time as many as 2.9 million live babies were born in the United States was 1942.)

A predictable reason for the decline in *adult* membership of the 1960s was the "birth dearth" of 1926–41. The unexpected development, as described earlier, was the inability of the mainline Protestant denominations to attract and retain adults who were born back in the baby boom that followed World War II.

The result was that by the early 1980s 16 percent of all Americans born before 1924 identified themselves as Methodists, but only 7.7 percent of those born in the 1958–65 era called themselves Methodists. Likewise slightly over 6 percent of the population born before 1924 are Presbyterians compared to only 3 percent born in the 1958–65 period. The figures are not quite as dismal for Lutherans, but the trend is the same. While 9.5 percent of those born before 1924 claim to be Lutherans, only 5.7 percent of those born during the 1958-65 era call themselves Lutherans. A similar pattern prevails for Epicopalians as slightly over 3 percent born in the first quarter of this century identify themselves as Episcopalians compared to 1.8 percent for those born during 1958–65.

By contrast, 13 percent of those born before 1924, 13 percent of those born during 1924–57, and 14 percent of those born in the 1958–65 era identify themselves as Southern Baptists.

Self-identified fundamentalists represented 11.8 percent of Americans born before 1908, only 7.8 percent of those born in the 1907–23 period but 12 percent of those born in the 1958–65 era.

The persons who identified themselves as "liberals" in religious terms constituted 3.3 percent of those born before 1924, 1.5 percent of those born in the 1941–57 era, but only 0.8 percent of those born in the 1958–65 era.[23]

In simple terms, one of the reasons for the numerical decline of the mainline Protestant denominations is they are running out of inventory. The generations that filled the churches in the 1950 era are dying off and replacements are not arriving in equal numbers from younger generations. A simple illustration of that point is in the findings of *The Presbyterian Panel*, a regular survey of members initiated by the former United Presbyterian Church in the U.S.A. In 1973 the typical Presbyterian was a forty-eight-year-old white married woman. Nine years later the *Panel* reported the typical Presbyterian was a white married woman in her early fifties. The *Panel* also reported the proportion of United Presbyterians who were fifty-five or older increased from 31 percent in 1973 to 41 percent in 1981.

While it may not be a representative cross section of the membership, the Survey of United Methodist Opinion reported that nearly 70 percent of the lay members of the panel were past forty-four years of age. (Of all Americans age fourteen and over approximately one-half are under thirty-eight years of age and 39 percent are past forty-four years of age.)

Given (a) the defection of the children born after World War II to families who were members of mainline Protestant churches, (b) the loss of 6 million members by death, (c) the decision not to use the strategy of starting new congregations as the means of reaching the new immigrants, (d) the sharp decline in the number of new congregations organized to reach a new generation of theologically more conservative people born after 1955, (e) the birth dearth of the 1926–41 era, and (f) the fact that forty-year-old women have an average life expectancy of forty-one more years compared to thirty-five years for forty-year-old males, it is not surprising that the typical mainline Protestant congregation has a disproportionately large number of members who are women born before 1925.

One consequence is that the twenty-six-year-old seminary graduate who leaves school to become the pastor of a small or middle-sized Anglo congregation often will have more difficulty making friends among members of his or her own age than did the twenty-six-year-old pastor of 1956.

A second consequence is a predictable decline in the number of infant baptisms and in the number of children in the Sunday school.

A third common consequence is the dream of finding a dynamic young pastor who will come in and reverse the aging of that congregation's membership.

The Catholic-to-Protestant Migration

When a Catholic married a non-Catholic back in 1950, the chances were about three out of four that the non-Catholic spouse would become a convert to Catholicism. During the past three or four decades two changes have altered that pattern. The first is the increase in the proportion of Catholics marrying non-Catholics, a change from approximately 20 to 25 percent in 1950 to at least 40 percent in 1985. The second change is that today for every two non-Catholics who join a Catholic parish as a result of marrying a Catholic, three Catholics leave when they marry a non-Catholic. [24] The reasons why people leave a particular church or denomination are myriad, but conversations with ex-Catholics who are now members of Protestant congregations suggest at least seven influential factors behind the move: (1) the desire by both husband and wife to be members of the same congregation, (2) the ban on artificial birth control in the Catholic Church, (3) the refusal by many Catholic priests to allow a divorced person to receive Holy Communion and/or the priest's refusal to officiate at the wedding of a person who has been divorced, (4) the attitude of Catholic policy-makers toward the role of women in the church, (5) the discovery by the Catholic while visiting a Protestant congregation that worship can be an exciting, joyous, and inspiring experience rather than simply the fulfillment of an obligation, (6) the increase in the number of young people who have been living together before deciding to seek a church wedding, and (7) the opposition of the Catholic Church to abortion.

For many Catholics this switch to a Protestant congregation has been eased by the ecumenical movement that flourished in the 1960s. As Protestants and Catholics began to acknowledge and affirm the legitimacy of the other's religious convictions, as Catholics watched as a Protestant minister and a Catholic priest shared in officiating at an interfaith marriage, as Catholics and Protestants studied together in the same theological seminaries, as Catholics and Protestants shared in worship services and retreat experiences, as a sharply decreasing proportion of Catholic children are being educated in Catholic parochial schools, as old prohibitions on Catholics such as abstaining from meat on Fridays were removed, and as the Charismatic Renewal Movement emerged as the most ecumenical experience in American history, it became easier for Catholics to find a new church home in a Protestant congregation. Naturally, this change would be far easier for the Catholic whose formative years coincided with this breakthrough in Catholic-Protestant relationships and for those Catholics marrying a Protestant than it would be for Catholics born before 1940 and for those who attended a Catholic parochial school as a child.

For generations it was widely assumed the Episcopal Church was the place for ex-Catholics who had married a Protestant spouse. By the mid-1950s that role as a "bridge church" was being challenged by the Christian Church (Disciples of Christ) which offers the Lord's Supper every Sunday. In more recent years, however, it is not unusual to hear a Presbyterian or Lutheran or Methodist or Baptist pastor report that between one-fifth and one-half of all new adult members received in the past year had been reared in the Catholic Church. One survey conducted by the Southern Baptist Convention reported that 14 percent of all new members were former Catholics and that four

87 ▪

Catholics joined a Southern Baptist congregation for every Baptist who left to become a Catholic.

Without this influx of adult Catholics it appears the numerical decline of the mainline Protestant denominations would have been far greater, perhaps a difference of 1 to 3 million members, for the nine largest denominations. Even more significant, however, the aging of these denominations would have been more pronounced without this influx of ex-Catholics born after 1945.

While the absence of detailed figures makes impossible anything more than an estimate, it appears the majority of ex-Catholics are not to be found in the churches affiliated with the mainline Protestant denominations. They appear to be more likely to be found in charismatic or Pentecostal churches, in Baptist or Assemblies of God congregations, among the Mormons and in that growing number of nondenominational or independent churches that place a great emphasis on an experiential, rather than a rational approach to the Christian faith. The congregations that represent what was described earlier as the Southern California religious subculture appear to be attracting many former Catholics.

The implications and consequences of this Catholic-to-Protestant migration can best be described from the perspective of the year 2015 rather than from today's far more limited view.

One obvious change is that the Roman Catholic Church no longer is receiving as many new members through marriage as it did in the 1950s. As fewer people marry into the Catholic Church, the church's conversion rate has dropped from 4.3 converts per 1,000 Catholics in 1950 to 2.1 in 1969 to 1.6 in 1979.

From the perspective of the leaders in the typical Protestant congregation a more pressing question may be summarized, Do we want to encourage more former Catholics to come to our church, and if we do, what will that mean?

In pondering that question, it may help to reflect on what appear to be the distinctive charcteristics of those congregations that are receiving a disproportionately large number of former

Catholics as new members. It should be understood that very few congregations display all of these characteristics.

Perhaps the most common is that the sacrament of Holy Communion is offered every Sunday morning. This is the custom in every Christian Church (Disciples of Christ) congregation, of many Episcopal parishes, and of a growing number of Lutheran and United Methodist churches.

A second characteristic, which is far from universal, is a warm, joyous, inspiring, affirming, and uplifting worship experience every Sunday morning. A great many former Catholics also strongly emphasize the attractiveness of enthusiastic congregational singing. This emphasis on an inspiring worship experience and lively singing is heard most frequently in those large nondenominational churches and Assemblies of God congregations that include hundreds of ex-Catholics in the membership. Overlapping this is the widely acknowledged fact that the quality of preaching in Protestant congregations frequently is far superior to that found in the typical Catholic parish. The combination of the size of the work load carried by the typical Catholic priest and the absence of a tradition of great preaching in Catholicism means many ex-Catholics are surprised by and delighted with the quality of the preaching they hear when they first visit a Protestant church.

For many ex-Catholics the role of women in worship has great symbolic importance and repeatedly they refer to the highly visible woman liturgists and/or to the role of women as elected officers in that parish and/or to the fact that this church is served by a woman who is an ordained minister. Those congregations seeking to be open to Catholics may want, if the list includes several women, to print the names of the officers and the church council on the back of the Sunday morning bulletin.

Dozens of pastors insist that the critical factor is not Holy Communion every Sunday morning, but rather is the openness of the members to a generation of younger adults. These pastors insist the central issue can be summarized in four words, Do we trust people? Many of these pastors also contend that is the critical factor in reaching the generation born after the end of World War

89 ▪

II, regardless of whether they grew up in a Catholic parish, a Protestant home, or no church at all.

A great many self-identified former Catholics also lift up their appreciation of the greater emphasis on the role of the laity they encounter in Protestant churches. Specific examples range from the influence of the laity in decision making on policies, finances, and administration to the lay liturgist to the Bibles in the pews so they can read along as the minister reads the Scripture lessons for the day to the Sunday school to the fact that the congregation selects and calls their own minister rather than having a pastor appointed by a bishop to the greater emphasis on world missions.

Obviously few of the people who constitute this migration are choosing a new church home on the basis of denominational loyalty or an inherited preference. Some pick a Protestant church on the basis of the spouse's allegiance, many more make the choice on the basis of the meaningfulness of the worship experience. Others are heavily influenced by the personality and belief systems of the pastor. This helps explain why the churches with an exceptionally large proportion of ex-Catholics in the membership also tend to have the benefit of a long pastorate.

While they represent a minority of any sample, a significant number of these new members expressed appreciation for the fact they were not asked to renounce their own religious heritage. One quoted his Lutheran pastor as saying, "We're not asking you to disavow your roots. We both come from the same tradition. The only difference is some of us left earlier than you did."

A significant number of the people this writer talked to were Catholics who had married into a Protestant church when they picked a spouse and did not display any particular interest in doctrinal issues. A far larger proportion, however, see themselves on a religious pilgrimage and express great eagerness to learn more about the teachings of this particular church. In some of these churches the majority of the participants in the adult Bible classes are people who come from a Catholic background even though they represent only a minority of the total membership. The churches receiving a disproportionately large number of new members coming from a Catholic heritage usually place great emphasis on a strong teaching ministry. This is most visible in those very large nondenominational churches in which one-third or more of the members were reared in a Catholic home. (While it may surprise some and produce dismay in others, it is not unusual to find a large number of women who grew up in the Catholic Church in those congregations that place great emphasis on the subservient relationships of the wife to the husband.)

Finally, while it really is of minor significance, it was interesting to hear comments such as this, "Mother was so pleased when I wrote her that I had found such a wonderful church home and so many new friends here at St. Paul's. She was so delighted to learn I was going to church every Sunday I didn't have the heart to tell her it's a Lutheran church." Those parishes named for a saint do have an advantage.

Many ministers, especially several Southern Baptist pastors, have raised another issue. Will we make them (the former Catholics) like us or will they make us like them? In more specific terms this semi-humorous question refers to: (a) doctrinal and policy questions about infant baptism and "getting the baby done to please Grandma," (b) admission to and the frequency of the Lord's Supper, (c) the traditional high esteem in which the office of pastor is held in the Catholic Church and the deference granted the Catholic priest as contrasted to a much lower view of the pastoral office in several Protestant denominations, (d) the title to be used by the laity in addressing the pastor, (e) policies and content of the teaching for the instruction of children about to be confirmed, and (f) the level of stewardship (the typical Protestant family gives twice as much to the church every year as the typical Catholic family). It was easier to be a pastor when most of our adult members either were unchurched and completely open to what we taught or came from a denominational and belief background similar to ours!

For many more pastors, however, the influx of new members who were reared in the Roman Catholic Church is a welcome breath of fresh air and a signal that "our church can reach that *91* •

generation born after 1940—we do not simply have to watch ourselves grow old together."

For those ministers who were taught in seminary that the appropriate leadership role for a pastor is to be a facilitator or an equipper or an enabler, another change is more disturbing.

The Reemergence of the Independent Entrepreneur

If you were admitted to the hospital as a patient in 1953, you almost certainly went to a church-related or a municipal or a university-connected hospital, incorporated as a not-for-profit corporation. If you looked out the window when the garbage truck came by to pick up your garbage and trash, you probably watched municipal employees doing the work. If your house caught on fire and you called the fire department, you would most likely have seen a municipal fire truck respond. If you listened to a sermon on the radio, the chances were about three out of four you were hearing a minister from one of the mainline Protestant denominations. If you ordered curriculum materials for your Sunday school or colorful bulletin covers for the Sunday morning service, your order probably was filled by a not-for-profit denominational supply house. If your child had an accident and needed medical care, you probably rushed to the emergency room of the local not-for-profit hospital for care. If a pastor urged a parishioner to accept God's call to the ministry and go off to seminary, in all likelihood that pastor recommended a denominationally related seminary. If you wanted to participate in a regular exercise program, you probably went to the YMCA or to a municipal park.

Today, unlike the 1950s, the chances are increasing every day that a patient will be cared for in a proprietary hospital, the garbage and trash will be picked up by a profit-making waste disposal company, the fire truck you see on the street belongs to a private fire protection company which seeks to make a profit, the preacher you watch on television is not related to any of the mainline Protestant denominations, and an independent or nondenominational supply house will provide the bulletin covers or the stewardship materials or the curriculum resources you seek. More and more people seeking emergency medical care are turning to one of the "Doc-in-a-box" franchises rather than going to the emergency room of the local hospital, and a remarkably large number of people are enrolled in private profit-making health clubs.

These and many other changes are the result of the reemergence of the independent entrepreneur. The natural and predictable bureaucratization of the many governmental and not-for-profit organizations has tended to make the staff or the employees the number-one client. One result is many of these long-established agencies no longer are able to compete, in terms of costs, creativity, efficiency, or quality of services with this new generation of entrepreneurs. Twice as many new businesses were incorporated in 1985 as in 1972.

The parallel is that as the churches become more concerned with the care of their own members, housekeeping matters, pensions for the clergy, or the issues that are important to the staff, it becomes increasingly difficult to attract new members. Along comes the independent entrepreneur who places the religious needs of the "client" at the top of the list of priorities and new members begin to flock to that church.

It would be much easier to rationalize what is happening if a clearly defined line separated "us" (the mainline Protestant churches) from "them" (the new or recently revitalized congregations led by a minister with a magnetic personality and obvious entrepreneurial gifts and skills). The issue is far more complicated than that, however, because an increasing number of those large and rapidly growing Presbyterian, United Methodist, Reformed, Lutheran, and Christian (Disciples of Christ) churches are members of "our denominational family" and are led by a senior pastor whose ministerial standing is in our denomination.

The issue is further complicated by the fact that the self-identified enabler-pastor often is not attracting new members, and that was the leadership role taught in many seminaries in the 1950–75 era. All too often the congregations served by the *93* ▪

self-identified enablers are faced with an agenda filled with survival questions while the congregations served by the entrepreneurial pastors are able to allocate a far larger proportion of resources, both human and financial, to missional objectives. To be faithful and obedient to what was taught in seminary may mean an agenda filled with questions on institutional survival and diminishing numbers on Sunday morning. Is that what God intended? By contrast, the pastor of the 1950s, who had been in school in the 1930s or 1940s, rarely was faced with that trade-off. Back in the 1950s it did not seem to matter where you had gone to school, or even whether or not you had graduated from seminary. Your congregation, like most other non-profit organizatons of the 1950s, usually attracted more people year after year.

Is it acceptable in the eyes of the Lord for a pastor today to abandon the role of enabler or equipper and accept the role of an initiating leader? For a great many pastors that transformation cannot be accomplished without strong feelings of guilt, some of which are self-induced, some of which are induced by longtime friends, and some of which are a remnant of a heritage from seminary. It was easier to be a pastor back in the 1950s when one did not have to feel guilty or apologize because the congregation was larger this year than it was a year earlier. That was consistent with the numerical growth of the denomination. By 1980 it often was seen as a sign of disloyalty or worldliness if a pastor reported substantial numerical growth while the denomination was continuing to shrink in numbers. It is always easier to go with the majority.

Guilt over growth, however, is only one of the stresses experienced by many of today's pastors that was not a part of the religious scene of the 1950s.

Stresses and Choices

Perhaps the most stress-producing consequences of the trends described here are those felt by congregational leaders in churches related to the mainline denominations. Should we follow in the direction recommended by our denominational leaders and watch as our denomination shrinks in numbers and resources? Or should we maintain a loyal stance, but seek to work from within to change the culture, value system, priorities, and direction of the denomination? Or should we largely ignore our denominational ties and model our approach to ministry after what we see appears to be working with those big independent churches that are reaching so many younger adults today? This third alternative becomes more and more attractive to some as year after year they see an increasing number of Presbyterian, Methodist, Reformed, Lutheran, and American Baptist congregations following that route and reporting substantial numerical growth. What is even more compelling is when members come back from a Sunday morning or Sunday evening visit and report with a combination of envy and awe on the vitality, friendliness, dedication, and enthusiasm of the members they met. Frequently, these reports also emphasize the youthfulness of the members in the congregation that was visited.

Back in the 1950s it was possible to be a loyal follower of the denominational policies, support the denominational benevolence and missionary programs, purchase and use the denominational hymnal,* utilize the denominational resources and models in the Christian education program, accept the denominational model for staffing the congregation and incorporate the denominational polity in the organizational structure of the congregation, and be somewhere between pleased and satisfied with the results.

It is a different world today and many of those systems, techniques, and structures that were appropriate for the 1950s do not work today. What met the religious needs of the adults who were a product of the baby boom of 1914–25 frequently do not work with the adults who were born in the 1946–65 era.

---

*The difficulties confronting anyone seeking to produce a hymnal that will please everyone in every congregation are illustrated by the results of a survey in which members were polled on the hymns they wanted retained in the new United Methodist hymnal and also on the hymns they wanted deleted. The same hymn, "How Great Thou Art," topped both lists.

What should pastors and congregational leaders do? In scores of cases, particularly Presbyterian and Lutheran, the decision has been made and implemented to take that congregation out of the denomination. That is a completely unacceptable course of action, however, for the vast majority of ministers and lay leaders. Their denominational ties run too deep to do that. The 1970s and 1980s witnessed these discussions in hundreds of Assemblies of God, Reformed Church in America, Lutheran Church—Missouri Synod, United Presbyterian, Southern Baptist, Presbyterian Church U. S., and United Methodist congregations. For most of the participants in these debates the pain and guilt over leaving greatly outweighed the promised benefits of a fresh start in a different religious subculture.

There are no easy answers to this question. The course chosen by many, to drop into a stance of passively ignoring the larger denominational context, also appears to be unacceptable to the majority of ministers and lay leaders.

The issues that create these intradenominational stresses include: (1) policies on ministerial placement, (2) affirmation or disavowal of the Charismatic Renewal Movement, (3) the philosophy of world missions, (4) the philosophy and content of curriculum resources for the Sunday school, (5) the adoption of a new hymnal, (6) the choice of a basic strategy described earlier (inclusiveness versus evangelization) in seeking to reach the new immigrants, (7) the ordination of women, (8) the age at first confirmation, (9) the use of quotas in choosing denominational officials and staff, (10) the role of the Christian Day School, (11) the right of a pregnant woman to an abortion on request, (12) American foreign policy, (13) models for new church development, (14) the philosophy of theological education, (15) the stance on interchurch cooperation, (16) the priorities in granting financial subsidies to congregations, (17) the ordination of self-avowed homosexuals or their employment in denominational agencies, (18) the relocation of the denominational headquarters. (19) the role of men in the church, (20) the priorities in allocating benevolence funds, (21) the increased use of inclusive language, and (22) the consequences of our minister getting a divorce.

The stress has been enhanced by the difficulty in being able to identify clearly and unequivocally what is the "liberal" or the "conservative" position on each of these issues, but that is the subject of the next chapter. Before moving to that, however, it may be useful to look briefly at four approaches for reducing the stress and minimizing the conflict.

The first, and for many the most difficult is to answer a simple question. The question is, What year is it? If we agree we are near the last days of the Christian era, we will respond differently than if we agree we are living within the very early centuries of what we assume will be at least a 50,000-year era. If we believe we are in the dying stages of the history of our denomination, we will bring a different perspective to these discussions than if we believe we are in the early formative years of the history of our denominational family. Is this year number 205 in a 250-year account or is it year number 205 in a 10,000-year history? That perspective makes a big difference.

Second, unlike the 1930s, this is now a society that offers people more than the traditional two choices of "take it or leave it." Much of the stress can be alleviated by intentionally giving people several positive choices. (See chapter 9.)

Third, if instead of viewing our denomination as a collection of identical service centers or our congregation as a gathering of people at the same point on a religious pilgrimage, if we can identify and affirm the diversity among the churches and among the members, it will be easier to understand why what is applauded by some is not acceptable to everyone else. The 1960s taught people how to be indignant. The great need for the balance of this century may be to teach people to be compassionate. When compassion is stronger than indignation, the stresses will be less pronounced.

Fourth, many of the stresses are a product of a world view that places at the top of the agenda the distribution of resources. The classic definition of politics is the allocation of scarce resources among competing demands. The stronger the scarcity interpretation of reality (shortage of talent, money, members, space, pastorates, prestige, power, missionaries, time, gifts), the more likely the decision-making process will be politicized.[25] A remarkably effective response to that sequence is to raise the expectations of what everyone is expected to contribute. The higher the expectations of what people can and will contribute in terms of talent, creativity, time, energy, sacrifices, money, commitment, and other resources, the higher the morale of the total group and the less pronounced the internal divisiveness. That is the message of the Christian faith, the story of the great schools, the theme of the great churches, and the glue of unified societies.

By contrast, raising the expectations of what people will be given invariably tends to politicize the decision-making processes, increase the stress level, and encourage divisive arguments about who is receiving a fair share and who is being cheated out of a fair share.

This is a central reason why the denomination that sees itself shrinking in numbers and resources naturally tends to suffer severe internal divisiveness as the decision-making processes become increasingly politicized.[26] That is one reason why it was easier to be a pastor back in the 1950s when nearly everyone agreed the pool of resources was increasing every year and would continue to grow. The greater the emphasis on receiving, rather than on contributing, the more likely the number of unhappy people will increase.

NOTES

1. For a discussion of the origin and various meanings given to "mainline" see Martin E. Marty, A Nation of Behavers (Chicago: University of Chicago Press, 1976), pp. 52-79.

2. Edwin Scott Gaustad, Historical Atlas of Religion in America (New York: Harper & Row, 1962), p. 4.

3. Ibid., p. 5.

4. Ibid., p. 26.

5. Ibid., pp. 42-111.

6. Bernard Quinn, et al., Churches and Church Membership in the United States 1980 (Atlanta, Ga.: Glenmary Research Center, 1982), pp. 1-3.

7. Will Herberg, Protestant-Catholic-Jew: An Essay in American Religious Sociology (New York: Doubleday & Co., 1955).

8. George Gallup, Jr., Religion in America, 50 Years 1935–1985 (Princeton, N.Y.: The Gallup Report, 1985), p. 27.

9. Reginald W. Bibby and Merlin B. Brinkerhoff, "The Circulation of the Saints: A Study of People Who Join Conservative Churches," *Journal for the Scientific Study of Religion*, vol. 12, 1973, pp. 173-83.

10. Dean M. Kelley, *Why Conservative Churches Are Growing* (New York: Harper & Row, 1972). This edition includes Kelley's reflections on the initial responses to his book.

11. Another insight-filled book on this same subject is Carl Dudley, *Where Have All Our People Gone?* (New York: The Pilgrim Press, 1979).

12. William H. Willimon and Robert L. Wilson, "The Seven Churches of Methodism" (unpublished manuscript, Duke Divinity School, 1985).

13. Perhaps the best consistent evidence of the gap between the people in the pew and the clergy is *The Presbyterian Panel*, published by the Research Unit of the Support Agency of the Presbyterian Church (U.S.A.). Repeatedly the poll reveals the members to be at the conservative end of the spectrum, the pastors closer to the middle, and the clergy in specialized ministries to be closer to the liberal end of that spectrum. For a succinct review and summary of the documentation of this "headquarters-pew" gap see A. James Reichley, *Religion in American Life* (Washington, D.C.: The Brookings Institution, 1985), pp. 264-85.

14. Tom W. Smith, "America's Religious Mosaic," *American Demographics*, June, 1984, pp. 19-23.

15. Ibid., p. 23.

16. Meyrowitz, *No Sense of Place*, pp. 115-49.

17. Arthur Hertzburg, "The Triumph of Jews," *New York Review of Books*, November 21, 1985, p. 21.

18. One of the influential books on this "melting-pot" or assimilation theory of the 1960s was Nathan Glazer and Daniel Patrick Moynihan, *Beyond the Melting Pot* (Cambridge, Mass.: The MIT Press and Harvard University Press, 1963). Mr. Moynihan has since publicly stated that the melting-pot theory no longer describes American society.

19. For an elaboration of this point see Lyle E. Schaller, *Growing Plans* (Nashville: Abingdon Press, 1983), pp. 140-45.

20. Smith, "America's Religious Mosaic," p. 23.

21. Wade Clark Roof, "Alienation and Apostacy," in *In Gods We Trust*, ed. Thomas Robbins and Dick Anthony (New Brunswick, N.J.: Transaction Books, 1981), pp. 87-99.

22. Andrew M. Greeley, "Religious Musical Chairs," in *In Gods We Trust*, ed. Thomas Robbins and Dick Anthony (New Brunswick, N.J.: Transaction Books, 1981), p. 104.

23. Smith, "America's Religious Mosaic," p. 22.

24. An excellent analysis of membership changes in the Catholic Church was sponsored by the National Conference of Catholic Bishops, directed by a Presbyterian minister and published by a liberal Protestant denomination's press. Dean R. Hoge, et al., *Converts, Dropouts, Returnees* (New York: The Pilgrim Press, 1981). See also Dean R. Hoge, "Interpreting Change in American Catholicism," *Review of Religious Research*, June, 1986, vol. 27, pp. 289-99.

25. A fascinating account of how the decision-making process in a liberal arts college can be politicized is Elizabeth Lilla, "Who's Afraid of Women's Studies?" *Commentary*, February, 1986, pp. 53-57.

26. An exceptionally comprehensive analysis of the growth of the evangelical wing of American Protestantism and the search for a new consensus in the mainline churches is Richard G. Hutcheson, Jr., *Mainline Churches and the Evangelicals* (Atlanta, Ga.: John Knox Press, 1981).

WHAT IS THE LIBERAL POSITION?

Back in the 1930s and 1940s the educational reformers of that era urged that small public school districts be consolidated into much larger units and they were remarkably successful. The number of elementary school buildings dropped from 238,306 in 1930 to 65,800 in 1971, and the number of school districts plunged from 118,368 in 1941 to 14,851 in 1982. The one-room, one-teacher public elementary school almost disappeared as the result of school consolidation and their numbers shrank from 149,282 in 1930 to 798 in the all-time low year of 1982. The liberal reformers had prevailed and public education in America was transformed in scarcely more than one generation. (This writer graduated from high school in a class of 12. Our youngest son graduated in a class with 440 other seniors.)

The conservatives who fought that war lost. They were overwhelmed by the more progressive educational leaders and the professionals of the day.

The liberal educators of today have rediscovered the values of the one-room school—the deliberate mixing of grades so older children teach younger pupils, a greater emphasis on the basics, the frequent opportunities for one-to-one interaction between the teacher and the student, the value of repetition, and the positive effects of peer pressure. The prominent child psychologist, Bruno Bettelheim has declared, "The one-room school was the best school we ever had."

The one-room school is making a comeback. In the fall of 1985 three new one-room public schools were opened in Montana. From rural Nebraska to uptown Manhattan the concept of a "community," which the one-room school epitomizes, is being seen as the best environment for learning. The big growth, of course, is in the hundreds of private one-room elementary schools operated by the Amish, the Hutterites, by a growing variety of fundamentalist churches in rural America, by liberal Protestant churches in the inner city, and by the founders of non-sectarian private schools.

What is the liberal position today in regard to the one-room, one-teacher elementary school?

One of the most remarkable achievements of the past 150 years in the United States has been the increase in the number of children enrolled in school. As recently as 1920 more than a fifth of all children ages 5-13 were not enrolled in school. By 1985 approximately 98 percent of the children in that age group were enrolled in school, thanks largely to the compulsory school attendance laws supported by, among others, liberal church leaders all across the nation. (Most of that remaining 2 percent were five-year-olds who were not enrolled in kindergarten.)

In recent years a rapidly growing number of parents have decided to teach their children at home in defiance of the compulsory school attendance laws. What is the liberal position on that question? To support the rights of parents, many of whom are very liberal on social, economic, and political questions? Or to support the enforcement of compulsory attendance laws?

The mid-1980s witnessed a remarkable level of agreement among liberals, neoliberals, conservatives, and neoconservatives *101* ▪

that the huge federal deficit posed a threat to future generations and taxes must be raised in order to maintain the level of public, social, and educational services demanded by the general public. The issue, however, was which elected officials should bear the onus of raising taxes. Local officials? State officials? Congress? What is the liberal position on that issue?

One interpretation of recent political history by a scholar who supported the Equal Rights Amendment to the Constitution is that the liberal support for abortion rights killed ERA.[1] That proposed amendment was approved, within two years of its introduction, by 33 states when the 1973 Supreme Court decision, *Roe vs. Wade,* established a constitutional right to abortion. In the next decade only three additional states approved ERA. Could a liberal both support the ERA and oppose abortion on demand? Could a liberal support the ERA and oppose the *Roe vs. Wade* decision, thus increasing the chances for approval of the ERA? The linking of the two may have been the primary reason that amendment was not approved.

In the 1970s the liberal position clearly called for the support of the antitrust laws and the divestiture of the American Telephone and Telegraph Company. The Bell system kept residential rates low by *(a)* charging businesses and long distance users above cost fees so residential charges could be kept below actual cost and *(b)* deferring many charges to future generations through thirty- and forty-year depreciation schedules so charges could be kept low for the current generation of uses. These facts were apart of the public record early in the trial. What should be the liberal position? To subsidize telephone use for low income residential users or to charge full cost? The liberal position of the 1970s was to eliminate the subsidy for low income residential users. The liberal position of the 1980s is to provide a subsidy for low income residential users.

In 1982, for the first time in its history, the College Entrance Examination Board (CEEB) released the data that revealed the median scores of black students were two hundred points below the median scores of white students on the Scholastic Aptitude Test. In the 1960s it was thought that it would be a racist position to reveal that gap. In the 1980s it was deemed to be racist to conceal it.

What is the liberal position on the military draft? To protest it as unfair, unjust, and a support of militarism? Or to endorse it on the grounds that without it the male enlisted personnel of the armed forces will be drawn largely from low income Blacks and whites? As the number of nineteen-year-olds drops from 4.2 million in 1980 to 3.1 million in 1992, that will become a major issue for church leaders.

What is the liberal position on keeping alive, as physicians are now able to do, the baby born with only a fragment of a brain who can never achieve any cognitive ability?[2] Should the hospitals keep that baby alive or allow it to die?

Frequently the choice is between equality or freedom. What is the liberal position?[3] Should freedom be sacrificed in the effort to promote equality? Or should the enhancement of individual freedom be the goal, even when part of the price is inequality?

This conflict between freedom and equality can be illustrated first by looking briefly at the issue of public versus nonpublic schools and second by subsequently examining the growing intergenerational conflict in American society. Both issues illustrate why it has become increasingly difficult to define a "liberal" or "conservative" position. Both issues also illustrate why it is more difficult to be a pastor today than it was in the 1950s.

Public Schools or Nonpublic Schools?

In 1848 the Reverend George H. Atkinson, a graduate of Andover Theological School and a Congregational minister, arrived in Oregon as a missionary for the American Home Missionary Society. His assignment was to create "churches, schools, whatever would benefit humanity—temperance, virtue, the industrial, mental, moral, and religious training of the young, and the establishment of society upon sound principles by means of institutions and religion and learning."

Within two years Atkinson had persuaded Governor Lane to *103* •

establish a public school system, drafted the governor's message to the legislature on that subject, written the basic legislation, seen it adopted by the legislature and signed into law by the governor, and been appointed the first school commissioner from Clackamas County. By the time he died in 1889 Atkinson was widely credited with being the father of the common school in Oregon.[4]

During his lifetime, and despite his role as a proponent of the common school, Atkinson founded private sectarian academies in Oregon and Washington. Drawing on the resources of their eastern supporters, Atkinson and his fellow Protestant ministers of the nineteenth century did not perceive a firm distinction between public and private schools. For Atkinson and many others the educational world was divided in two spheres. One contained God, the Bible, virtue, public schools, private academies, the Sunday school, Anglo-Saxon values, the church, the family, and the Protestant ethic. The other sphere contained the Roman Catholic Church, the devil, the Pope, immigrants from southern Europe, and the Catholic parochial schools. For example, in a speech he made to the National Education Association's convention in 1888 Atkinson urged educators to use the Bible as a textbook in the public schools and to teach Protestant values.

A broader example of this mixing of Protestant doctrine and public education can be seen in the work of the American Sunday School Union (ASSU) founded in 1824 to plant Sunday schools. This pan-Protestant organization frequently enlisted teachers from the free "weekday" public schools to teach the Sunday school held in that same building. The literature produced by this evangelical parachurch movement also was widely used in the public schools.[5]

During the eighteenth and nineteenth centuries, as public schools gradually began to replace the sectarian schools, the Protestant ethic and value system dominated the curriculum. With the increasing immigration of Roman Catholics to America in the second half of the nineteenth century this took on a bitter anti-Catholic tone. *The McGuffey Readers*, which sold an average of 1.5 million copies a year for nearly a century, contained a clear Protestant bias. *The New England Primer* was clearly an anti-Catholic reader.

As the Catholics lost the battle over which religious view should be taught in the public schools, they established their own parochial schools. In accordance with the dictum, "Every Catholic child in a Catholic school," adopted by the Third Plenary Council of Baltimore in 1884, the Catholic schools grew very rapidly in the East and Midwest. For a hundred years following 1860 close to 90 percent of all children in private schools were enrolled in Catholic parochial schools.

Concurrently with the growth of the Catholic parochial schools the value system taught in the public schools gradually changed from an evangelical Protestant emphasis to a nondenominational Christian value system to the current secular value system.[6]

When the public schools in the United States taught a religious value system that was unacceptable to Catholics, the Catholic Church in America concluded it had no alternative but to create its own private school system. This was met with great resistance by those who believed the public schools should teach "American values" and every child should be in a public school that taught those values. In the early years of the twentieth century a strong anti-private school movement set out to close all private schools including the German Lutheran schools. In 1922 in Oregon, where the common school movement had been founded by evangelical Protestants, a state-wide referendum, supported by the Ku Klux Klan, requiring children to attend only public schools was approved.

For more than two centuries a central issue has been to determine which value system should be taught in the public schools. When members of the mainline Protestant denominations controlled public policy, the decision was to teach an evangelical Protestant ethic in the public schools, so the Catholic structure created its own school system. While this was resisted by the proponents of equality, the emphasis on freedom allowed the Catholics to create their own educational system. As *105* ▪

the nation became more pluralistic, the shift was to teach a nondenominational Christian ethic. Thomas Jefferson, Horace Mann, Horace Bushnell, and George Cheever were among the early proponents of that change. The reformers of the early years of this century advocated the elimination of any religious teaching from the public schools. The 1962 decision by the United States Supreme Court that officially mandated prayer in a public school was unconstitutional is often cited as the end of an era. The public schools today, with a few exceptions in the South, no longer teach a Protestant value system.[7]

Thus, in one sense we are back to where we were in the pre-Civil War years. Evangelical Protestant parents still want their children to be educated in schools that teach a value system the parents can endorse. The two big differences are: (a) one hundred fifty years ago that could be and was accomplished through the growth of the public school system; today it is happening through the emergence of a series of networks of private Protestant schools and (b) in the nineteenth century Congregationalists, Baptist, Presbyterians, and Methodists (and some Lutherans) dominated the evangelical Protestant movement (which included the formation of the American Sunday School Union and the sending out of missionaries such as George Atkinson); today most of those who are organizing private Christian schools are not members of the mainline Protestant denominations.

What Are the Alternatives?

Today's parents who are dissatisfied with the value system taught in the public schools usually see themselves with five alternatives. One is to reform the public schools. These efforts have been unsuccessful and the number-one victims of the failure of the public school system currently are blacks in large central cities.

The second alternative has been followed by millions of white and a comparatively small number of black parents who have moved to suburbia where parents can exercise a substantial degree of influence over values and goals in the public schools and benefit from what some would call a tax-supported private school system.

A third alternative is followed by many Asian parents who are convinced that closely knit family ties and a strong and supportive home environment when combined with the "immigrant ethic" will enable their children to secure a good education in those same large urban school systems where poor whites, poor Hispanics, and poor blacks leave school without an adequate educational foundation.

The fourth alternative is home instruction. In 1975 an estimated 10,000 children were being taught at home by parents. By 1986 that number had grown to 160,000. Today nearly every state is prepared to grant official recognition for home instruction. This alternative is being followed in disproportionately large numbers by parents who identify themselves as "very liberal" or "very conservative." The growth of home instruction raises again the question, What is the liberal position on this issue? Which is the superior value, freedom or equality?

The fifth alternative can be seen in the increasing number of Protestant parents who are sending their children to private Christian schools. This increase is greatest among Baptist parents, both black and white.

What Is the Issue?

One of the reasons this is such a divisive question is the impossibility of obtaining an agreement on a definition of the central issue. This can be illustrated by seven different, but very common, definitions of the basic issue.

For at least a century a central theme of the attack on private schools has lifted up the theme of equality over the value of freedom. Frequently, this has been expressed in the claim that the physical facilities were substandard and/or the classes were too large and/or the teachers were not adequately trained. Most states enacted laws regulating those areas of concern, but some of *107* ▪

the legislation has been perceived as an effort to close the religious schools.

Back in the late 1950s and the 1960s the basic issue appeared to be very clear to many church leaders. Do you support the idea of racially integrated public schools? Or do you support the segregated private academies?

The majority of church leaders, both North and South, found it very easy to decide which position they supported. Some argued the dominant value was freedom while their opponents contended equality must override freedom. In the South, however, a substantial number of church leaders protested the issue was far more complicated.

Consistently parents have argued that the central issue is the value system taught in the public school, not the quality of the physical facilities or the training and certification of the teacher.[8]

In recent years a growing number of people have concluded that the central issue is money and economic issues. This frequently is offered as an argument against federally funded vouchers for parents who could take that voucher and cash it in at the school of their choice, either public or private. Opponents of vouchers contend this would starve low quality public schools. Should freedom or equality be the criterion for deciding that issue?

A fifth debate centers around the question of how to reform large and complex bureaucracies. Can that be accomplished from within? Or can it be accomplished only by external pressures? As the public schools gradually have evolved from educational institutions subsidized in part by the poorly paid teachers to employment centers for adults, the question is raised, How can you make the students, rather than the teachers and the administrators, the number-one client for that enterprise? No one has yet come forward with a workable solution. Some proponents of private schools contend that is the natural evolutionary pattern of any huge institution and the only way to have pupil-centered schools is to organize the emergence of new institutions. It is unrealistic to expect reform to come from within

▪ *108* a massive bureaucratic structure. Supporters of this view point out that most of the leaders in the recent efforts to reform the public schools have been governors and employers (consumers of the product), not professional educators (producers of the product).

When this becomes the definition of the issue, it is easy to agree that Martin Luther and John Wesley were right. It is much easier to start a new organization than to reform a long-established and very large institution!

Another group of people who are concerned about the growing underclass in America (see chapter 6) contend the central issue is to make the schools competent to inculcate the values that often are not taught in the home. This idea of making the public school a substitute for an inadequate home environment also was a major theme of urban reformers in the 1870–1920 era.

Perhaps the most widely neglected definition of the issue focuses on how the public schools are organized. In a brilliant book on leadership John P. Kotter argues that educators "have a large responsibility for the development of leadership capital," but they create a setting that makes students dependent on the teachers and minimizes helping the student learn how to relate to peers. Others argue the public schools teach, not democracy, but subservience to authority figures.

Once upon a time the American high school was organized to be separate from work and provide educational experiences prior to entrance into the labor force. The high school was preparation for adulthood. In recent years the high school has shared the student with the workplace as a larger and larger proportion of the sophomores, juniors, and seniors carry part-time jobs during the school year. The curriculum has been modified to train students to be consumers. For many students, if one counts the hours, the job, not the school, is the primary instructor. On that part-time job in the fast-food restaurant or as a clerk in the store the high school student learns that a job is something one must endure to produce money, not something to be enjoyed.

The students see school as something society has imposed on them, not as an opportunity to learn and practice critical thinking or to conceptualize abstract ideas or to enjoy creative tasks. *109* ▪

Consolidation made the typical high school too large to be a social center and as a decreasing proportion of students participate in those extracurricular activities that once were the incubator for the next generation of the nation's leaders, the paycheck has replaced the report card as the source of self-evaluation. The part-time unskilled job has replaced work on the student newspaper as a place to find meaning in life. When homework is perceived as optional, those who feel the most inadequate in verbal skills look for a part-time job to fill the hours while those with the greatest commitment and the highest skills benefit the most.[9]

As an increasing number of parents recognize the changed role of the large consolidated high school, more and more of them are deciding to make the financial sacrifices necessary to send their children to a high school that operates on a different set of basic organizing principles. Should they have the freedom to do that or does the demand for equality override the issue of freedom?

At this point the pastor also begins to see why it is more difficult to organize and direct a high school youth group than it was thirty years ago. It is a different world for high school students today!

An overlapping definition of the central issue in this debate can be traced back to the fact that during the past quarter century researchers have been presenting some very persuasive evidence that suggests the large consolidated high schools cause the student to feel unneeded. "A school should be small enough that students are not redundant."[10]

A review of the research on American high schools reported that a recurring theme of these research reports is that a four-year high school should have an enrollment of five hundred or less.[11]

The proponents of private schools frequently cite their relatively small enrollment as an asset, but rarely is size identified as the central issue in the debate, except by parents when administrators propose expanding an existing school in order to double the enrollment.

If agreement could be reached on a definition of the central issue in the debate over public vs. nonpublic schools, it would be ▪ *110* easier for churches to decide on their position. Perhaps the most significant achievement in recent years among the professional educators and policy-makers in the public vs. nonpublic school debate has been to encourage a higher level of tolerance of one another.[12] Thus far governmental agencies have made more progress in encouraging toleration of diversity than have the mainline denominations.

The Church Growth Dimension

One aspect of this debate that frequently is overlooked when denominational policy is being discussed concerns the role of the Christian day school as a vehicle for church growth. With the exception of a few denominations, such as the Lutheran Church—Missouri Synod, the Prebysterian Church in America, the Christian Reformed Church, and the Seventh-Day Adventists, this rarely receives serious attention.

The experiences of congregations in these and other denominations, as well as a growing number of nondenominational or independent churches suggest the Christian day school can be a remarkably effective vehicle for reaching at least five groups of people.

While they do not represent huge numbers, the first of these groups consists of families who include a developmentally handicapped or emotionally disturbed child who has not been able to adapt to life in the public schools. In scores of communities across the nation the public school system pays the tuition of children it is not able to accommodate when they enroll in a private school. The church-sponsored private school for these students can be an extraordinarily redemptive ministry.

The largest group, in proportion to their numbers in the general population, are black parents in families in which one or both parents are employed in the public school system and have strong upwardly mobile ambitions for their children. In several large cities a third to one-half of the parents employed in the public school send their children to private schools.

The largest group in actual numbers consists of those husband-wife couples, both black and white, who place a high *111* ▪

priority on their children's education. They want their children to be educated in a school that provides an overt teaching of Christian values, a disciplined environment, and commendable adult role models, is clearly pupil-centered rather than employee-dominated, and does not have a large enrollment. As one parent said, "I know that when my child encounters a member of the faculty or administration in the corridor, that adult will be able to address my child by name correctly. That is the best way to maintain discipline and it also reinforces my child's self-esteem and sense of importance as a person."

A fourth group that overlaps the second and third consists of both husband-wife couples and single parents who are willing to make substantial personal sacrifices in order to provide what they see as the best available educational experience for the child. A growing proportion of this group are the single parent mothers with only one or two children and an annual income over $20,000.

The fifth, and perhaps the most visible group, is composed of parents who state very clearly that the primary reason they send their children to a Christian day school is because they want their children taught (a) by a person who sees teaching as a Christian vocation rather than as a source of a paycheck, (b) in a classroom setting that openly teaches a Christian value system, and (c) in a setting in which the Bible is viewed and taught as the word of God, not simply as a piece of great literature.

Parents in all of these five groups recognize that in today's world most children between ages six and eighteen spend more time with teachers than with their parents. Therefore, they want their children in a school where the teachers are desirable role models, teach a value system that coincides with the value system of the parents, and see their calling as a Christian vocation.

The congregation seeking to reach and serve the people represented by one or more of these five groups may want to give serious consideration to organizing a Christian day school.

Who Attends?

For those concerned with (a) enabling their denomination to become more racially inclusive or (b) responding to the agenda of black parents or *(c)* the numerical growth of their own congregation, it may be of interest to look at the changing enrollment patterns. The most highly visible change has been the decline in the enrollment in Catholic schools from 5.6 million in 1965 to less than 3 million in 1985. The number of Catholic schools stood at 12,893 in 1960, rose to 13,292 in 1965, dropped to 9,559 in 1980, and to slightly under 9,300 in 1985. In 1965 89 percent of all students enrolled in private elementary and secondary schools were in Catholic schools. By 1985 that proportion had dropped to 64 percent. When allowance is made for the growing number of children enrolled in Catholic schools (especially black children) who do not come from Catholic families, a reasonable guess is that by 1986 Catholics accounted for less than one-half of the private school enrollment in the United States.

While the number of Catholic schools has declined from 13,292 in 1965 to 9,300 in 1985, the number of non-Catholic private elementary and secondary schools has doubled from fewer than 7,000 in 1965 to well over 15,000 in 1985. The enrollment in the private non-Catholic elementary and secondary schools had quadrupled from a half million in 1965 to approximately 2 million in 1985.

The third set of figures that should interest those who see the private Christian schools as racist academies is that between 1965 and 1985 the white enrollment in private schools dropped from approximately 6 million to 4 million while black enrollment increased from 230,000 in 1964 to nearly 400,000 in 1985. In California, for example, blacks are enrolled in private schools in twice their proportion of the state's population. In the District of Columbia black enrollment in private schools nearly doubled between 1970 and 1983.

These enrollment figures suggest Protestant church leaders, especially those seeking to reach black families, may want to take a second look at the Christian day school.

Which Side Appeals to You?

The larger debate, however, should be seen as no longer being a Catholic-Protestant issue or a public school-nonpublic school   *113* ▪

question or simply the segregationist-integrationist polarization, but rather as a serious discussion of which values are to be reinforced through education. It is a complex issue and it has become a basic dividing line in our society. This was illustrated by the national poll commissioned by the *New York Times* in 1983 asking adults whether they would send their children to neighborhood public schools if the cost of private schools was not a factor. Of those responding 37 percent chose the private school while only 53 percent chose the public school alternative. One-third of the families with an income under $10,000 annually chose the private school.[13]

This means, to go back to the central theme of this chapter, that it has become increasingly difficult to define the liberal position on public education. By and large the Democratic Party has come out on the side of the professional interest groups within the realm of public education. This was clearly the position of both Jimmy Carter and Walter Mondale. They became defenders of the status quo. Does that represent the liberal position of 1990?

Today's conservatives are the crusaders for reform and change, but they are divided into at least two camps. One group sees education as an extension of the family. Some in this group choose to keep their children out of school and educate them at home. Others want the public schools to reflect and proclaim the values of the parents. Another faction within this extraordinarily heterogeneous group is persuaded that the Christian day school is the answer, and their numbers include fundamentalist Protestant ministers, Pope John Paul II, many of the advocates of tax credits or vouchers, a growing number of black parents who are employed in the public school system, thousands of white working-class parents with upwardly mobile ambitions for their children, and many of the proponents of bilingual education.

The other group of advocates of radical change in the educational system are convinced this can be done in the public schools by installing a core curriculum, by establishing uniform standards, by raising the level of competence required of public

school teachers, and by placing a greater emphasis on the basic communication skills in the English language.[14] Their leaders tend to be the consumers of the "product" of the public schools and include governors, employers, university teachers of the liberal arts and humanities, a growing number of law enforcement officials, and social workers and ministers as well as some parents.

In summary, that version of the debate divides the world into three parts, the protectors of the status quo in public education, the parents, and the consumers of the products of the public schools. When you pick the group with which you identify, you can receive ready made arguments to support the position of that group, but it still will be hard to identify the "liberal" or "conservative" point of view.

A second way of looking at this issue is to ask, Which is the number-one goal, to preserve the public school system or to provide every child and youth with a meaningful and productive educational experience? Once upon a time those two goals were perceived as coterminous. Today they are viewed by many as conflicting objectives that may be mutually exclusive.

A third point of view that cannot be ignored because it has been attracting influential adherents in recent years is that the conflicting interest groups, ranging from textbook publishers to teachers' unions to state boards of public instruction, each with a major stake in the public schools, now neutralize one another. This point of view insists that volunteer reform will have little impact. The only road to reform, innovation, and improvement will come when the ground rules are changed so economic rather than political pressures dominate the decision-making processes. This means economically rewarding the entrepreneurial administrators who create the best schools, as measured by what happens to the students.[15] This point of view clearly places freedom above equality in the hierarchy of values. Is that a liberal or a conservative position?

Another perspective for looking at this issue is in terms of the change from the day when it was widely understood that the older generation willingly made sacrifices on behalf of a younger generation to today when it is increasingly assumed that the *115* ▪

younger generation should make sacrifices on behalf of an older generation.

From Obligations to Adversaries

> Among the first objects of those who wish well to national prosperity, to encourage and support the principles of religion and morality, and early to place the youth under the forming hand of society, that by instruction they may be moulded to the love of virtue and good order.

This is quoted from the preamble of the act of the legislature of Georgia, adopted in 1785, that chartered the University of Georgia. This was the first charter issued in the United States for a state university.

For most of its history a central value in the United States has been for each generation to seek to improve the lot of succeeding generations. The Georgia legislature obviously was motivated by a concern for future generations when that first state university was chartered.

For generations, older people sacrificed on behalf of their children's future. Until recently it was assumed that parents would scrimp, sacrifice, and save to send their children to college. Mothers went back to work, fathers found a second job, vacations were postponed, and a secondhand car was purchased instead of a new one in order for Johnny or Mary to go off to college.

Back in the 1950s the typical pattern for the new congregation was to postpone for a decade or two construction of the permanent sanctuary in order to be able to build attractive classrooms for the children's division of the Sunday school. As the congregation grew in size and the program staff was expanded, the first positions to be added to the payroll often were a youth director and/or a director of children's ministries.

Relatively large proportions of both state and municipal budgets of the 1950s were allocated to programs for children and youth including education, recreation, and the care of children without parents.

■ *116*   One of the most remarkable responses by American churches to a presidential plea came following Abraham Lincoln's Second Inaugural Address. On March 4, 1865, Lincoln asked, "With malice toward none, with charity for all, with firmness in the right as God gives us to see the right, let us strive on to finish the work we are in, to bind up the nation's wounds, to care for him who shall have borne the battle and for his widow and his orphan." The churches responded by founding scores of orphanages, many of which still exist as homes for emotionally disturbed or developmentally disabled children. The adults of that day were asked to sacrifice on behalf of these children.

The past three decades have brought a revolutionary shift in this concept of intergenerational obligations. The historic pattern placed the primary burden on the older generation of sacrificing for the younger generation. The major exception to that pattern could be seen in homes where the aging grandparents lived with their children, or a couple took in and cared for an elderly relative. The dominant pattern, however, called for older people to sacrifice on behalf of younger people.

One illustration of that was the federal regulation that placed a ceiling on the interest financial institutions could pay savers. Savers come in disproportionately large numbers from among mature adults while borrowers come in disproportionately large numbers from among a younger generation. This policy meant that people born before 1900 and in the early years of the twentieth century subsidized the loans that fueled the housing boom and the new church construction boom of the 1950s and early 1960s. That national policy was reversed in the 1980s.

A parallel illustration, for those with long memories, were the discounts offered by trains, airlines, theaters, schools, motels, and buses for children. Today most of the widely advertized discounts are for senior citizens.

Today American society is being reorganized on the principle that younger people should sacrifice on behalf of an older generation. The prime illustrations of this, of course, are Social Security, Medicare, and federal guarantees of private pensions. Another example of the current expectation that younger people will subsidize older people is the change in financing the repairs *117* ▪

of the nation's highways and bridges. Until recently these repairs were financed out of user taxes, with the gasoline tax being the major source of revenue. Today many states and municipalities are selling bonds, to be retired by future generations, to pay for highway improvements to be enjoyed by today's users. Today's children will be expected to pay for fixing the potholes created by their parents' driving in order to avoid raising taxes on those parents.

Part of the argument for this shift in intergenerational obligations was that aging Americans had sacrificed in their working years on behalf of a younger generation and it was now time to compensate the elderly for their sacrifices. This also was justified on the premise that "elderly" and "poor" frequently were synonyms. The political attractiveness of this change lay in the combination of (a) the increased life expectancy of Americans, (b) more voters of 1988 being born in the 1910–25 era than were born in the 1930–45 era, and (c) the fact that persons age fifty and over are far more likely to vote in congressional and presidential elections than are persons under age thirty.

The Churches Follow the Trend

In the 1960s, again in response to a plea from the federal government, the churches began to construct and manage housing projects for the elderly rather than create new facilities for children. The capital expenditures by the churches in the 1970s and 1980s were more likely to be for better facilities for adults than rooms for children. The weekday preschool program that filled so many church rooms from Monday to Friday during the 1960s and 1970s was being supplanted in the 1980s by the aerobic dance classes for adults. The new wave for the 1990s will be the adult day care center. The focal point for the weekday nursery school of the 1970s was the child. The number-one client for the day care centers of the 1980s is the middle- and upper-income mother, and the child is the number-two client.

This shift in who benefits from intergenerational obligations from the younger to the older was facilitated by the aging of the membership in several denominations, most notably the former United Presbyterian Church, The United Methodist Church, and the Christian Church (Disciples of Christ). In each of these three denominations the process for the selection of policy-makers was designed to increase the influence of mature adults, and thus it was easier to reverse the old priorities.

What Follows Success?

While the impact of the Great Society programs of the 1960s on blacks, on families on welfare, and on the younger poor is still widely and vigorously disputed,[16] it is hard to argue that federal programs have not benefited the elderly. The average after-tax per capita income of persons over age 65 is now 13 percent higher than it is for the rest of the American population. Two-thirds of all couples in which the head of the household is past 65 own their own home without any mortgage. Americans past 50 years of age control 7 trillion dollars worth of wealth or more than two-thirds of the net worth of all households in the United States. In 1986 the 12 percent of the American population age 65 and over received over one-half of all governmental expenditures for social services. The Social Security system alone transfers over $210 billion every year from the young to the old. In 1970 an elderly person was more likely than a child to be living in poverty. By 1986 that had changed so that a child was 6 times more likely to be living in poverty than a person over 65. Over half of all discretionary income is now received by households headed by someone over 50. The 1986 federal budget called for domestic transfer payments, most of which go to the elderly, of $375 billion, 30 percent above the 1980 budget, after allowing for inflation. In 1983 the median household income in the United States was $20,873 per year, but one-fourth of all Social Security payments in 1983 went to families with total income over $25,000 annually. In 1900 two-thirds of all Americans over 65 lived with relatives; in 1985 84 percent lived by themselves. The elderly today not only are better off financially than ever before in American history, they are financially better off than the rest of the population. Nearly one-half of all women, age 65 and over, who are widowed, divorced, or never married have their own private pension. Nearly two-thirds of all elderly female heads of household own their own homes, according to the Bureau of the Census. In 1973, before this huge increase in the income of the elderly, persons age 65 and over saved 15 percent of their income. By 1985 their savings had dropped to less than 6 percent of their income. Why save for the benefit of the next generation? They also are far better off in terms of health than their counterparts of a generation ago.

This reversal of the historic pattern in which older people sacrifice on behalf of younger people has produced a generation of the healthiest and wealthiest mature adults in American history.

The Emergence of Adversarial Relationships

This reversal of intergenerational obligations also has produced some other consequences that inevitably will enhance the adversarial relationship between generations. This can be illustrated by several interesting contemporary incidents and statistics.

In 1985 the taxpayers of California were paying Governor George Deukmejian a salary of $49,100. They were also paying former Governor Edmund G. (Pat) Brown a pension of $62,314 that was scheduled to rise to $107,880 in 1986. A member of the California Board of Equalization, who received a salary of $73,780 a year in his last year in office, was scheduled to receive an annual pension of $187,839 upon retirement.[17] The taxpayers of 1999 will have to pay for the pensions that were promised these elected officials by an older generation of voters.

In Birmingham, Alabama, the older workers at a steel plant voted against a proposed union contract favored by the younger workers. The terms of the existing contract meant that if the plant closed they would be financially better off in retirement than they would be if they continued working under the new contract. The younger workers voted for a more moderate contract, but lost their jobs when the proposed contract was rejected and the plant closed.

In 1900 63 percent of all American males past the age of 65 were still in the work force. By 1985 that figure had dropped to 15 percent. As recently as 1950 87 percent of all men age 55-64 were still working. By 1982 that had dropped to 70 percent.[18] The General Accounting Office reported that by 1983 the median age for retirement was 62 years and that three-quarters of those drawing Social Security benefits for the first time in 1981 were under 65. One quarter of all men in the 55-59 age bracket identify themselves as retired. This combination of (a) earlier retirement, (b) longer life expectancy, (c) increased benefits for the retired, and (d) rising health costs produced an estimate by a former chief actuary for the Social Security Administration that in the year 2050 41 percent of all compensation for all workers will have to be siphoned off for Social Security taxes and other benefits for the elderly.

The new contract signed by major league baseball players in the summer of 1985 guarantees an annual pension of over $90,000 for the player who retires with 10 years of major league experience. It did not, however, provide any pension benefits for an earlier generation of players who retired before the pension system was created. The argument was today's generation of baseball players do not have any obligation to those earlier generations who made the game the national pastime. The players could argue they were observing the old value of older people sacrificing for a younger generation.

While a number of young couples in which the husband is an enlisted man in the United States Army live in near poverty, a report by the Center on Budget and Policy Priorities reported that in 1982 60 percent of the military pension benefits go to retired military personnel who are among the wealthiest 20 percent of all American households.[19]

After allowing for the impact of inflation, the average Social Security check increased by 25 percent between 1970 and 1985 while the dollar amount of the average check for Aid to Families with Dependent Children (AFDC) dropped by a third. The *121* ▪

national policy favors the retiree who winters in the Sunbelt and expects the twenty-nine-year-old grandmother (see chapter 6) to pull herself up by the bootstraps.

Perhaps the most useful statistical indicator of the demographic pressures behind these intergenerational changes can be summarized by two simple statements. In 1940 only 37 percent of all 50-year-old women had a living mother, but by 1980 that proportion had risen to 65 percent. Second, in 1900 the average woman spent 19 years as the mother of a dependent child, but only 9 years as the daughter of a dependent parent. In 1985 the average woman spent 18 years of her life as the daughter of an elderly parent. Dozens of nursing homes today have as residents the elderly parent and the elderly daughter of that parent.

Consequences and Questions

It would be impossible for a society to experience such a revolutionary change in priorities without enormous consequences. Several of these help explain why it is more difficult to be a leader in the churches today as conflicts over priorities dominate the agenda and pit the wants of one generation against the needs of another generation.

One reason it is so difficult is that the time frame for planning has been shortened. In the business world the pressure is to be able to show the elderly investors and the directors of the pension funds that this company will show an improvement in profits this quarter regardless of the impact on the company five years hence.

As society has become "results oriented," the pressures have increased to sacrifice long-term benefits in favor of short-term gains. That generalization applies to the president of the business as well as to the president of the labor union who is negotiating a new contract. It applies to the research departments in corporations, medical schools, and governments. It applies to the policy-makers who set the payout schedules for Social Security and to the coaches recruiting athletes for the university football team. In the 1950s a mortgage was something to be paid off; today a mortgage is something one holds while waiting to trade it in on a new mortgage.

The fifty-nine-year-old grandparent in 1933 saved to help pay for the college education of the twelve-year-old grandson. Today that grandson, now retired, tours the national parks in a recreational vehicle with a sign on the back that proclaims, "We're spending our children's inheritance."

"Instant gratification" has become a contemporary cliché that explains both the television commercial that advises, "You only go around once," and the increasing number of twenty-nine-year-old grandmothers.

This change in the nature of intergenerational obligations also helps explain why in several denominations the allocations of member contributions for ministerial pensions has increased at a far faster rate than the increase in member contributions for world missions.

This change in the intergenerational obligations also helped explain the sharp decrease in the number of new congregations organized for Anglos by several mainline Protestant denominations after 1960. The primary beneficiaries of new church development, except for a few places in the Sunbelt, are younger adults. Most of the initial financial costs are borne by older members of long-established congregations.* This is an acting out of the traditional emphasis on older people sacrificing on behalf of the next generation. The decline in new church development coincided with the change in priorities as more resources were allocated for taking care of people who had passed their sixtieth birthday.

Space does not permit a thorough analysis of all the many consequences of this change; however, five specific ones can be lifted up here to illustrate the theme that life for a church leader is more difficult today than it was in the 1950s.

---

*The two big exceptions to that generalization are: (a) those denominations in which new congregations covenant to start a new mission within a decade or less, and (b) those denominations that are concentrating on starting largely or completely unsubsidized new churches to reach blacks, the new immigrants, and lower and lower-middle income Anglos.

Perhaps the most obvious and measurable of these changes concerns new church development. This change can be summarized by the question, Who will subsidize the interest rate for new church development? Back in the 1950s and 1960s national policy called for savers, mostly older people, to subsidize borrowers. Federal regulations placed a comparatively low ceiling on interest rates that could be paid savers. Thus the new congregation of the early 1950s could borrow $100,000 for construction of a new building and the interest on that loan might average approximately $450 a month. The cost of constructing an equivalent building in 1986 was approximately 5 times the 1953 cost. Thus, a mortgage for $500,000 in 1986 at 10 percent interest would require over $4,000 a month in interest payments, approximately 9 times the 1953 figure. If one assumes the median income of the families in a new congregation had climbed at the same pace as median family incomes for the American population—from approximately $4,400 in 1953 to approximately $26,000 in 1986—it becomes clear the rise in interest costs has had a serious impact. Interest costs have increased ninefold while income is only 6 times the 1953 figure.

When the cost of the land is added to the equation, the burden on the new mission is even more onerous. The new congregation of 1953 may have purchased a three-acre site—the recommended size in 1953—for $10,000. The interest on that loan at 6 percent was only $50 a month. By 1986 experience indicated the minimum sized parcel of land for a new church should be five acres, not three. (As the years have passed, the decreased size of the average family and the sharp increase in the number of one- and two-person households means it now requires more cars to bring the same number of people.) This five-acre parcel of land may have cost $150,000 in 1986. The interest on that loan at 10 percent comes out to $1,250 a month—compared to the $50 a month for the new mission of 1953.

The savers of 1953 subsidized that 6 percent interest rate. Who will subsidize the interest costs for the new churches to be organized in the remaining years of this century? It is reasonably safe to predict the savers of today are not interested in subsidizing today's borrowers! Few of the retirees in Arizona who received a 15 percent interest rate on their certificate of deposit purchased in 1981 are eager to loan money at an interest rate of 4 or 5 percent for new church development in 1989.

This scenario is further complicated by the erosion of denominational loyalties. Back in 1953 it was easier to persuade other congregations of that same denomination to pick up the cost of that $10,000 site and make an outright gift to the new mission. When the new congregation founded in 1953 is approached to help pay the cost of new church development, one response may be, "Well, we did receive $10,000 toward the purchase of our land, so we'll contribute $10,000 toward the purchase of a site for another new church." A less generous response may be, "We paid for our land and building. Why can't they pay for theirs?" In a few cases the response will be, "We no longer belong to that denomination."

A second, and far more common question that illustrates the change in intergenerational obligations is, We are now large enough in size and our program is so much more complex today than it was twenty years ago that we must expand our paid program staff. What should we add? Thirty-five years ago the chances were good that the debate would have been between a youth director and a director of Christian education specializing in children's ministries.

Today one group may urge adding a trained pastoral counselor to the staff, others want someone who can build and oversee a ministry with formerly married adults, a few will insist the most urgent need is for someone to work with children, more will favor a youth director, some will place a part-time, semi-retired minister of visitation who will call on shut-ins at the top of the priority list. A few will plead for hiring someone to organize and direct an adult day care for people in the earlier stages of Alzheimer's disease, some may plead for a part-time church nurse,[20] several will urge replacing the part-time choir director with a full-time minister of music, someone else may advocate bringing a business administrator in to free more of the pastor's time for pastoral work, several will urge hiring someone to organize more programs for senior *125* •

citizens, a couple of others may support the case for filling that vacancy with a recreation leader while the pastor really would like an associate who is a generalist.

Usually it is more difficult to choose from among ten or twelve courses of action, each of which has a strong lobby, than it is to choose between two alternatives. That scenario also is complicated by the question of which generation of members will be the winner. It was easier when the choice was between a youth director and a children's worker and all adults agreed the next generation deserved top priority.

A third question is reflected in the problem of setting the priorities for capital improvements. Which is the higher priority, renovating the women's rest room or modernizing the nursery? Remodeling the parlor or creating a youth room? Installing an elevator or buying a bus for youth ministries? Renovating the sanctuary or remodeling the children's wing? Fencing in that last parcel of grass for a playground for children or paving it to increase the off-street parking? Buying new furniture and a new carpet for that room used by the largest adult Sunday school class in the church or remodeling the room for four- and five-year-olds? If we divide that huge room at the end of the hall on the second floor, who will have the first claim on that space? As intergenerational rivalries have replaced the sense of intergenerational obligations, the pastor finds it difficult to please everyone.

A fourth and parallel question has arisen in many regional judicatories. If a new staff position is to be added, should the top priority be to find someone to specialize in new church development? Or in helping churches develop an adult day care center? Or to expand the camping and travel program for children and youth? Or to help churches create new ministries with mature adults? Or to concentrate on community affairs and social action? Or are we looking for someone who will call on the mature members and encourage them to remember their churches and/or our denomination in their will? Which generation will receive most of the new staff person's time?

A fifth consequence of this change in the orientation of our society is more subtle and can be seen in the reward system for volunteers. Readers with reasonably long memories can remember when the typical Protestant congregation had two focal points for lay volunteers. One consisted of that network of administrative and program committees that were responsible for the general oversight of congregational life. Some people volunteered to serve on those committees because they enjoyed it, others because it was a chance to meet and make new friends and/or to learn new skills, and many volunteered out of a sense of obligation, "Someone has to do it and I guess it's my turn." The second focal point was staffing the Sunday school. Some teachers volunteered out of a sense of parental obligation, a few because they felt it kept them young and active, and many because they felt a sense of obligation to that next generation.

Recent years have brought a tremendous increase in the number of adult-oriented groups and classes in the churches ranging from adult Bible study classes to drama clubs to adult handbell choirs to book study circles to aerobic dance classes to softball teams to marriage enrichment retreats to Mothers' Clubs to trips to the Holy Land to theater parties to co-ed volleyball leagues to parenting classes to investment seminars. When asked why they allocate time and energy (and frequently substantial amounts of money) to participate in these and similar events, their responses are more likely to cluster around the theme, "Because I enjoy it," rather than around the explanation, "I feel an obligation to help others."

This is simply a reflection of the change that has been taking place in all of American society. When asked how they spend their discretionary time, today's adults are far more likely to list self-help classes, jogging, recreation, shopping, traveling, and watching television than participation in the traditional clubs, organizations, and programs of yesteryear that were organized so that volunteers could help others in general and a younger generation in particular.

Those responsible for enlisting volunteers in programs designed to help a younger generation have a far more difficult task than their counterparts of the 1950s.

The Big Issue

The biggest, and potentially most divisive, issue concerns the prophetic voices of the churches. In seeking to influence public and denominational policy, what should be the position of the churches on this change in intergenerational obligations? This issue can be illustrated by looking briefly at a dozen specific questions.

1. On January 14, 1986, a lawsuit was filed in federal court in Washington, D.C., by two state attorney generals, one Democratic and one Republican, and the National Taxpayers Union, charging that the deficit spending policies of the federal government in the 1980s benefit today's adults at the expense of the youth and children of today who will have to bear the burden of the interest charges on that debt. The suit argued that by forcing the children of today to assume responsibility for the debts incurred by today's fiscally irresponsible adults, the children are being denied their constitutional right to the equal protection of the laws under the Constitution. The suit argued that since children cannot vote, this constitutes "fiscal child abuse."

What is the appropriate response of the churches to this issue?*

2. An increasing number of union contracts call for a two-tier salary schedule. New employees are hired on a lower salary schedule than the one that applies to long tenure employees. In some contracts the new employees always will be paid at a lower level and never will reach parity with the older generation of employees.

What should be the position of the churches in two-tier salary schedules? Should they be adopted in denominational agencies? If not, should the churches affirm their use elsewhere?

3. Should Social Security benefits be taxed? Recently the federal government began to tax one-half of the Social Security benefits received by individuals and couples above a certain

---

*When studying this issue, it should be noted that only since 1976 has the United States Treasury been issuing a consolidated financial statement. The statement for the fiscal year ending September 30, 1984, revealed that federal liabilities, including accrued pension and Social Security obligations and borrowing from the public stood at 4.7 trillion dollars while assets totaled 9 trillion dollars for an accumulated position of 3.8 trillion dollars in net liabilities.

income level. The justification was *(a)* the median income of those recipients was above the median income of the American population and *(b)* the employer had contributed one-half of the payments on behalf of that employee. Since the employee does not pay federal income taxes on those employer contributions, it is only fair that one-half of the benefits received by the recipients should be taxed.

Inasmuch as ministers have been classified for Social Security purposes as "self-employed," and therefore pay a higher rate of Social Security tax, should one-half of the Social Security benefits received by the clergy and other formerly self-employed retirees be exempt from that tax? Since the recipient paid federal income taxes on the entire contribution, should there be a special provision for the retiree who formerly was self-employed? Or should *all* benefits be taxed on the assumption that the average retiree's benefits from Social Security far exceed what both the recipient and the employer paid into the fund including the accrued interest?

Will the churches side with the generation paying Social Security taxes or the generation receiving the benefits?

4. Should a means test be used to determine who receives Social Security benefits? Perhaps one-third of the recipients desperately need those checks, at least a fourth do not need Social Security benefits, and the 40 percent in the middle may find that Social Security makes the difference between comfort and "just getting by."

Or, to state it more precisely, in 1984 the elderly received $235 billion (an average of $8,000 per person) of the $320 billion the federal government transferred from one group of people to another group of citizens. While the child population is double the size of the elderly population, Social Security payments were ten times as much as was paid for Aid to Families with Dependent Children (AFDC) in 1984. Should a smaller proportion of those transfer payments be made to the elderly so a larger proportion can be used to help the children and youth who will constitute tomorrow's generation of adults?*

---

*In 1986 the federal budget included a 30 percent increase in transfer payments, after allowing for inflation, over the amount in the 1980–81 federal budget.

5. Should national policy be designed to encourage people to save or to spend?

The needs analysis system used by most colleges and universities to determine which students will receive financial aid is biased in favor of the family that buys a large house with big mortgage payments and takes costly vacations every year. It is biased against the family that buys a small house, limits vacation expenditures, and lives very frugally in order to save for their children's college expenses.[21]

The decision to tax one-half of the Social Security benefits received by couples and individuals above a certain income level stands out as a clear economic incentive to spend rather than to save.

Should the churches attempt to influence national policy on this question?

6. According to a 1980 survey by the United States Department of Housing and Urban Development approximately one-quarter of all rental units are not available to families with children. Dozens of residential communities have been developed in the South and West which categorically prohibit all children under age twelve or eighteen.

Should the churches take a position on this issue as these prohibitions are challenged in the courts?

7. Unquestionably the most sensitive of these issues arises from the fact that medical science now is able to prolong the life of the terminally ill person for months and perhaps even years.

If it costs an average of $700 to $2,000 a day to prolong the life of a terminally ill person for another 60 days, should that be done? Who will pay that $60,000 to $100,000? Who will make the decision on what should be done?

In 1985 the American population included 6 million people age 80 and over. That number will rise to 10 million by the year 2000.

Should the churches support those who want to make it easier for the terminally ill to choose death? Or should the churches support those who insist the dying must be kept alive, even against their own wishes, for as long as is scientifically possible?

Should public expenditures for children, for education, and

for job training be reduced so the number could be 12 million in the year 2000 instead of 10 million? Will the votes of the 44 million recipients of Social Security in the year 2000 (compared to 26 million beneficiaries in 1970) offset the appeal of the 44 million children under age thirteen in 2000, none of whom will be able to vote? Will the churches speak on behalf of those who can vote or on behalf of those who are too young to vote?

8. Two contradictory trends already are having an impact on the system for ministerial placement and retirement.

One trend, as has been pointed out before, is earlier retirement. The median age of retirement in the private sector was sixty-two years in 1985 according to the Bureau of Labor Statistics. The other trend is that because of better health and increased life expectancy many people are choosing to work until age seventy or older.

In those denominations and regional judicatories that are now experiencing a surplus of pastors and seminary graduates and a shortage of pastorates, what should be the policy?

Should veteran ministers be encouraged, perhaps by supplementing their Social Security and pension income, to retire early? Should ministers be encouraged to continue to serve after reaching the age of sixty-five? Should an aggressive new church development program be launched to create a need for more pastors? Should the larger congregations that have been replacing ordained staff members with lay paraprofessionals (see chapter 7) be discouraged from doing that in order to create more positions for seminary graduates? Or should persons contemplating going into the ministry be discouraged with warnings of a shortage of jobs?

That is a far more difficult question for policy-makers to resolve than the problems their counterparts faced in the 1950s when there was a shortage of pastors!

9. In the 1860s and 1870s the churches built orphanages. A century later the churches constructed housing complexes for the elderly. In the 1980s the call was to create day care centers for the benefit of the working mother.

Geriatric psychologists estimate that mental impairment doubles in frequency every five years after age sixty-five. The *131* •

symptoms are present in over 1 percent of the sixty-five-year-olds, nearly 3 percent of the seventy-year-olds, close to 6 percent of the seventy-five-year-olds, 12 percent of the eighty-year-olds, and at least a fourth of the eighty-five-year-olds.

Should the big new program for the churches for the 1990s be adult day care centers for the closely supervised care of the elderly who need that assistance and for the benefit of their close relatives who need relief from the twenty-four-hour-a-day burden?

Or should that space and those resources be devoted to the enrichment of the young children born during the second biggest baby boom in American history that began in 1977 and is expected to last until 1990?

Very few congregations can do both. Which should be the higher priority? If the answer is, "Let some congregations focus on children and encourage others to open and operate adult day care centers," it may be important to look at the probable consequences. The congregation that includes the Early Childhood Development Center as part of its ministry with families that include preschool children is far more likely to experience numerical growth and to attract a new generation of younger members than the congregation that subsidizes and staffs an adult day care center. That could influence how congregational leaders respond to that set of choices. What is the primary value? Responding to an unmet need? Or institutional survival? Or taking care of the longtime members and their dependents?

10. Those with long memories may recall the promises of the mid-1960s of a "peace dividend." It was assumed that if the conflict in Vietnam could be brought to an end, the federal government would have huge financial resources available that could be redirected from military to social needs.

President Kennedy's last budget allocated three dollars to military expenditures for every dollar for social programs. The 1985 federal budget called for one dollar for the military for every two dollars for social programs and transfer payments. The "peace dividend" was paid. A rough estimate is that close to half of it went to state and local governments as revenue sharing, a huge chunk of it went to increase Social Security payments, perhaps a third of it paid interest on the national debt because of the rise in interest rates, a fifth of it was allocated as aid to higher education, including aid to students, a third of the peace dividend went to farmers, at least 200 percent went to pay the unanticipated high costs of Medicare, and perhaps a tenth of it went to increase benefits for children. The net result, of course, was years of unprecedented high deficits by the federal government.

Should the churches seek to change the allocation of the peace dividend? If so, should fairness or equality or precedents or votes be the primary criterion? Which generation should receive the larger share? Those born before 1930? Or those born after 1975?[22]

11. For many residents of rural America the big change brought by the 1980s was the new wave of consolidation of farms. The farm population dropped from over 32 million in 1935 to 19 million in 1955 to slightly under 9 million in 1975 to 5 million in 1986. More significant, the number of farms in the United States dropped sharply. In 1880, for the first time in American history, the number of farms passed the 4 million mark and by 1900 that number had jumped to 5.7 million. For the next 50 years the number of farms ranged between a low of 5.7 million and the high of 6.8 million reached in 1935. Farming and farm families were the stable foundation of the economy of rural America as the movement westward to the frontier was replaced by the urbanization of the nation. Tens of thousands of one-room schools, small Protestant churches, and retail stores were built to service that farm economy.

Between 1950 and 1969 the number of farms had been reduced by more than one-half to 2.7 million. Between 1969 and 1986 that number had been reduced once again by nearly one-half.

What should be the position of the churches as efforts are undertaken to rebuild the economic base of these rural communities where agriculture can support no more than one-fourth, or perhaps only one-seventh, as many people as it did in 1955?

The popular call, of course, is to recruit employers who will   *133* ▪

create the jobs that "will help us keep our young people here." The search is for "high tech" or "clean" industries that will provide these jobs.

Should the clergy and the churches concentrate their resources in helping recruit new industry? Or would it be more productive to pursue other courses of action to expand the economic base of what once were farming communities? In many rural communities the comparatively low cost of housing makes them attractive retirement centers. The retired couple can sell their home in a metropolitan county, purchase a house of equivalent size and quality in one of these rural communities and have $40,000 to $100,000 left to invest to supplement their income. The farms and the factories, which once were the basic components of the local economy, could be replaced by the post office which delivers the Social Security, pension, interest, dividend, and disability checks. In some of these communities the post office already is bringing in more "outside" money to the local economy than the farms and factories combined. Is that a future the churches can endorse?

In other communities the tourist industry offers promise as vacations become longer, as retirement comes earlier, and as more and more families own and use two homes. Most of the jobs created by the tourist industry, however, are at the low end of the wage scale and many are seasonal. Many of these jobs, however, may be more attractive to the semi-retired than to teenagers or to young adults.

A third alternative, which already is becoming more and more visible, is built on five assets to be found in many rural communities. These are: (a) low land costs, (b) comparatively low construction costs, (c) a large supply of caring people with a strong work ethic who want to continue to live and work in that community, (d) a surplus of managerial capability, and (e) good transportation to metropolitan centers only two or three hours away. This helps explain the increase in the number of nursing homes being constructed in rural communities. Frequently they are able to offer better care at a substantially lower cost than the nursing homes located in larger cities. The employees really care for the residents, and they learn and remember the names, idiosyncrasies, and unique needs of each of the residents. The staff earns the respect and admiration of the members of the families of the residents. Both the residents and their families appreciate the love, the concern, the dedication, and the continuity of the staff.

Should denominational and congregational leaders support and encourage efforts to build more nursing homes in rural America? Should pastors be encouraged to learn the skills necessary to organize and operate a nursing home? Should congregations take on the responsibility of building nursing homes in rural America?

All three of these alternatives illustrate the intergenerational issue. Should the churches in rural America concentrate their efforts and resources on increasing the proportion of the population born before 1935? That would be the result of emphasizing the role of these ex-farming communities as retirement centers or as tourist attractions or as places to locate new nursing homes? Or should the churches ally themselves with those who believe the high tech industries will leave the university centers for rural America and that light industry is the way to "keep our people here in this community"? Will the primary goal to be retain and welcome adults who have celebrated their fiftieth birthday? Or to build the future on the generation born after 1970? What is the liberal position on that choice? What is the conservative position?

12. Finally, as adversary relationships replace the traditional definition of intergenerational obligations, the churches need to examine their position on the general spread of adversary relationships in the entire society.

Examples include: *(a)* the relationships between major league baseball owners and players, *(b)* the physician-patient relationship, *(c)* the competition between the elderly and the young for a larger share of the transfer payments in the federal budget, *(d)* the relationships between congregations and the national (or regional) denominational headquarters, *(e)* the deteriorating relationships between taxpayers and the Internal Revenue

Service, (f) the stance of many mainline Protestant leaders toward the federal government, (g) the internal adversary relationships that dominated the Lutheran Church—Missouri Synod in the late 1960s and 1970s, (h) the struggle between the "conservatives" and "moderates" in the Southern Baptist Convention in the 1980s, and (i) the predictable adversarial relationship that normally evolves between the recipient of any financial subsidy and the source of that subsidy.

In seeking to understand the context for these deepening adversarial relationships, it may be useful to keep in mind four basic generalizations:

1. Historically, nearly all religious movements have been led by very strong-willed and authoritarian leaders in their early days. Examples range from Moses to Martin Luther to John Wesley to Cotton Mather to Mary Baker Eddy to Annie Semple McPherson to Louis Farrakhen.

When those leaders disappear and the movement becomes a permanent organization, the leadership role may be assumed by another powerful and influential individual or, more frequently, by a bureaucratic structure, or the movement may begin to drift into a series of semi-autonomous bodies that are loosely knit together.

2. As long as that movement is able to focus most of its resources and most of the time and energies of the followers on that initial cause that brought it into being, it is unlikely adversarial relationships will emerge.

After the movement becomes an organization, it is easy for the original cause to become a secondary goal and questions of power, orthodoxy, patronage, control, and priorities usurp the agenda. Internal adversarial relationships surface easily and quickly (all readers who believe in the doctrine of original sin at this point will respond, "Naturally!"). This pattern can be seen in military alliances as the war comes to an end, in the history of organized labor, in political parties, in the civil rights movement of the 1955-85 era, in the feminist movement, and in public education as well as in the churches.

3. Religious organizations often thrive as the members unite

against an external enemy (another church or denomination, the Devil, a council of churches) but tend to be torn apart when an internal adversary (the liberals, the fundamentalists, national headquarters, homosexuals, the seminaries) is identified.

4. The American legal system is built on the concept of adversarial relationships. While a few efforts have had modest success to introduce a greater emphasis on reconciliation and to alter that basic win-lose emphasis (such as divorce proceedings, labor negotiations, and small legal claims), they have met with limited success. Reconciliation is foreign to the basic system.

This means that when a religious body resorts to the civil courts to settle disputes, it is moving into a system built on adversarial relationships.

What is the liberal religious position on encouraging the concept of adversarial relationships in the churches and expanding adversarial relationships in our society? What is the conservative religious position on that and on the other issues raised here?

NOTES

1. Gilbert Steiner, *Constitutional Inequality: The Political Fortunes of the Equal Rights Amendment* (Washington D.C.: The Brookings Institution, 1985). For two other perspectives see Jane J. Mansbridge, *Why We Lost the ERA* (Chicago: University of Chicago Press, 1986) and Mary Frances Berry, *Why ERA Failed* (Bloomington: University of Indiana Press, 1986).

2. Two provocative books on this issue are Jeff Lyon, *Playing God in the Nursery* (New York: W. W. Morton, 1985) and Helga Kuhse and Peter Singer, *Should the Baby Live?* (New York: Oxford University Press, 1986).

3. In his book *Socialism and America* (San Diego: Harcourt Brace Jovanovich, 1985), veteran socialist Irving Howe laments the fact that nowhere on this planet is there a socialist government in a society that is free and democratic. For a lucid discussion see James P. Sterba, "Recent Work on Alternative Conceptions of Justice," *American Philosophical Quarterly* vol. 23, January 1986, pp. 1-22.

4. David Tyack and Elisabeth Hansot, *Managers of Virtue* (New York: Basic Books, 1982), p. 39.

5. Ibid., pp. 34-44.

6. For a more extensive discussion of this transformation see Chester E. Finn, Jr., "The Politics of Public Aid to Private Schools," in *1982 American Education Finance Association Yearbook* (Cambridge, Mass.: Ballinger Publishing Co., 1982), pp. 183-210 or Patricia M. Lines, "The New Private Schools and Their Historic Purpose," *Phi Delta Kappan*, January, 1986, pp. 373-79.

7. For a carefully documented account of an earlier effort by reformers to make the public schools a system for inculcating the values that were deemed appropriate for an industrial society see Marvin Lazerson, *Origins of the Urban School* (Cambridge, Mass.: Harvard University Press, 1971).

8. A persuasive argument for this definition of the issue is offered by Lines, "The New Private Schools and Their Historic Purpose."

9. John P. Kotter, *Power and Influence* (New York: The Free Press, 1985), pp. 184-90. A similar thesis is offered by Benson R. Snyder, *The Hidden Curriculum* (New York: Alfred A. Knopf, 1971) and by Arthur G. Powell, Eleanor Farrar, and David K. Cohen, *The Shopping Mall High School* (Boston: Houghton, Mifflin Co., 1985). An excellent brief definition of an effective school is Diane Ravitch, "A Good School," *The American Scholar*, Autumn, 1984, pp. 481-93. Those interested in a brief but provocative essay on a parallel theme about higher education can find it in Andrew Hacker, "The Decline of Higher Learning," *New York Review of Books*, February 13, 1986, pp. 35-42.

10. Roger G. Barker and Paul V. Gump, *Big School, Small School* (Stanford, Calif.: Stanford University Press, 1964), p. 202.

11. Harvey Passow, *Secondary Education Reform: Retrospect and Prospect* (New York: Teachers College Press, 1976).

12. Phyllis L. Blaunstein, "Public and Nonpublic Schools: Finding Ways to Work Together," *Phi Delta Kappan*, January, 1986, pp. 368-72.

13. Judith Cummings, "Non-Catholic Christian Schools Growing Fast," *New York Times*, April 13, 1983.

14. A somewhat different statement of the issue can be found in Chester E. Finn, Jr., "Our Schizophrenic Educational System," *Wall Street Journal*, October 23, 1984, from which this basic outline has been drawn. Another statement of a parallel concern in a broader context is James Q. Wilson, "The Rediscovery of Character: Private Virtue and Public Policy," *The Public Interest*, Fall, 1985, pp. 3-16. An excellent newsletter that focuses on youth, rather than on institutions, is *Character II*, with the editorial office at 1245 W. Westgate, Chicago, Ill. 60607.

15. For an introduction to this marketplace approach see the brief essay by a professor of education, Myron Lieberman, "Why School Reform Isn't Working," *Fortune*, February 17, 1986, pp. 135-36.

16. For an introduction to this debate see Charles Murray, *Losing Ground* (New York: Basic Books, 1984), Daniel Patrick Moynihan, *Family and Nation* (San Diego: Harcourt Brace Jovanovich, 1986), pp. 124-35, and Jesse Jackson and Charles Murray, "What Does Government Owe the Poor?" *Harper's*, April, 1986, pp. 35-47.

17. Based on a front page article in the *San Francisco Chronicle*, January 27, 1986. The coming conflict between the generation born before 1940 and the generation born after 1950 over the rising costs of Social Security is described by Philip Longman, "Justice Between Generations," *The Atlantic Monthly*, June, 1985, pp. 73-81.

18. Jarold A. Keifer, *Gaining the Dividends of Longer Life: New Roles for Older Workers* (Boulder, Colo.: Westview Press, 1984).

19. *New York Times*, March 3, 1985.

20. For a plea for this new vocation see Lyle E. Schaller, "Why Not a Minister of Health?" *The Clergy Journal*, January, 1985, pp. 22-23.

21. For a more extensive discussion of the policy on financial aid see Denis P. Doyle and Terry W. Hartle, "Facing the Fiscal Chopping Block," *Change*, July/August, 1985, pp. 8-56. In a similar fashion several denominational executives are raising questions about the large debts owed by recent seminary graduates.

22. During the 1970s the national tax policy of the United States was changed to reduce the burden on corporations, single adults, and childless couples. The tax rate on married couples with children was raised substantially to offset this change. Should the churches support an anti-family or a pro-family national tax policy? See Allan C. Carlson, "What Happened to the 'Family Wage'?" *The Public Interest*, Spring, 1986, pp. 3-17.

THE NEW MAJORITY

For the ninth time in twenty minutes Albert Brown got up from the rickety kitchen chair to go press his ear against the closed bedroom door on the first floor of this thirty-five-year-old farmhouse. Just as he thought he heard the cry of a baby, the door opened and there stood the family doctor with coat and tie off and his sleeves rolled above his elbows.

"How's my wife?" cried Albert in an anxious voice. "She's fine and you're the father of a handsome baby boy," replied the doctor.

The year was 1920 and the baby was named Benjamin.

Thirty years later that boy, now a married man, sat in the waiting room of the municipal hospital anxiously waiting as his wife was about to give birth to their first child in the delivery room a few yards away. After what seemed hours, the obstetrician opened the door and walked up to Ben and announced, "Mr. Brown, your wife just gave birth to a seven-pound, ten-ounce baby boy."

"How is he?" asked Ben. "Is the baby O.K.? Is he all right?" *139* •

"Yes, he's as healthy as can be and you may come in now and see your wife." They named the baby Charles.

Thirty years later Charles, dressed in a green hospital gown and his face covered with a mask, stood by the birthing table as his wife, Vicki, was getting ready to give birth to their first child. "Is it a boy or a girl?" cried Charles as the baby emerged from the womb.

These three births in one family tree illustrate two of the most remarkable changes of the twentieth century. In 1920, when Benjamin was born, 799 out of every 100,000 births were accompanied by the death of the mother. The woman who gave birth to five children had one chance in twenty-five of not surviving. Ben's father had cause to be concerned about his wife. The chances were that he knew two or three or four men who had been widowed when their wives died in childbirth. By 1950, when Charles Brown was born, the maternal birth rate had dropped from 799 per 100,000 births in 1920 to 83 or fewer than one maternal death per thousand births. By 1980, when Charles became a father for the first time, the number of women dying in childbirth had dropped to 9.2 per 100,000 births or less than one per 10,000 births. By 1985 the rate had dropped to less than 7 per 100,000 births—a 99 percent decrease from the 1920 rate.

The second half of that extraordinary change was the decrease in the infant mortality rate. In 1920, when Benjamin was born, 41 babies out of every thousand did not survive for as long as one month, and another 86 died before their first birthday. By 1950, when Charles was born, those figures had dropped to 21 and 29 respectively. By 1980 the rate had declined to 8.5 neonatal deaths (within four weeks of birth) per 1,000 births and an additional 12.5 deaths per 1,000 births during the next eleven months. The law of averages in 1920 gave Benjamin an 87.3 percent probability of being alive a year from his birth. For his grandson, sixty years later, the chances had increased to a 97.9 percent probability. In 1985 98.3 percent of all babies born that year in the United States survived to their first birthday.

Today many parents take for granted the mother's survival, assume the baby will be healthy, and are most interested in
whether it will be a boy or a girl.

Another influential change can be expressed by three sets of numbers. In 1830 nearly three-quarters (72.5 percent) of the immigrants coming to the United States were male. In 1914, the peak year for immigration into the United States, nearly two-thirds (65.6 percent) of the 1.2 million immigrants to the United States were male. Between 1950 and 1980 only 46 percent of the 10 million immigrants to the United States were male.

■ ■ ■

A third influential change of the twentieth century is reflected in the life expectancy tables of forty-year-old adults. In 1920 the average forty-year-old male could expect to live another thirty years, one fewer than for the average forty-year-old female. By 1950 the life expectancy of the average forty-year-old man had been increased by only sixteen months, but for women the increase had been fifty-six additional months. Today the average forty-year-old white male can expect to survive until his seventy-fifth birthday, but it is four years less for the average forty-year-old black male. By contrast, the average forty-year-old white woman still has over half of her life (an additional forty-one years) ahead of her and the average forty-year-old black woman can expect to survive for two years beyond the death of the average forty-year-old white male.

At this point the reader may think, "That's interesting, but what difference does it make?"

The Significance of 1944

For most of American history males have constituted a majority of the population of the United States. As recently as 1920, for example, the American population included 2 million more males than females. One reason, of course, was the large number of women who died in childbirth. A second was that up until 1930 the majority of immigrants to the United States were males. (In every year since 1929 males have constituted a minority of the immigrants to the United States.) The third *141* ■

reason has been the great advances in prolonging the life expectancy of mature adults. Two-thirds of the advances have produced an increase in female life expectancy.

While the gap has narrowed in recent years, 60 percent of all accidental deaths are males, 70 percent of the victims of homicide are males, 70 percent of all suicidal deaths are males, approximately 55 percent of all deaths from cancer are males, and in well over 90 percent of all deaths resulting from military service the victim is a male. As women account for a larger proportion of the consumption of cigarettes, alcohol, and cocaine, as more women drive more miles annually in an automobile, and as more women enter stress-producing jobs, the odds may even out.

The Bureau of the Census conducts a complete census every ten years. In 1940 males outnumbered females in the American population by 454,000. By 1950 females were in the majority and outnumbered males by over a million. After allowing for deaths in military service, immigration, and changes in life expectancy patterns, a reasonable guess is that 1944 was the year when women became the new majority in the United States.

POPULATION OF THE UNITED STATES (thousands)		
Year	Male	Female
1820	4,847	4,742
1850	11,838	11,354
1860	16,085	15,358
1870	19,494	19,065
1890	32,237	30,711
1900	38,816	37,178
1920	53,900	51,810
1930	62,137	60,638
1940	66,062	65,608
1950	74,833	75,964
1960	87,865	90,600
1970	98,926	104,309
1980	110,053	116,493
1985	119,000	126,000

The normal cultural lag between the creation of a radically new idea or the invention of a new method of producing food or fiber or the adoption of a new form of transportation is twenty to thirty years. Many of the original patents, for example, had expired before Xerox was able to market a significant number of office copying machines. Therefore it is not surprising that it was twenty years after women became the new majority when the feminist revolution began to be felt all across the nation. It was forty years later before white males became a minority in the nation's labor force. It was forty-two years later when the Bureau of Labor Statistics announced that women outnumbered men in the nation's 13.9 million professional jobs. It was thirty-six years before the first woman was elected to the office of bishop by a predominantly white mainline Protestant denomination and it was forty-one years later when the bishop of one mainline denomination was married to a spouse who was an ordained minister in a different denomination. It was thirty-five years later when, for the first time in peace time, women constituted a majority of the undergraduates enrolled in America's colleges and universities. It was forty years later before the slogan, "Women will elect the next president of the United States," became a popular rallying cry and it was forty years after they had become a majority of the population before women outvoted men in a presidential election.

A Decade of Radical Change

The 1970s brought the most striking changes for women. The proportion of women in the 25-34 age bracket with a college degree increased from 12 percent in 1970 to 21 percent in 1982. The number of women aged 25-34 who were enrolled in college tripled between 1970 and 1982. This new majority, who constitute 53 percent of the adult population, accounted for 59 percent of the increase in the civilian labor force between 1970 and 1982.

Between 1972 and 1981 the proportion of accountants who were women rose from 22 to 38 percent, the proportion of women economists doubled from 12 percent of the total in 1972 to 25 percent in 1981, the proportion of seminary students who are female climbed from 10 percent of the total enrollment in 1972 to 23 percent in 1981 to 26 percent in 1985. The proportion of women among bartenders nearly doubled from 28 percent in 1972 to 48 percent in 1981.

143 ·

The number of women graduating from medical schools was 534 in 1950, dropped to 331 in 1955, doubled to 699 in 1970, and jumped to 4,903 in 1985. By 1986 17.2 percent of all physicians were female. The number of women graduating from dental school jumped from 34 in 1970 to 700 in 1980. A parallel trend occurred in the law schools as 801 graduated in 1970 compared to 10,754 in 1980. In 1970 526 women received an engineering degree, up from 191 in 1950, but in 1984 10,761 women were granted a degree in engineering. Women now outnumber men in such professional positions as psychologists, editors, reporters, teachers, statisticians, and public relations specialists.

In 1970 only 2.8 of all lawyers were women; by 1985 that had jumped to 18.1 percent. The number of women physicians doubled between 1970 and 1980.

Today between 25 and 40 percent of the persons in professional schools (medical, dental, law, theology, veterinary medicine, and accounting) are women. The lowest proportion is among those studying for the ordained ministry.

A poll conducted by the *New York Times* on November 11-20, 1983, reported that only 26 percent of the women questioned cited motherhood as being "one of the two or three most enjoyable things about being a woman today." That was exactly one-half the proportion that lifted up motherhood in 1970. In 1970, 43 percent listed "homemaker" as one of those two or three best things available to women. In 1983 only 8 percent lifted up that role. In 1983, 26 percent of the women surveyed placed "a career, a job, and the pay" among those top two or three, which tripled the percentage of 1970.

This same survey also asked, "If you were free to do either, would you prefer to have a job outside the home, or would you prefer to stay home and take care of your house and family?" The response of white women in 1983 was: 42 percent chose "job," 50 percent chose "home." The response of black women was exactly the opposite as 61 percent chose job and only 30 percent chose home and family. Women who were in professional and

managerial positions chose job over home by a 63-27 margin

while women in blue-collar jobs chose home over job by a 49-43 margin. (Some women did not respond to that question or replied, "Don't know.")

To a significant degree that poll revealed that people get what they want, for working women chose job over home by a 58 to 33 margin and women not employed outside the home chose home over job by a 62 to 31 ratio.

The changing role of women is also reflected in two other mirrors of our society. The traditional housewife, a role once played by Lucille Ball and Harriet Nelson among others, has almost disappeared from television programs. "Good old mom" has been replaced on television by pregnant unmarried women, female detectives, divorced women, elderly widows sharing an apartment, and women engaged in professional or managerial employment such as airline pilots or lawyers or physicians or newspaper reporters.

A parallel change came in the comic strips when Lois Flagstone of "Hi and Lois" fame took a job selling real estate in 1980. The problems of women in the workplace, either married or unmarried, constitute the theme of "Sally Forth" and "Cathy." Miss Buxley in "Beetle Bailey" can make jokes about old men that would be totaly unacceptable if made by a young male in a comic strip about an elderly female. Those who are seriously interested in the pace of social change can be kept up-to-date by "Mary Worth" who may be the most adaptable counselor in modern history.

Those with long memories may bring up "Winnie Winkle" or "Tillie the Toiler" or "Brenda Starr" from an earlier era, but the issues they faced were completely unlike those confronting "Cathy" (the creation of Cathy Guisewite) or "Sally Forth" or "Hello Carol."

Television and the comic strips agree it is a different world for women today than it was in the 1950s, but so do readers of the sports pages.

In 1970, for example, a man won the New York Marathon in 2 hours, 31 minutes, and 38 seconds. No women were among those who finished that grueling race of 26 miles and 385 yards. *145* ▪

Nine years later the first of many women to cross the finish line in the New York Marathon did so in 2 hours, 27 minutes, and 33 seconds, 4 minutes faster than the time of the man who had won in 1970. In 1985 the first woman to finish ran the distance in 2 hours, 28 minutes, and 34 seconds.

The decade of the 1970s also brought many other changes to women. The number of married women, living with a husband, who were employed outside the home jumped from 4.2 million in 1940 to 18.4 million in 1970 to nearly 25 million in 1980. In percentage terms, the striking difference was between younger married women and single women. In 1980 82 percent of all single women age 25-44 were employed outside the home as were 66 percent of the single women aged 45-64.[1] That represented a *decrease* from 1960 when those proportions were 83 percent and 80 percent.

By 1982, in one out of eight of those families in which both the wife and the husband were employed, the wife's income exceeded that of her husband. This can complicate matters when the husband, who is a pastor, receives a call to a new church and they agree the wife cannot afford to leave her job.

By contrast, the proportion of younger married women, living with a husband, who were employed outside the home climbed from 33 percent in 1960 to 43 percent in 1970 to 60 percent in 1980 for those aged 25-44. The change was less significant for women aged 45-64. In 1960 36 percent of the women in that age bracket who were living with their husband were employed outside the home. That proportion climbed moderately to 44 percent in 1970 and to 47 percent in 1980. For married women past age 65 who are living with their husbands the proportion employed outside the home has remained stable at approximately 7 percent for over a quarter of a century.

Who Went to Work?

Before moving on to a brief review of many other changes that occurred among women during the 1970s, it is important to look at the women who represent most of this increase in proportion to the women employed outside the home. A remarkably well-documented beginning point is to turn first to a small city in middle America.

In their study of Muncie, Indiana, in the early 1920s Robert and Helen Lynd found that 44 percent of working-class wives were employed outside the home in 1924. When the same study was replicated a half century later, it was discovered that 48 percent of the working-class wives of Muncie were employed outside the home in 1978, a very moderate increase. During the Lynd's five-year visit to Muncie in 1920–24, they had found only one business-class wife employed outside the home—her husband was unemployed. By 1978, however, 42 percent of the business-class wives in Muncie were employed outside the home. In 1924 three-quarters of the women in Muncie who were employed outside the home stated, when interviewed by the Lynds, that economic pressures were the reason for their entrance into the labor force. By 1978 both working-class wives and business-class wives agreed that paid employment is more satisfying than housework, but economic pressures still were a strong motivating factor.[2]

For the nation as a whole, among married women living with their husbands and with at least one child under six years of age, the proportion employed ouside the home climbed from 12 percent in 1950 to 19 percent in 1960 to 30 percent in 1970 to 51 percent in 1986.

The proportion of married women living with a husband and with children in the 6-17 age bracket, who are employed outside the home, has always been higher than for women with preschool-age children. The proportion of employed women with school-age children climbed from 28 percent in 1950 to 39 percent in 1960 to 49 percent in 1970 to 63 percent in 1983.

Mothers of school-age children, with no preschool-age children at home, are far more likely to be employed outside the home than are married women who do not have any children under eighteen. Only slightly over half of this latter group are employed outside the home. Likewise, among divorced women those most likely to be employed outside the home are those with school-age children and no children under six. For the past two decades six out of seven women in this last category have been in the labor force.

For those who are (a) quickly bored with too many paragraphs filled with statistics and (b) more interested in consequences than numbers, it is important to lift up four basic generalizations about this unprecedented increase in the number of women employed outside the home. First, a large part of that growth is the sharp increase in the number of women in the labor force who are married to business- and professional-class husbands. Second, the sharp increase in the number of formerly married women with school-age children has been an influential factor behind this change. Third, another large slice of that increase is composed of younger childless women who have decided to work for several years before beginning a family. Fourth, the larger proportion of high school graduates going to college and the rapid escalation in the costs of going to college have forced many mothers to find a job.

From an historical perspective it should be emphasized that the big change has been in the entrance of *married* women into the labor force. In 1890 one single woman was an employed member of the labor force for every seven men. By 1955 that had dropped to one single woman in the labor force for every nine men. It was not until World War II that the number of married women living with their husbands and employed outside the home exceeded the number of single women in the labor force. In 1985 men outnumbered single women in the civilian labor force by slightly over a five-to-one ratio. Married women living with their husbands and employed outside the home in 1985 outnumbered all single, widowed, divorced, and separated women in the labor force by a five-to-four ratio. This distinction is important for an understanding of some of the consequences of this movement of more women into the labor force.

Among the most highly visible consequences for the churches are (1) the increasing number of women in the labor force who are married to pastors,[3] (2) the increase in the number of women serving as pastors of churches,[4] (3) the shortage of volunteers in those churches that traditionally have depended largely on housewives to fill volunteer roles, (4) the decline in participation by younger women in the women's organization (see chapter 9 for a more detailed discussion of that point[5]), and (5) the feminization of several of the mainline Protestant churches, but an examination of that subject must be postponed for a few more pages.

What Else Changed?

In addition to the changes already identified, several other changes are influential parts of the context for those concerned about the new role of women in American society. For example, the number of legal abortions tripled from an estimated 586,000 in 1972 to 1,554,000 in 1980.* Births by Caesarean section jumped from one in twenty in 1970 to one in five by 1984. The number of currently divorced women rose from 115,000 in 1900 to 823,000 in 1940 to 2.7 million in 1970 to 6.9 million in 1982. In percentage terms that meant that out of all living women who had been married, by 1982 7.1 percent currently were divorced (another larger group had been divorced and had remarried). That compared to 3.9 percent of all married women who were currently divorced in 1970.

Nearly one-half of the women marrying for the first time in the 1960–64 era reported they did not engage in sexual intercourse until after marriage. That proportion of virgins at marriage had dropped to 21 percent for women who married for the first time in the 1975–77 era. For women marrying for the first time in the 1975–79 era 45 percent of the Hispanic women said they were virgins when married compared to 22 percent for white women (compared to 53 percent for white women first married in 1960–64), and 5 percent for black women (compared to 12 percent for black women first married in the 1960–64 era).[6]

The number of currently (not remarried) widowed women increased from 3.9 million in 1920 to 9.6 million in 1970 to 10.8

---

*For those interested in such comparisons it should be noted that in the United States in 1984 there was one abortion for every two live births while in Russia there were two abortions for every live birth.

million in 1980 while the number of widowed men who had not remarried dropped from 2.3 million in 1950 to 2.1 million in 1970 to 1.9 million in 1982. It appears that the principal beneficiaries of the increased number of divorced or widowed women are (a) divorced men and (b) widowed men. Both groups now have a greater range of choices for remarriage than was available in 1960 or 1970 and the widowers have less competition.

Single parent mothers with children under eighteen almost doubled from 2,858,000 in 1970 to 5,400,000 in 1980. That contrasts with a 10 percent increase between 1970 and 1980 of women who were married and living with their husbands.

The 1970s saw an increase of 3.3 million in the number of currently divorced women and an increase of 2.3 million currently divorced men (that figure is lower because men tend to remarry sooner after divorce). The 1970s also brought an increase of 4.7 million among single never-married women (compared to an increase of 6.2 million in the number of never-married men in that decade), an increase of 1.1 million widows (contrasted to the slight decrease in the number of widowers referred to earlier), and a net increase of 4.9 million married women.

What that all adds up to, very simply, is the number of women age eighteen and over in the American population increased by 13.8 million during the 1970s, compared to an increase of 13.2 million in the male population for the decade. The new majority has become an even larger majority. Nearly one-half (6.2 million) of the increase in the adult male population was accounted for by the increase in the single never-married men.* The increase in the female population was divided almost exactly into three equal sized groups, a net increase of 4.8 married women, a net increase of 4.4 formerly married women, and a net increase of 4.7 never-married women.

The tendency of the younger women of today to postpone

---

*It should be recognized that a tiny proportion of single men who tell the census enumerator they have never married are lying in the hopes of evading child support responsibilities.

marriage explains why most (65 percent) of that increase in the adult female population over age eighteen was composed of single women.

A Return to the Good Old Days

While it has been erroneously publicized as a new trend, largely because few of today's trend watchers have firsthand recollections going back to 1900, one of the most significant changes affecting women really is a return to the patterns of a hundred years ago in regard to marriage. American women born in the 1928–42 period, unlike those born in the 1860–90 era and unlike those born in the 1950–65 era, were more likely to marry than any other generation of women in American history, and they married earlier in life than any other generation of women before or since. This remarkably strong affirmation of marriage by women born in the 1928–42 era has distorted the comparison base used by many decision-makers.

PROPORTION OF WOMEN NEVER MARRIED		
Year	Age 20-24	Age 25-59
1890	52%	25%
1900	52	28
1910	48	25
1920	46	23
1930	46	22
1940	47	23
1950	32	13
1960	28	11
1970	36	11
1980	50	21
1983	56	25

By 1983 the percentage of younger women in the 20-24 age bracket who had never married was double the proportion in 1960, and slightly higher than it had been in 1890 or 1900.

The proportion of women in the 25-29 age bracket who had never married more than doubled from 1960 to 1983 and was back up to what it had been in 1890.

Perhaps the most far-reaching consequence of this for program planning in the local church were the decisions made a generation or two ago to use marital status as a primary criterion in dividing adults into groups and classes.* The results often included classes for younger couples, for middle-aged couples, for empty-nest couples, and for widows. Later, in the 1960s and the 1970s, the idea of organizing special groups for singles began to spread and was a remarkably popular concept in the 1965–82 era. (See chapter 9 for a more detailed discussion of this approach.)

More and more churches are finding it far more effective to organize new groups around the theme of "what we're going to do together," rather than by age or marital status. Examples range from the weekend bicycle trip to an in-depth study of the Gospel According to John to a trip to the Holy Land to the work camp mission trip for adults to the special committee to plan and oversee the remodeling of the building to staffing the vacation Bible school to a bazaar or mission festival to going as a group to see a play. Another productive approach is to distinguish among several distinctively different audiences.[7]

For many congregational and denominational policy-makers the most baffling consequence is to decide on the appropriate response to the woman who declares, "I've never been married, I do not expect I ever will marry, but I see no reason why I should not become a mother." Sometimes this is a preface to a request by the mother to the pastor to baptize her baby. More often it is the uncomfortable silence expressed by members when they learn that a close friend in the church is now a grandparent, but there is no son-in-law to congratulate. What is the proper response to make to this new life-style?

A third consequence is what to say to the influential and widely respected leader born in the 1930s who is proposing a course of action or a program that was appropriate for that generation that married early in life, but simply does not fit in today's radically different world? How does the fifty-nine-year-old pastor politely

---

*By contrast the adult Sunday schools in the late nineteenth century and first decade of the twentieth century were organized by age and gender rather than marital status.

tell the fifty-one-year-old person chairing a program committee, "Sorry, but you're out-of-date"?

A fourth consequence facing the younger women in the new majority who have decided to postpone marriage in favor of a college education and a career can best be summarized as a shocking discovery for some, but not for all women.

Where's My Husband?

The widely publicized changes of the 1970s, including the decision by many women to postpone marriage in favor of a career, have focused largely on this amazing increase in the number of women in vocations formerly filled by men. That is only a part of the total picture. The majority of women born since the end of World War II see no reason why that should be an either-or choice. They want both a career and marriage. The figures in an earlier section were cited to document the point that many will not have that both-and option available to them. There is a national shortage of husbands.

The situation is most serious for older women and for black women. For persons aged 25-29, for example, white men in 1984 outnumbered white women by 88,000, but black women outnumbered black men in that age group by 157,000. (In part that was due to an undercount of black men by the Bureau of the Census, in part because of the high death rate among young black men, and in part because women outnumber men among immigrants to the United States.) In the age bracket 30-39 white women outnumbered white men by 36,000 in 1984 while black women outnumbered black men in that age bracket by 329,000. (In comparing those figures it should be remembered that whites in the United States outnumber blacks by a 7-1 margin.)

This shortage of potential husbands for the new majority is far greater than it first appears because at least 8 percent of the 30 million men born in the 1952–67 era will never marry. Futhermore, since eight out of nine grooms marry a younger woman, the women born back when the birth curve was climbing (1946–61) will be faced with a more severe shortage. *153* •

For example, the number of women born in 1953 exceeded the number of men born in 1950 by nearly 100,000.

The good news is for younger women seeking a husband. Those born on the down side of that birth curve (1962–73) have more choices among slightly older men. The 1.8 million women born in 1966 can rejoice in the fact that three years earlier nearly 2.1 million boys were born. The world is filled with people who lament the fact they were born too soon.

At age 40–49 white women outnumbered white men by 263,000 in 1984 while black women outnumbered black men in that age group by 252,000.

At this point it may be appropriate to point out that not every black single woman is elated with the improvement in race relations in American society. Black women tend to be more aware of the fact that between 1970 and 1984 the number of white women with a black husband nearly tripled from 41,000 to 111,000 while the number of black women with a white husband increased only from 24,000 to 64,000. Those white women were using up a scarce commodity in the black community.

A recent study by three university professors predicted that college-educated women who have not married by age twenty-five have only a fifty-fifty chance of ever marrying and only one in five of all college-educated women who have not married by age thirty will ever do so. The odds drop to one in twenty for college-educated women who have not married by their thirty-fifth birthday. This study predicted that 22 percent of the college-educated women born in the mid-1950s will never marry compared to 9 percent of the college educated born in the mid-1930s.[8]

Because of the tendency of white women to marry men who have more formal education, the increasing proportion of women with a college degree has changed the dynamics of the marriage marketplace. One scholar has estimated that for every 223 unmarried women in the 40-49 age bracket there are only 100 unmarried men in that same age group and for every 10 women in the 40-49 age bracket who have a college degree there

are only 3 men who are not married, older, and better educated.[9]

As will be pointed out in the next chapter the impact of this shortage of husbands is far more serious for black women than for white women.

Separating Marriage and Motherhood

This national shortage of husbands has many consequences. The one that has had a profound impact on society and also is beginning to transform ministry and program development in the local church is the separation of marriage and motherhood. One expression of this change is that in 1982 19 percent of all babies were born to women without husbands, up from 5 percent in 1970.

Another is that marriage no longer is followed rather quickly by motherhood. For three hundred years approximately one-third of all brides were pregnant on their wedding day. Thanks to improved methods of birth control and legalized abortion, that proportion has dropped to one-sixth in recent years.

As marriage and motherhood no longer are as closely related as they once were, five trends have emerged that influence the life and ministry of local churches. The first is the postponed birth of that first child. In 1982 a total of 137,000 women gave birth to their first child after the mother's thirtieth birthday. That was more than triple the 1970 figure of 42,000. In 1982 562,000 gave birth to their first child after the mother's twenty-fifth birthday, more than double the 269,000 total for 1970. Among other consequences this means (a) many more young childless couples and a need for the churches to take that into account in program planning ("couple classes" rarely attract both couples with two or three children and childless couples of the same age), (b) a need to create Mothers' Clubs for the new mothers in their late twenties and early thirties who have left behind the friendship circle and the mutual support groups they enjoyed while employed, (c) a need to recognize the value of more attractive nurseries (what was an acceptable level of quality in 1967 no longer is acceptable to many of today's new mothers), and (d) a need to develop the capability within the nominating committee *155* •

to identify and understand the gifts, skills, and experiences this new generation of mothers can bring to volunteer positions in the church after a decade, more or less, in the labor force.

The second change is of far greater significance to the congregation oriented to the traditional nuclear family. In the early 1950s three out of five American households consisted of an employed father, a mother not employed outside the home, and a couple of school-age children. By 1985 that family unit represented not 60 percent of all households as in 1955, but only 8 percent. Only four out of ten children born in the late 1980s will experience all three of these characteristics of what traditionally has been defined as a "normal" childhood:

1. Their mother and father were married and living together when that child was born.

2. The mother and father will not separate or be divorced before that child reaches age eighteen.

3. Both parents will survive until after the child's eighteenth birthday.

If a fourth is added, growing up in a home with at least one brother or sister, the proportion drops to one out of three children who will enjoy all four of those experiences.

That suggests it is a new world for those in charge of the Sunday school, the vacation Bible school, the youth program, the weekday early childhood development center, and the Sunday morning nursery. Their assumptions about the home life of the children must change from what were the valid assumptions of 1955.

One response by many churches has been to concentrate on the traditional nuclear family that stays together and "wonder why our membership is shrinking." A second, and far more threatening, approach is to explore that new frontier and plan ministries and programs on the assumption it is a different world today. A third response has been chosen by a large proportion of white males born in the late 1950s and the early 1960s. That is to choose not to go into the pastoral ministry—the proportion of

twenty-three-year-old white males enrolled in a theological

seminary in 1985 was approximately one-third the proportion of 1955.

For some pastors the most disturbing of these five trends that have surfaced with the separation of marriage and motherhood is a relatively small but rapidly growing phenomenon. An increasing number of women who have concluded they do not want to mix marriage and a career now see no reason why motherhood and a career should be mutually exclusive goals.

To place this in perspective it should be noted that in 1970 the number of families headed by a never-married mother was 234,000. In 1982 that total had jumped to 1,092,000. The number of children living with a never-married mother rose from a half million in 1970 to 3.3 million in 1983—2 million are Black children, 9 million are Anglo, and 3 million are Hispanic.

Many of these families conform to the general stereotype of unwed mothers, but a growing number, still to be counted by some inquisitive demographer, are financially self-supporting women who are single mothers by choice. They recognize the biological clock is running. They do not see any prospects of marriage or they do not want to marry.[10] One estimate is that 7 percent of the clients of one sperm bank are women who want to be mothers but do not want to marry. Another sperm bank claims over half of its clients fit this category. Typically, they have a good job with an income sufficient to pay for child care during the working hours. Some are self-employed. Many are able to work at home. Many do want to be part of a mutual support group. They do not want to be seen or to see themselves as unique. They understand this is not always an easy and comfortable life-style. They seek a chance to share experiences with others in the same circumstances. A mutual support group, called Single Mothers by Choice, was formed in New York City in October 1981.

How many women's organizations in local churches have organized similar groups as a part of their effort to reach and include more younger women? What is the position of the churches on this issue? Should the churches, in the face of the growing shortage of husbands, encourage artificial insemination   *157* ▪

of single women who do not want to be denied the chance to be mothers? Or should the churches encourage these women to adopt children? Or is the appropriate Christian response simply, "That's too bad you didn't find yourself a husband before the inventory was exhausted." The traditional alternative of completely ignoring the subject no longer is available.

The fourth of these five trends is a product of several factors, and it can be identified in reasonably precise terms, but the consequences are still highly speculative. The trend represents a combination of (a) a sharp increase in the number of children who are the firstborn child to that mother and (b) the increasing number of children being reared in one-parent homes or with a stepparent.

Both trends are increasing. In 1960 only a fourth of all babies were the firstborn child to that mother. By 1985 that proportion had jumped to 43 percent. A lot is known about how adults tend to display characteristics that reflect their place in the family constellation.[11] What no one yet can tell with a high degree of confidence is what society will be like when four out of ten adults display the characteristics that typically are found among firstborns. Heretofore the vast majority of adults have been persons who displayed the friendliness, extroverted personality, tolerance for others, and the ability to get along with other people that marks the middle-born child or the capability to ignore the expectations placed upon them by others that charcterizes last borns. Whether the nation can survive the day when more than 40 percent of all adults are lonely onlies or perfectionist firstborns is yet to be demonstrated. Those promise to be trying days, for both the surrogate parents and those who do not seek surrogate parents.

Perhaps the more serious issue, and one about which even less is known for sure, is what will happen in a society in which a majority of the adults grew up in a home that (a) did not include a father, or (b) saw the parents separate or seek a divorce during the child's formative years, or (c) the only resident parent was the father, or (d) the child had to greet a new stepparent on one or more occasions. The early evidence to come in is far from encouraging.

Finally, the combination of the increase in the divorce rate, the shortage of husbands for divorced women who want to remarry, and the separation of marriage from motherhood suggests this is not only a different world from the one in the 1950s, it is also far more complicated than anyone had anticipated, and it is not necessarily a fairer place.

A well-documented illustration of that point can be found in an extensive examination of the impact of no-fault divorce laws by a well-known scholar.[12] The trade-off appears to have been that in minimizing the faultfinding, bitterness, and acrimony that traditionally accompanied a divorce proceeding, women lost a powerful bargaining tool. As a result, this study suggests, one year after divorce the average divorced woman had experienced a 73 percent decline in her standard of living while the average divorced man experienced a 42 percent increase in his standard of living. Who promised that reforms always increase fairness? Every change has a price tag and many of the changes women have experienced during the past couple of decades have had unexpectedly high price tags.

It is a new world for women, and it is still too early to be able to predict all the consequences of women becoming the new majority, but some of the changes already are very obvious. One is that the congregation served by a woman as the pastor is far more likely to be without a minister's spouse in the congregation than is the congregation served by a male pastor.

Another is the rapid pace at which the roles of women have been changing, despite the fact that many of the traditional expectations and restrictions have not completely disappeared. In the good old days people had the opportunity to die of old age before they became obsolete. In this world the pace of change is so fast people must endure changes they once could have avoided by death.

Motherhood vs. Feminism?

Until recently one of the most carefully ignored subjects has been whether motherhood should be perceived as a trap that   *159* ▪

severely limits the freedom of women or as a legitimate and socially acceptable role for women. To some extent this has been an intergenerational issue with the women born in the 1928–42 era struggling for full equality with men while the women born before 1928 and after 1955 are more likely to have a pro-motherhood and pro-child perspective. In recent years several younger mothers have come out with a strong affirmation of marriage and motherhood that have aroused sharp negative reactions from among many of the older feminists.[13] This is a highly emotional debate that can be extremely divisive and frequently divides people along generational lines.

While students of generational theory probably would not find this to be unusual, many church leaders have been surprised to discover that congregations attracting a disproportionately large number of women born before 1928 and an even larger number of mothers born after World War II usually display a strong pro-motherhood attitude and often reinforce this with a weekday early childhood development center, a vigorous women's organization, a redundant affirmation of marriage, parenting classes, mutual support groups for new mothers, or classes for newlyweds.

One of the reasons it is more difficult to be a pastor today is because some believe it is impossible to be a supporter of such traditional values as motherhood, marriage, and the family and also support the movement for women's rights.

The Changing Roles of Women

"Would you be willing to finish out the school year teaching a third-grade class for us?" pleaded an administrator from the public school system in a south Texas city. He was addressing the wife of the senior minister of a large church in that city. Since he also was a member of that congregation, he knew the pastor's wife had a degree in elementary education and had been a classroom teacher.

"One of our teachers is pregnant and cannot finish out the year. We have these three choices. One is a woman who has taught only physical education. The second is another woman who has taught only in high school. The third is you. Would you help us out?" continued the school administrator.

"Why, yes, I think I might," replied the minister's wife, "but I cannot give you an answer right now. Could you give me two days to talk to my husband and to think about it?"

The next morning the president of the women's organization called on this minister's wife and asked, "What's the problem? Isn't this church paying your husband as much as it should?"

"I don't know what you mean," replied the minister's wife.

"Well, I just heard that you were going back to teaching school and the only reason I could think of that would cause you to do that is our church isn't paying your husband as much as we should," declared the visitor. "We've never had a minister's wife who worked."

Before the day was over, several other members of the women's organization had called questioning whether it was true she planned to go back to teaching school. In the face of these questions and objections, the minister's wife decided to reject the plea that she finish out the school year teaching third-graders in the public school. She disliked turning down the request for a favor from a parishioner, but she also did not want to offend those parishioners who were convinced the minister's wife should not be employed outside the home.

A couple of months later the governing board of that congregation voted to adopt a motion that declared, "The minister's wife has a right to do anything she wants to do."

The year was 1967.

Twenty years later six out of ten women married to parish pastors are employed outside the home as schoolteachers, physicians, secretaries, travel agents, bank officers, sales managers, social workers, nurses, architects, typists, college professors, sales persons, dentists, realtors, proprietors of their own businesses, veterinarians, clerks, attorneys, and other vocations.

■ ■ ■

In 1968 a female undergraduate at Barnard College violated that school's housing regulations by living off campus with her boy friend. That story was front page news in the *New York* *161* ■

Times, which ran nearly two dozen articles on the subject before it no longer appeared to be news. Today thousands of college students live off campus with a boy friend or girl friend and no one, except for some parents, sees that as a news story.

. . .

For more than a century women married to diplomats employed abroad in the Foreign Services of the United States Department of State were expected to be active partners with their husbands. They stood in line with husbands at official receptions smiling and shaking hands. They helped represent the United States in other countries by writing invitations, planning and serving dinners and receptions, and serving as hostesses without pay. These Foreign Service wives were evaluated annually in regard to their social activity and their skills at entertaining. The wife's rating would be considered as a part of the report on the husband's overall performance. That process evaluation of wives was abandoned in 1972. In 1986 Congress was asked to consider a proposal that wives of Foreign Service officers be paid for their work, a policy followed by two dozen nations. As of early 1986 Congress had not acted on that proposal.

. . .

While it is not of earthshaking importance, one of the interesting consequences of this change in the role of women can be seen in the announcement of engagements and weddings. On November 21, 1965, for example, the *New York Times* ran 75 such announcements which were long enough to include occupations, but only 29 percent listed the occupation of the bride. Ten years later, on November 23, 1975, 75 percent of the 36 wedding notices listed the bride's occupation. In the 37 notices carried in the November 24, 1985, issue of the *Times* only one bride's occupation was *not* listed, and she was an Andorran who was married in London. That Sunday's list included among the 36 brides reporting their occupation four bankers, four lawyers, two architects, and two curators. It is a different world from what it was in 1965!

One of the many consequences of this remarkable change in
the number and variety of employment opportunities open to

women can be seen in the changing mix of the program staff in many of the large churches. It is not uncommon today for women to constitute a substantial majority of the program staff in large churches. (See chapter 7.)

A second interesting change is the increase in the number of nuns in the Roman Catholic Church who, while they cannot be ordained as priests yet, are serving as resident "pastors" of small rural Catholic parishes not able to secure the services of a priest.

Perhaps the most amusing impact of this change in the role of women in the churches is the increasing difficulty many congregations have had in securing volunteers to staff the kitchen. This is less pronounced in working-class congregations, but increasingly common in those Protestant churches that serve a constituency drawn from the top fourth of the social, economic, educational, and income ladder. In one such congregation, which serves breakfast from 7 to 8:15 every Sunday morning, 100 percent of the volunteers in the kitchen are male. This responsibility is the central organizing principle of that men's fellowship.

A far more significant consequence of the professionalization of women in the labor force is that huge numbers of these working women are bringing the competencies, the verbal skills, the organizational concepts, and the self-confidence they have acquired in the marketplace back into their local churches, into their denominational involvement, into their political party, and into local government.

This combination of (a) the fact that women now constitute a growing majority of the American population, (b) the remarkable increase in the life expectancy of forty-year-old women, (c) the rapid progress toward full equality in the labor force, (d) the fact that most Christian churches are able to attract single women in far greater numbers than they are able to attract single men, (e) the increase in the proportion of women who will never marry, and (f) the reward system in most churches that places a premium on verbal skills—an area in which women as a group tend to be superior to men—leads to a discussion of another significant trend. *163* ■

The Feminization of the Churches

From the perspective of those who are most concerned with what is happening in local churches the big change that has accompanied this emergence as the new majority can be seen in the increased participation of women in all aspects of congregational life and administration as well as in corporate worship.

The Muncie studies referred to earlier reported that in 1890 59 percent of all married women were "regular" attenders (according to their daughters' recollections three decades later), that proportion dropped to 23 percent in 1924 and was back up to 48 percent in 1978. Married women in Muncie who "never" attended church climbed from 30 percent in 1890 to 53 percent in 1924 and tobogganed to 17 percent in 1978.[14] The Lynds asked ministers to complete a questionnaire on church attendance for November, 1924. This revealed that Sunday worship attendance was 61 percent female and 39 percent male in 1924.[15]

A pair of nationwide surveys using the identical methodology indicated that in 1952 church attendance in the United States was approximately 53 percent female and 47 percent male, but that by 1965 the ratio had changed to 61 percent female and 39 percent male.[16] The Gallup Poll reported that 43 percent of the women interviewed in 1983 and 37 percent of the men declared they had attended church in the past week. This was based on an equal number of interviews with women and with men.[17] When the fact is taken into consideration that women constitute a majority of the adult population by a 53-47 ratio and a slightly larger majority of all church members, the Gallup figures suggest that women contituted *at least* 58 or 59 percent of all adults present for corporate worship on the average Sunday in 1983. As was pointed out in chapter 3, in several of the mainline Protestant denominations men account for less than 40 percent of the adult worshipers on the average Sunday morning.

A far greater change, however, has come in recent years as more and more churches allow women to hold policy-making positions once held by men. It is not uncommon today for women to constitute 70 to 80 percent of those in attendance at a meeting of the Council on Ministries or the Administrative Board in a United Methodist congregation or three-quarters of those present at the monthly meeting of the church council in a United Church of Christ congregation. While the proportions often are not as overwhelming, an increasing number of Presbyterian, American Baptist, Lutheran, and Christian Church (Disciples of Christ) congregations report that women constitute a majority of those in attendance at the monthly meeting of the governing board. It also is not unusual today to attend a regular meeting of a committee on missions or Christian education or music or worship or social concerns or hunger at which all or nearly all of those present are female. Even the last three strongholds of male majorities (ushers, trustees, and finances) now may have a minority of males present at the meeting or ushering on Sunday morning.

As women have become the new majority in the population, they also have become, by an even larger margin, the majority of both worshipers and leaders in a growing number of congregations. Can that trend be reversed? Do people want it to be reversed? Will it be necessary to create once again some all-male enclaves within each congregation to reverse that pattern? Or is it a systemic issue which will require a radical restructuring of congregational life in order to attract more men? (Advocates of this point of view, including this writer, contend that most congregations, both Catholic and Protestant, are structured to attract women and repel men.) Or will that discrepancy disappear as a new generation of men, who were reared in a more egalitarian society, come along to replace the men who were born into and grew up in a male-dominated society? Or is the heart of the issue a theological distinction as the theologically conservative churches attract a larger proportion of men while it is the theologically liberal congregations in which women usually outnumber men by a two-to-one margin? Or is this the hand of God at work in the world? Or is the subject too complex with too many different facets to be resolved here? Or is anyone still *165* •

reading a paragraph that has become this long and is filled largely with question marks?

A simpler issue is to second-guess the past rather than to attempt to solve contemporary problems.

What Happened to That Next Baby Boom?

Back in the early 1960s most of the demographers and population experts predicted another baby boom in the 1970s and 1980s as the babies born after World War II became parents. That anticipated baby boom never materialized.

While many factors were at work, several of which have been elaborated on earlier in this chapter, four explain why the 1980s turned out to be a different world from the one that was anticipated back in 1960. One was the decision by millions of women born in the later 1940s and the 1950s to postpone marriage and motherhood and to enter the labor force on a long-term basis. For a couple of million women that will have the unexpected consequence that they will never marry.

A second was the desire of many parents for smaller families. The typical family of three to six children was replaced by the typical family of one to three children. The number of one-child families at least doubled.

A third factor was the completely unforeseen rise in the divorce rate, from 377,000 divorcees in 1955 to 2.4 million in 1980, which meant a lot of marriages were terminated before baby number one or two or three was born. While rarely identified in these terms, divorce has become a very influential factor in birth control.

A fourth factor, and the theme of this chapter, is that while it took two or three decades for the changes to surface, as women became the new majority the world for women changed dramatically. One of the changes was the growing shortage of husbands. Among other consequences that meant a lot of divorced women did not and will not remarry. Some do not want to bear children. Others who may want to have more children cannot afford to do so.

Overlapping these are the widely publicized advances in

artificial birth control techniques and the legalization of abortion. A reasonable projection, based on the world of 1955, forecast that at least seven, and probably as many as 8 million American women, would become pregnant in 1980. Out of those projected 8 million pregnancies it was reasonable to expect possibly that 600,000 of them would end in an illegally terminated induced abortion, 1.8 million would be terminated by a natural miscarriage, and 5.6 million would result in the live birth of a baby. In fact, at least 1 million of those projected pregnancies did not occur because of the pill and other new birth control techniques; perhaps another million did not occur because of the sharp increase in the number of divorces; 1.6 million were terminated by an induced abortion*; slightly over a million were ended by a natural miscarriage and, as a result, only 3.5 million live babies were born in 1980. Abortion has become an important form of birth control in the United States.

That meant a smaller enrollment of first-graders in 1987 and fewer second-graders in 1988 than was anticipated a quarter century earlier. It also meant fewer children in Sunday school and a decrease in the undergraduate enrollment of the nation's colleges and universities.

Perhaps most significant of all the consequences, however, was that unfulfilled projection of over 5 million births each year in the late 1970s and 1980s meant that the population of the United States would grow older, instead of growing younger, that fewer workers would be around to support the retirement life of the "baby boomers" born after World War II who would retire after the year 2015, that the mainline Protestant churches would shift away from their child orientation of the 1950s to a greater emphasis on adult concerns, and that pastors and other church leaders would have to become more creative in planning ministries to meet the new needs of a radically different era. It is harder to be a pastor when the old formulas become obsolete.

---

*In the typical year 7 out of every 1,000 women in the Netherlands under the age of 18 have an abortion, and in Canada 18 out of every 1,000 women under age 18 have an abortion. In the United States the annual rate is 60 abortions for every 1,000 women under age 18.

What Do You Count?

Perhaps the most widely overlooked consequence of the unfulfilled forecasts of a huge baby boom in the late 1970s and 1980s coincides with the decrease in family size. Public school officials, population control experts, and demographers have concentrated their attention on the far smaller number of births than was anticipated. From the local church perspective the number-one client is the parent, not the baby. Few one-year-olds or two-year-olds come to church by themselves, especially in cold weather. Nearly all are brought by a mother.

Therefore it is important to note that while the number of births decreased from 4.3 million in 1961 to 3.7 million in 1970 to 3.1 million in 1975, before climbing back up to 3.5 million in 1980 and 3.7 million in 1986, this was not a result of fewer women becoming mothers. The birth *rate* went down because the huge increase in the number of women of childbearing age was not accompanied by a record number of babies being born, but as families shrank in size, more mothers were required to produce a smaller number of children.

In 1960, for example, only 1.2 million mothers gave birth to their first child, but 4.2 million babies were born that year. By contrast, in 1980, when only 3.5 million babies were born, more than 1.4 million women became a mother for the first time. The number of babies was shrinking, but the number of mothers was increasing as family size shrank.

One consequence of this, since most parents tend to be more anxious that child number one receives better care than child number five, is the level of expectations was raised. This increased level of expectations has meant that many church nurseries that were acceptable in 1955 are now perceived as inadequate. It has changed the classroom style of the Sunday school, influenced the approach to youth ministries, and created a new demand for Mothers' Clubs. It also means the churches should be counting new mothers while the public school officials count births.

- *168*   The changes described thus far have reshaped American society and change always carries a price tag. Most observers would agree it is a better world today than it was thirty-five years ago, but the price tag is increased complexity. This means many of the issues facing local church leaders are far more complex than the issues on the agenda in 1950 or 1955.

Who Will Care for the Kids?

Perhaps the outstanding issue confronting the churches that illustrates the increase in complexity is the call for high quality day care for children of parents employed outside the home.[18] Frequently this is cited as a need in response to the growing number of working women. That oversimplifies the issue. As was pointed out earlier, there has been only a modest increase in the proportion of working-class mothers employed outside the home in the past seventy years. The big increase has been in the proportion of women with full-time employment who are married to professional, managerial, and business-class husbands. In 1986, 51 percent of all wives with a child under one year of age were employed ouside the home, compared to 31 percent in 1975.[19]

A second factor behind the increased demand for subsidized high quality day care has been the increase in the number of single parent mothers employed outside the home, from 600,000 in 1970 to 1.1 million in 1982. (That compares with an increase of 2 million in the number of women employed outside the home who are living with a husband and have children under six—that number climbed from 3.9 million in 1970 to 5.7 million in 1982.)

A third source of the increased demand for high quality day care centers comes from mothers who want the best for their firstborn child.

A fourth, and perhaps the most influential factor, has been the increase in the level of expectations by people born after 1945.

Women born after 1945 who are married to professional and managerial-class husbands are more likely to (a) be college graduates, (b) be employed in a professional, technical, or *169* •

managerial position, and *(c)* be able to articulate more clearly and with greater force their expectations of the world. Likewise mothers of firstborns often seek more for that child than they do for their second child.

In addition, to a substantial degree the American political economy is designed to provide fairly generous governmental subsidies for the middle- and upper-class segments of the population. (Most fiscal experts agree that an income tax system that provides deductions for state and local taxes, for interest payments, and for charitable contributions represents a decision to subsidize middle- and upper-income taxpayers. Likewise Social Security benefits go in disproportionately large amounts, if need is considered to be a factor, to middle- and upper-income recipients. Military and government pensions also go in disproportionately large amounts to the people above the median income level for that age group. Federal aid to college and university students is largely a subsidy for middle- and upper-income families. The list could go on for pages and would have to include farm subsidies and federally subsidized interest rates for home buyers.) This question of who will susidize day care is an issue that cannot be ignored because of the costs.

For many experts, however, the number-one issue is what is best for the child. On this question the evidence is mixed. Among the questions being raised by researchers are these. Do the children who spend several years in a day care center tend to be more aggressive as they grow older than children reared at home? Are children raised in a day care environment less adaptive to stress and less secure in relationships with adults than children reared in the home? Does day care stifle spontaneity and creativity? Are children in day care centers more likely to catch contagious diseases than children reared at home? Why are several European countries with long histories of day care reducing that emphasis in favor of allowances for parents? How important is the continuity and reassurance of a family's setting for a two-year-old on a day-after-day basis? How important is the continuity of having the same adult faces day after day? How

important is the continuity of the same children day after day in a small setting versus many different children in a large setting? How important is it for a parent, rather than a stranger or an acquaintance, to be the person who responds when an emergency means the two-year-old has to be taken from the child care center? It is possible to cite what appear to be scholarly studies to support either side of each of these questions as well as dozens of similar questions. One of the few points of widespread agreement is that children under one year of age should not be in day care centers; however, 38 percent of all single-parent mothers with a child under a year old are employed full-time.

Thus far the national policy in the United States has been to subsidize mothers with young children to stay home. The number-one legislative and financial expression of that policy is Aid to Families with Dependent Children (AFDC).* The number of families receiving AFDC increased from 803,000 in 1960 to nearly 3.6 million in 1975 and has remained on a plateau ever since. The total number of recipients of AFDC has hovered between 10 and 11 million since 1973. The dollar payments for AFDC have increased from $4.9 billion in 1970 to approximately $15 billion in 1985. Proponents of federally subsidized high quality day care apparently are determined to make day care centers the number-one priority aid to families in which the mother is employed outside the home. This raises an interesting policy issue for church leaders to decide what they believe should be the number-one priority in intergenerational subsidies. Should the top priority be given for financial grants to enable mothers to stay home with their children? That is the current national policy. Or should the number-one priority be to provide subsidized day care so the mother can be employed outside the home?

The increase of a trillion dollars in the size of the national debt during the first half of the 1980s suggests either (a) there is a limit on the taxes the American people are willing to pay for intergenerational transfers of income (except apparently there is

---

*The original legislation for Aid to Dependent Children was directed to help children of widows. Nearly 50 percent of the early beneficiaries were half-orphans. By 1985 one-half of the mothers receiving AFDC payments had never been married.

no limit on what Congress is willing to transfer to the present generation from future generations) or (b) there is a ceiling on the taxes which elected officials are willing to levy on the present generation of taxpayers. In the light of this apparent ceiling on intergenerational transfers, who should be the chief beneficiary of any change in that policy? Should those taxpayers born before 1965 pay more taxes in order to increase the benefits provided by the federal government to teenage mothers? In 1985 the cost for Aid to Families with Dependent Children, food stamps, Medicaid, public housing, foster care, and special education for families started by teenage mothers came to nearly $20 billion.

Or should the taxpayers born after 1925 be asked to pay more taxes in order to improve the care of the 1.3 million elderly Americans in nursing homes? In 1985 federal, state, and local subsidies for residents of nursing homes exceeded $17 billion.

Or should the taxpayers born before 1950, the childless couples, the family which forgoes one parent's income so that parent can be home with the children, and single adults be asked to pay higher taxes in order to increase the federal subsidy for day care from $4 billion in 1985 to at least $10 to $15 billion, if not to the $50 to $75 billion, required to reach the goal of "high" quality day care?[20]

Or should the federal government borrow this money for a larger subsidy for more and better day care today and let the taxpayers of 2017 and 2031 foot the bill? The ethical side of the question becomes more complex when one realizes that over half of that increased subsidy for day care centers undoubtedly will go to families with above average income.

If the staffing standards set by experts in early childhood development are met (one adult for each two children under age three and one adult for each four children over age three)* and if these staff members are paid at the median salary level paid public school kindergarten teachers in 1987, the daily operating costs (exclusive of the costs of constructing the facilities) would be between $35 and $50 for each child over age three and $60 to $80

---

*State requirements for licensed day care centers vary greatly and range from four children per adult to as many as twelve children per care-giver.

per child for each child under three. That would be the cost for what might be defined as "quality day care." "High quality day care" probably would cost at least $50 to $100 per day per child. Many single parents and low income parents will continue to leave their child with grandmother, a neighbor, or some other relative rather than pay that.

In addition, an undetermined amount of first-hand parental involvement would be required plus visits to the homes by staff. It is possible to keep those costs down by (a) increasing the number of children per staff member and (b) paying the staff at or near the minimum wage as is the practice in many licensed centers. A number of feminists have raised the issue, however, if it is fair to pay a woman $6,000 to $8,000 a year to care for the children of the parent who is making $20,000 to $60,000 a year.

One of the more widely overlooked questions for church leaders who believe their congregations should offer day care for children of working mothers concerns the type of care to be offered. The statistics suggest many parents have serious reservations about placing their children in an institutionalized setting. For every two preschool children in a licensed day care center (about half of which are profit-making ventures with the primary goal of making money and the care of children as a secondary goal), four or five children are cared for by a relative, neighbor, or friend.

If people's values are gauged by their actions, it appears the number-one preference of those parents who can afford it is in-the-home care. This can run as high as $10,000 to $15,000 a year. According to the American Council of Nanny Schools at least thirty schools in the United States are offering training to prepare women to serve as live-in child care specialists. The cost for a family with two young children usually is less than the actual costs of high quality institutional day care.

Perhaps the greatest frustration of the employed mother is the unexpected illness or accident which means the child cannot be with other children. If unmet needs are influential in planning ministries and programs, perhaps offering care for children   *173* ▪

recuperating from an illness or accident should be a high priority for churches seeking to offer child care. If the parents' preferences are influential, perhaps the highest priority should be given to finding and training adults who would like to offer care in their home and obtain a license to do that.

That option immediately raises the question of whether the churches should offer direct services or place a higher priority on equipping others to offer the services.

Many will urge the churches to accept a public advocacy role and lobby for the public schools to offer day care for children of all ages from early in the morning before school opens until late evening.* An impressive argument also can be made for the serious unmet need of the employed mothers of handicapped or developmentally disabled children who are not accepted by many day care centers. The fastest growing *need* is for *adult* day care inside the home and the second fastest growing need is for *adult* day care outside the home. That, however, would require a 180-degree shift in the intergenerational transfer of governmental and/or charitable funds for day care.

Questions to Be Asked

These comments are offered here, not as an attempt to analyze the day care issue, but rather to suggest it is a very complex problem. It is even more complicated in those states where the law prohibits the employer from inquiring about the past prison record of applicants seeking work in day care centers. The complexity also is enhanced by the rising costs of liability insurance.

Additional questions that complicate the issue include several others that come up repeatedly in churches offering day care for children of working parents. Do we charge for days when the

---

*In those states where school tax levies are determined by the voters, proponents of participatory democracy might be especially interested in this alternative since it allows the people to decide public policy rather than to leave that decision to elected officials.

child is absent? The public schools charge for "slots," not attenders. What should our child care center charge for, days or slots? Should the congregation as a whole subsidize it out of the budget or should the subsidy be from designated second-mile giving? Whom should we see as our number-one client? The parent? The child? The staff? (Whoever comes in third on that question will be expected to subsidize whoever comes in first.) What are the qualifications necessary to serve on the staff of our center? Should we offer this as a community service or as part of a larger ministry with families that include young children? Do we serve only preschool children or do we also offer an afterschool program for older children? (In 1986 before and afterschool programs operated by public schools cost $125 to $150 per month per student.) If we charge a fee based on a sliding scale that requires upper-income parents to pay full costs, will we be able to compete with other day care centers for these upper-income families? Do we need their children to provide a wider range of experiences for all children? Do we accept children from homes where the parent is not employed, but simply seeks convenient (and perhaps subsidized) baby-sitting services? Do we operate in the evenings to serve those single-parent families in which the parent works a night shift? Would we really do more good to take the money we plan to allocate to subsidize the day care center and provide "scholarships" for the care of the children of the most needy working parents in our community, so they can find the kind of child care they prefer, such as paying a grandmother or a neighbor? If, after several years we determine we may be doing more harm than good, how do we terminate the operation without dismissing employees who need their jobs? Who will do the evaluation to determine whether the children are benefiting or being harmed by spending a couple of thousand hours a year in our center?

Inasmuch as more children of working mothers are cared for in private homes than in day care centers and the costs are substantially less, does this suggest our church should consider offering that alternative rather than institutionalized care? Or are those choices to be available only to those who can afford them? *175* ▪

Questions on Subsidies

From a larger perspective on public policy the churches may have to take a position on subsidies for child care.

If the churches support current proposals for federally subsidized high quality day care for the children of working parents, that raises another series of questions. Should the subsidy go to the parent or to the day care center? If it is directed to the parent, may that parent take the grant to pay a live-in person to care for the child? Would that grant be subject to income tax? Or, like Social Security payments, would it be largely or completely a tax-free grant? If the grant is given to the day care center, would mothers who care for neighbors' children be eligible to receive those grants? Or is part of the long-term goal to minimize day care by neighbors and relatives in favor of institutionalized care? As was pointed out earlier, the current national policy is biased in favor of mothers caring for their own children in their own home. Should that bias be reversed in favor of parents who work outside the home? Implementation of some of the current proposals could mean a federal subsidy of $20,000 a year to the parent earning $50,000 a year. That is double the federal aid to the single parent rearing the same number of children in the home and substantially above the wages paid to the women providing the care. Or should there be a means test to restrict grants only to low-income parents?

If the congregation provides subsidized child care and subsidizes that out of the offering plate, should the subsidy be available to all or only to low-income parents? Or only to members? If the median annual income of the families in that congregation is $33,000, should families below that income level who do not have children be asked to subsidize the care of children from families where the total annual income of both parents is above $50,000?

Should the system be parallel to the federal aid program for university and college students of the late 1970s and early 1980s that was designed to ask low-income families to subsidize the education of children from higher-income families? Or should it be designed so higher-income adults subsidize day care for children of *only* low-income parents? (That probably means it would not receive approval in Congress.)

Or should the primary subsidy be paid by the employer as a fringe benefit? How can this be designed to meet the demands of those who insist on equal treatment for men and women in the labor force? Or should national policy deliberately be biased in favor of parents and against childless adults?

Who will make these policy statements on behalf of the churches? Pastors? Parents? Denominational leaders? Interde-nominational organizations?

Life was easier back in 1955 when the big annual venture into the field of child care was the annual vacation Bible school!

What About Men?

Some readers may ask why this long chapter lifts up the changes affecting women and largely ignores men. The answer is in the title of this book. Today it is a far different world for women than it was thirty-five years ago. When compared to women, in disproportionately large numbers men as a group continue, as in the past, to place a higher priority on work than on family relationships, avoid physicians, wear the same clothes two or more days in a row, drink, purchase overly expensive cars, lie, ignore their parental responsibilities, buy themselves toys they rarely play with, fish, live on the streets, get themselves killed in automobile accidents, seek political control over others and surrender that power only when forced to do so, watch football games on television, kill one another, die prematurely, kidnap other people, quickly find a younger replacement when the first spouse disappears and sometimes do that prematurely, deal drugs, vote Republican, be unwilling to ride on buses, physically abuse their spouses, not wash their own clothes, carry handguns, eat too much, abandon their children, not read books, gamble, drop out of church before graduating from high school, be unfaithful to their spouses, try to hold two full-time jobs at the same time, sexually molest children, embezzle, drop out of school, borrow more money than they will be able to repay, *177* ∎

prefer to express their creativity through their hands rather than through verbal skills, beat up on one another, snatch the purses of old ladies, sexually harrass persons to whom they are not married, chew tobacco or use snuff, join the Communist Party, not listen when others speak, get poor grades in school, ride motorcycles, commit arson, not attend Sunday morning worship, sin, not learn to type, drive big trucks in order to scare motorists in small automobiles, cheat, explore new frontiers, play handball, seek to prove their masculinity by impregnating young women and girls, commit suicide, bet on the World Series, race automobiles, give out unsolicited advice, and write books about women.

In other words, for most men the world has not changed as much since 1950, even since 1400, as it has for women since they became the new majority.

In two areas of life, however, men have moved into new roles in larger numbers than have women. One is the role of absentee parent. The second is as a member of the growing urban underclass which draws its constituents in disproportionately large numbers from young unemployed males who have dropped out of school, but have not joined the labor force. One result of those two changes is the rapid growth in the number of twenty-nine-year-old grandmothers.

NOTES

1. For a remarkable account of middle-class single women see Martha Vicinus, *Independent Women: Work and Community for Single Women* (Chicago: University of Chiago Press, 1985).

2. Theodore Caplow, *Middletown Families* (Minneapolis: University of Minnesota Press, 1982), pp. 97-100.

3. For an excellent analysis of the changing role of women married to pastors see Donna Sinclair, *The Pastor's Wife Today* (Nashville: Abingdon Press, 1981).

4. For a brief on behalf of the movement of women into the pastoral ministry see Lyle E. Schaller, ed. *Women as Pastors* (Nashville: Abingdon Press, 1982).

5. A brief analysis of the central organizing principles of a local church organization for women can be found in Lyle E. Schaller, *Getting Things Done* (Nashville: Abingdon Press, 1986), pp. 52-53. See also chapter 9 on choices in this book.

6. Christine A. Bachrach and Marjorie C. Horn, "Marriage and First Intercourse, Marital Dissolution, and Remarriage: United States, 1982," *Advance Data*, April 12, 1985.

7. For a more creative approach to dividing adults into classes and groups see Warren J. Hartman, *Five Audiences* (Nashville: Abingdon Press, 1987).

8. William R. Greer, "The Changing Women's Marriage Market," *New York Times*, February 22, 1986. Also see *Newsweek*, June 2, 1986, pp. 54-61.

9. Laurel Richardson, *The New Other Woman* (New York: The Free Press, 1985).

10. When the Air Force Academy began to prepare to admit women cadets in 1976, the most perplexing issue was what to do when the first woman cadet became pregnant. Dozens of scenarios were proposed but no one could anticipate what actually happened. The first woman among the cadets to become pregnant did not appear to be carrying a child and categorically denied it until less than a week before the baby was born. Judith Hicks Stiehm, *Bring Me Men and Women* (Berkeley, Calif.: University of California Press, 1981), pp. 208-9. So much for those who expect to be able to anticipate every future contingency.

11. A very readable introduction to the subject and to the subject of birth order is Kevin Lehman, *The Birth Order Book* (Old Tappan, N.J.: Fleming H. Revell Co., 1984). An earlier introduction to the subject is Lucille Forer and Henry Still, *The Birth Order Factor* (New York: David McKay Co., 1976). An excellent research report is Walter Toman, *Family Constellation* (New York: Springer Publishing Co., 1976).

12. Lenore J. Weitzman, *The Divorce Revolution: The Unexpected Social and Economic Consequences for Women and Children in America* (New York: The Free Press, 1985). See also Eugenie Ladner Birch, ed. *The Unsheltered Woman: Women and Housing in the '80s* (New Brunswick, N.J.: Center for Urban Policy Research, 1985).

13. Two books for mothers, one by an economist and the other by a linguist, that have aroused negative responses from feminists are Sylvia Ann Hewlett, *A Lesser Life: The Myth of Women's Liberation in America* (New York: William Morrow & Co., 1986) and Deborah Fallows, *A Mother's Work* (Boston: Houghton Mifflin Co., 1985). Also see *Fortune*, August 18, 1986, pp. 16-23.

14. Theodore Caplow, et al., *All Faithful People* (Minneapolis: University of Minnesota Press, 1983), p. 306.

15. *Ibid.*, pp. 75-76.

16. Martin E. Marty, Stuart E. Rosenberg, Andrew M. Greeley, *What Do We Believe?* (New York: Meredith Press, 1968).

17. *Religion in America* (Princeton, N.J.: The Gallup Report No. 222, March, 1984), pp. 57, 95.

18. For a view of day care by a highly educated professional who also is a mother see Fallows, *A Mother's Work*. For a brief critique of some of the questions facing the churches see Brenda Hunter, "Breaking the Tie That Binds," *Christianity Today*, February 21, 1986, pp. 31-33. For an analysis of one commercial operation see Myron Magnet, "What Mass-Produced Child Care Is Producing," *Fortune*, November 28, 1983, pp. 157-74.

19. Howard Hayghe, "Rise in Mother's Labor Force Activity Includes Those with Infants," *Monthly Labor Review*, February, 1986, pp. 43-45. In March, 1985, 64 percent of all black married mothers with a child under one year of age were employed compared to 49 percent of the white mothers living with their husbands. It also should be noted that only 31 percent of the white mothers of preschoolers worked full-time on a year around basis compared to 47 percent of the black mothers of children under age three. One result of that was that the median income in 1984 of black wives with preschoolers was 50 percent higher than the median income of white wives who were employed outside the home and had preschool children.

20. During the 1980s Congress began to change this longtime policy of encouraging mothers to stay home with children by changing the tax laws to (a) penalize families with two or more children, (b) penalize families in which the wife remained home to rear the children while the husband worked, (c) reward childless couples, and (d) reward parents who choose to hire someone else to care for their children.

THE TWENTY-NINE-YEAR-OLD GRANDMOTHER

"**A**t the heart of the deterioration of the fabric of Negro society is the deterioration of the Negro family. . . . In a word, a national effort towards the problems of Negro Americans must be directed toward the question of family structure."

In these words, drawn from his monograph, *The Negro Family: The Case for National Action*, assistant secretary of labor Daniel Patrick Moynihan (by 1986 senior United States senator from the state of New York) challenged the nation to develop a policy that would break the vicious cycle that was resulting in the continued deterioration of the Negro family. Moynihan concluded that simply lifting legal barriers to full participation would not be sufficient to bring blacks into the mainstream of American life. The issue was "enhancing the stability and resources of the Negro American family," and a comprehensive jobs program. He contended that many of the children reared in a welfare dependency world would not be able to take advantage of equal opportunities if and when available. The report was completed in March 1965.

What happened?

Publication of the report in the summer of 1965 aroused a storm of indignation from politicians, civil rights organizations, social scientists, and church leaders.

In a famous commencement address at Howard University, which had been written by Richard N. Goodwin and Moynihan, President Lyndon B. Johnson addressed the problems facing blacks in northern ghettos and announced that he planned to call a White House Conference to address issues facing Negro Americans.

By early November, a week before the scheduled Conference, sixty representatives from churches and civil rights organizations in New York had met to demand that any references to "family stability" be deleted from the Conference's agenda.[1]

Twenty years later, in the Godkin Lectures at Harvard, Moynihan reflected on the bitter criticism aimed at his report. "There was a massive failure of nerve among whites. . . . There was seemingly no untruth to which some would not subscribe if there appeared to be the least risk of disapproval from the groupthink of the moment. This was notably so among churchmen."[2]

Twenty-one years later, in January, 1986, CBS presented a two-hour documentary, "The Vanishing Family: Crisis in Black America," that picked up the thesis presented by Moynihan, and the program received widespread approval from black clergy, black civil rights leaders, black politicians, black law enforcement officials, black academicians, and black journalists.

One reason for the change in the public response was that the events of the previous two decades had demonstrated the accuracy of Moynihan's diagnosis. In 1965 one-quarter of black births were out of wedlock, and he was widely criticized for using that as an indicator of the destabilization of the black family. In 1985, 58 percent of all black babies were born to unmarried mothers, some of whom were the babies born out of wedlock that Moynihan had referred to in 1965, or to their younger sisters.

181 ▪

One projection suggests that by the year 2000, 70 percent of all black families will be headed by a single woman.

In 1984, 81 percent of all white children under age eighteen were living with two parents. One out of eight white births was to an unmarried mother compared to nearly three out of five black births. Five percent of all black children live with relatives other than their parents compared to fewer than 1 percent of white children.

One study reported that out of every one hundred white teenage pregnancies in 1985, 47 were terminated by abortion, 35 resulted in a birth to a married mother, and 19 were births to an unmarried mother. By contrast, the black teenage girl was twice as likely to become pregnant as the white teenager. Out of every one hundred black teenage pregnancies in 1985, 41 were terminated by an abortion, 8 resulted in a birth to a married mother, and 51 resulted in a birth to an unmarried black mother.[3] Out of every thousand teenage black girls 85 will become an unmarried mother in an average year compared to 15 out of every thousand white teenagers.*

According to a study of Professor William J. Wilson of the University of Chicago in 1980, there were only 35 employed black men aged 18-19 for every 100 black women, aged 18-19, and only 45 employed black men, aged 20-24, for every 100 black women in that age bracket, down from 75 in 1960.[4] Potential fathers are more numerous than potential husbands among young black adults.

Perhaps the most sigificant single statistic that supports Moynihan's thesis is that in 1965 the average score of black students in aptitude tests was 68 percent of the average score of white students. By 1980 that ratio had fallen to 45 percent of the white score.

At the end of 1985 a total of 3.3 million children in America under eighteen years of age were living with a never-married

---

*It must be emphasized the big increase in births referred to here are to *unmarried* teenage girls. The birth rate for all women aged 15-19 in 1984 was the lowest since 1940 and was slightly over one-half the rate of 1955. Likewise teenage mothers accounted for only 13 percent of all births in 1984, the lowest proportion since 1957.

mother. Approximately 2 million of these were black children, 900,000 were white, and 300,000 were Hispanic. That figure of 3.3 million in 1985 is over six times the 1970 total!

Another, and perhaps more interesting, reason for the positive response to the CBS documentary was that the taboo of the 1960s had been broken. It no longer was considered to be a racist position to describe the deterioration of black families. This first became apparent as an increasing number of "grass roots" blacks openly identified the heart of the problem. Some were quoted in newspaper stories, others spoke up at neighborhood gatherings, and a growing number indicated their discontent by making major sacrifices to enroll their children in private Christian day schools which placed a strong emphasis on traditional family values. They were joined by the black clergy and by a growing number of outspoken black scholars such as Thomas Sowell, Walter Williams, Kay Hammond, Eleanor Holmes Norton, Glenn C. Loury, and Eddie N. Williams. In 1984 the National Urban League and the NAACP co-sponsored the first Black Family Summit Conference held at Fisk University in Nashville. By early 1986 most black leaders were publicly acknowledging that the decline of the family was a crucial national issue.[5]

For those interested in the process of planned change the response to the Moynihan Report in 1965 illustrated the classic syndrome of "kill the messenger who bears the bad news." All too frequently the person who diagnoses a troubled situation becomes the target of attacks by those who do not want to hear the bad news. By the time the CBS documentary was televised in early 1986 enough time had elapsed since the publication of Moynihan's monograph so that it was now possible to make this an issue of serious public debate. A huge array of monographs, books, articles, and policy papers have been published since 1965 that offer a supportive context for open discussions about what is referred to as the "underclass."[6]

What Are the Implications?

This brief chapter is not the place to attempt to offer a solution to that extremely complex subject of the deterioration of the black   *183* ▪

family. The central thesis of this book is that today's world is a far more complex place than the world of the 1950s and therefore the challenges facing both congregational and denominational leaders are far more difficult than were the challenges of the 1950s.

This increased complexity is illustrated by the deterioration of the black family in America. Charges of "racism," which were hurled at Daniel Patrick Moynihan in 1965, no longer are perceived as rational or useful responses to someone who comes up with a diagnosis of a problem. If one defines the issue as a problem of illegitimacy, it becomes clear that the distinctive variable is social class, not race. One study, for example, suggested that over half of the variations from one community to another in the rate of illegitimate births *among whites* can be explained by income and educational levels. Thus, in 1980 in Ohio the illegitimacy rate among white births in Shaker Heights was 1 percent compared to 25 percent of all white births in that year in Portsmouth. When black births were studied, income and educational levels appeared to explain 79 percent of the variance in rates of illegitimacy.[7] The increase in the number of twenty-nine-year-old grandmothers appears to be a predominantly black problem if one looks solely at the numbers. If one looks at underlying causes, such as the ability to cope with difficulties, it may be really an issue of social class. A persuasive argument can be made that the ability to cope, a strong future orientation, and a willingness to pay the price of deferred gratification are among the best indicators of social class,[8] and social class, not race, is at the heart of this issue.

As the complexity of the causes behind this increase in the number of twenty-nine-year-old grandmothers becomes more widely understood, it becomes apparent that simply increasing federal appropriations to relieve poverty may not be as useful as it was thought to be once. The tremendous increases in federal expenditures to reduce poverty have been remarkably effective in reducing poverty among the elderly. In 1960 "old" and "poor"

often were synonymous. Today the most common synonym for

poor is "single mother," but increased federal expenditures have not eliminated poverty in single-parent families.

In more specific terms this rapid increase in the number of twenty-nine-year-old and thirty-three-year-old grandmothers raises a half dozen complex issues that deserve the attention of church leaders.

The first is what is the role of the churches in inculcating a system of values in each new generation of young people? Black parents and grandparents in the inner city repeatedly argue that a greater emphasis on traditional family values is the only way to break the cycle of what the Reverend Jesse Jackson has described as "babies having babies."

In that famous speech at Howard University in June, 1965, President Johnson declared, "The family is the cornerstone of our society. More than any other force it shapes the attitudes, the hopes, the ambitions, and the values of the child."[9] Which is the more influential in shaping values? The family? The federal budget? The school? Which should be the number-one concern of church leaders? Which should be a secondary concern? Which is the easiest to address at the annual denominational convention?

Overlapping this is a second issue. Should the churches teach a particular value system? Or should the educational system in the churches be value free? What values should be taught in the weekday nursery school which meets in your building? What values should be taught in the high school youth group? What values should be modeled by the actions of volunteer leaders working with children and youth? What values should be taught in the public school system? (See the section on the Christian day school in chapter 4.)

This debate over values raises a third question. What is the central motivating force behind the rapid increase in recent years in the enrollment of private schools? In the later 1950s and early 1960s it was easy for liberal church leaders to define the issue as racism and segregation.

Today, with the decrease in white enrollment and the increase in black enrollment in Christian day schools, it is a far more *185* ▪

complex issue. What is the "racist" stance? Moving to white suburbia to escape the central city public schools? Sending one's own children to a private school? Opposing the creation of more Christian day schools in the central city in order to force black children to attend public schools? Requiring competency tests for teachers in the public schools? Offering church-sponsored scholarships and/or federally financed vouchers to enable black parents to send their children to private schools?

Thus a fourth question for consideration by church leaders is, What is the appropriate response for a Christian on this issue? Whether the debate centers on books by Charles Murray[10] or Lawrence W. Mead[11] or Daniel Patrick Moynihan[12] or vouchers or on public housing or teacher training or the teaching of values or church mergers or denominational subsidies or athletic scholarships, it is far more difficult to define, with a high degree of self-confidence, the racist position today than it was in the 1950s.

From the perspective of many pastors, both black and white, an issue that should not be ignored is the disappearance of men from the churches on Sunday morning and Sunday evening. While this is not as apparent in the churches that place high expectations on the members as it is on those that function as voluntary associations, it is easy today to find a white congregation in which on the typical Sunday morning 60 to 70 percent of the adults present are females. Likewise it is easy to find black churches in which 75 to 95 percent of the adults at worship are women. It is hard to believe this trend is not related to the deterioration of the family.

While this is of minor importance, one of the consequences of the efforts by the federal government to eradicate poverty has been the elimination of a favorite excuse in white churches for not undertaking a particular course of action. It used to be easy to rationalize, "We simply don't have the financial resources. So many of our members are elderly and on fixed incomes, we can't afford to do that."

It is difficult to demonstrate that the federally financed war on
poverty did much for families, either black or white, but it did

help the elderly move out of poverty. Twenty-eight percent of the federal budget ($235 billion) for 1984 was allocated to persons over age sixty-five, an average of $8,000 per mature adult. In 1984, 26 percent of all Americans were under age eighteen while 13 percent were sixty-five and over, but federal expenditures for the elderly exceeded federal expenditures for children and youth by a 10-1 ratio. As a group, the elderly in the United States now have a higher per capita annual income than the rest of the population and a far higher per capita amount of savings. In 1985 the average Social Security check was for an amount nearly five times the average check of 1970. Few church budgets increased at that rate. What should be the responses by the churches to this division of the federally financed social welfare pie?

For some, the most perplexing and frustrating consequences of these changes in American society has been the realization that simplistic answers to complex questions often are counterproductive. In the 1950s the traditional answer in the churches was to "take up a collection." In the 1960s many denominations concluded that was insufficient and a better course of action would be to lobby for massive federal aid. Whether the subject is the disappearance of the family farm, the declining quality of the public school system, the deterioration of the family, the recurring famines in Africa or the plight of the homeless, additional dollars do not appear to be the way to reduce the size of the problem. Today, for example, an increasing number of black leaders publicly contend that the solution for the increasing number of twenty-nine-year-old grandmothers must come from within the black community, but that is of little solace for the white suburbanite who is convinced "our church must help." The search for scapegoats and easy answers continues, but it is not as promising as it was twenty or thirty years ago. As compassion supplants indignation, it becomes more difficult to find easy answers.

A simple illustration of this is the history of the "missional priority" of The United Methodist Church to reach and to serve a larger number of Blacks, Native Americans, Hispanics, and Asians. During the dozen years following adoption of that *187* ∎

missional priority in 1975 more than $20 million was allocated to that cause. With the exception of a rapid increase in the number of Korean congregations, which many concede probably would have occurred without the missional priority, very little has been accomplished. The proportion of the Black, Native American, and Hispanic population who identify with the denomination has shrunk. By contrast, the Assemblies of God, the American Baptist Churches, and the Southern Baptist Convention have experienced a sharp increase in the number of non-Anglo members.

This example leads to the final, and for many including this writer, the most disturbing issue that is illustrated by the growing numbers of twenty-nine-year-old grandmothers. Hope, not money, makes the difference. The Christian churches have been remarkably successful in recent decades in raising money to help the needy, to feed the hungry, and to shelter the homeless. They have been even more effective in getting a larger share of governmental and corporate expenditures allocated to these and similar causes.

The churches, however, historically have been most effective in reaching, assimilating into a worshiping congregation, and serving those who have hope. One example is the success in recent years, particularly of Presbyterians, Southern Baptists, and United Methodists, of reaching the Korean immigrants. Another example is the upward mobility of the members—and churches—of American Christianity. Perhaps the most significant example of the same point is that the early New Testament churches apparently attracted the upwardly mobile, the ambitious, the persons filled with hope, the self-confident, and those willing to "break out of the ordinary social structures," but did not attract the destitute, "the poorest of the poor" or those without hope.[13]

The Synoptic Gospels state clearly and unequivocally the concern of Jesus for the poor, the oppressed, and the downtrodden. For those who take this literally the great

disappointment of the past several years has been the emergence of a rapidly growing underclass and the inability of the churches to reach these people.

The most difficult issue of today is not raising money to help the poor; it is instilling hope in those who have no hope. This may explain the successes of the Korean-American churches and the limited success of missionaries on Indian reservations. This may explain why so many black immigrants from the Caribbean Islands have been able "to make it" in the United States and Canada and why so many of the children and grandchildren of those twenty-nine-year-old grandmothers have not been able to enter into the mainstream of American society. This may help explain why women greatly outnumber men in those inner city churches. This may help explain why a majority of black babies are born out of wedlock. This may help explain why the typical Asian family is a more cohesive and supportive unit than are so many of those black families headed by a never-married twenty-nine-year-old black grandmother.

This may help explain why the departure of the black middle-class from the inner city has had such an impact. The presence of the black physicians, teachers, businessmen, lawyers, and other persons with hope in the future provided positive role models in the 1950s. They were replaced as role models in the 1980s by drug dealers, unemployed men spending the day on the sidewalk, pimps, prostitutes, unwed teenage mothers who had dropped out of school to have a baby, and the twenty-nine-year-old grandmother on welfare. What is the source of hope? That may help explain why Jewish immigrants have been more successful in overcoming discrimination than the great-great-grandchildren of blacks brought here as slaves. Hope may be the key reason why some black twenty-nine-year-old grandmothers are financially self-supporting and others are not.

How do the Christian churches instill hope in the hopeless? That question rarely was raised thirty years ago. That is one reason why it is a more difficult time to be a leader in the churches today.

What Has Not Worked?

No one should interpret what is written here to suggest this is a problem only with black families. The American population also includes an excessively large number of white never-married twenty-nine-year-old grandmothers.

In searching for answers, it may be useful first to look at what has not worked with either black or white families. To eliminate any basis for racist allegations the focus will be largely on white teenagers.

During the middle third of this century the social reformers, planners, and experts on family life appeared to agree on ten factors that could be altered to produce a favorable impact on children during their formative years. While this is far from a complete list, it may be useful to reflect on what has been the result.

1. During the late 1930s, the 1940s, and the early 1950s most experts agreed that "safe, sanitary, and decent" housing would greatly improve the lot of the poor. The number of low-rent public housing units climbed from slightly over a half million units in 1960 to over 2 million in 1985. One result has been an increase in the number of twenty-nine-year-old grandmothers, both black and white.

The clearest lesson has been that though upper-income families and the elderly can live comfortably in densely populated apartment towers, low-income families with children have not found apartment living a beneficial environment.

2. In more recent years it was concluded that income supplements such as food stamps, direct public assistance, subsidized housing, and subsidized medical care could be used to lift families with children at home out of poverty and provide a more promising world for teenagers.

The number of free school lunches served rose from 217 million in 1960 to 1.7 billion in 1981. Federal expenditures for food stamps rose from $33 million in 1965 to $12 billion in 1981. Aid to Families with Dependent Children increased from 800,000 families in 1960 to 3.6 million families in 1982.

One result of these and other programs was that the percentage of *white* sixteen- and seventeen-year-olds living in poverty (using 1.25 of poverty line defined by the Census Bureau as the cutoff point) dropped from 24.7 percent in 1960 to 9.9 percent in 1980—a remarkable improvement.[14]

3. For years a variety of studies have indicated that children reared in large families do not perform as well on tests of intelligence and achievement as do the children reared in smaller families, even after an allowance is made for differing socio-economic status of the families studied.

In 1960 one out of five youth, ages 16 and 17, lived in families with four or more siblings. By 1980 that proportion had dropped to less than one in seven.

4. The educational reformers of the 1930–60 era were nearly unanimous in their conclusions that larger schools provided a far better educational environment than offered by small schools.[15] The number of one-room, one-teacher schools dropped from 149,282 in 1930 to 798 in 1982 and relatively few high school students are enrolled in schools with fewer than 350 students today.

5. For decades it has been argued that longer academic preparation is necessary to produce better classroom teachers. As recently as 1960 fewer than a fourth of all teachers had earned a master's degree. Today well over half hold that degree.

6. A parallel argument has been that children learn better in smaller classes. The average number of secondary school pupils per class dropped from 28 in 1960 to 23 in 1980 according to the National Center for Educational Statistics.

7. Others have argued that a critical variable in the educational setting is the per capita expenditures. The schools that spend more were believed to offer better educational opportunities. After allowing for inflation, per pupil expenditures on schooling almost exactly doubled between 1960 and 1980—from $1,248 (in 1980 dollars) in 1960 to $2,491 in 1980 (also in 1980 dollars).

8. In more recent years greater emphasis has been placed on the influence of the home and of the parents' education in *191* ▪

attempting to determine why some children perform better than others in school.

A dramatic improvement took place between 1960 and 1980 in regard to the educational attainment level of the parents. In 1960, 57 percent of all mothers of sixteen- and seventeen-year-old youths were not high school graduates. By 1980 that proportion had dropped to only 24.4 percent. Likewise the proportion of fathers living with sixteen- and seventeen-year-old children who had graduated from high school also improved greatly. In 1960 nearly two-thirds (64 percent) of these fathers had not graduated from high school. In 1980 only 27 percent were not high school graduates.

9. Nearly everyone has noted that the decrease in the speed limits on the nation's highways to 55 miles per hour has been accompanied by a decrease in the number of deaths attributed to automobile accidents from 54,600 in 1970 to 45,900 in 1975. The lower speed limit should mean fewer teenage deaths on the highways.

10. Finally, many people agreed that teenagers could benefit from part-time jobs during the school year. This would introduce them to the work ethic, provide pocket money, enable them to save to go to college and keep them busy. As a result by 1982, 43 percent of all white sixteen- to nineteen-year-olds *enrolled in school below the college level* had either part-time or full-time jobs, double the proportion of 1960. The average weekly income of all sixteen- to nineteen-year-old youth in 1984 was nearly $50 per week.

A review of these ten changes would suggest the typical sixteen- or seventeen-year-old of the 1980s had many advantages over the adolescents of 1960. What happened?

1. The death rate from automobile accidents for white adolescents ages 15-19 climbed from 35.5 per 100,000 persons in that age group in 1960 to 50.4 per 100,000 in1980—a 42 percent increase.

2. The homicide rate for white youth aged 15-19 jumped from 2.2 per 100,000 in 1960 to 7.3 in 1980.

3. The suicide rate for that same age group of white adoles-

cents climbed from 38 per 100,000 in 1960 to 9.1 in 1980.

4. Despite the availability of the pill and other birth control devices the birth rate nearly tripled from 6.6 per 1,000 *unmarried* white women aged 15-19 in 1960 to 15.9 in 1980.

5. This dramatic increase in the birth rate occurred despite a sharp increase in abortions. In 1973 for white women ages 15-19 out of every 1,000 pregnancies that were ended with either a live birth or an abortion (thus not counting pregnancies terminated by a spontaneous miscarriage) "only" 280 were terminated by an abortion. Six years later in 1979 that ratio had changed to 444 abortions for every 556 live births.

6. The delinquency rate for ten- to seventeen-year-olds more than doubled from 20.1 per 1,000 persons in that age group in 1960 to 46.4 in 1980.

7. In 1972 only 7 percent of all white youth aged 12-17 admitted they were using drugs. By 1979 that proportion had jumped to 16.7 percent. In 1972 only 24 percent of all white youth aged 12-17 admitted they were currently drinking alcoholic beverages. By 1979 that proportion had climbed to 37.2 percent.

8. The SAT scores for college-bound high school seniors dropped from 477 in 1960 on the verbal test to 424 in 1980 while the average score on the math test dropped from 498 in 1960 to 466 twenty years later.

While someone may argue that conditions would be far worse today without all of the "improvements" of the past quarter century, those "improvements" and reforms were initiated with the expectation of raising the quality of living, not preventing a decline or reducing the rate of decline. Once again the conventional wisdom failed to fulfill expectations.

These data are not offered to present a pessimistic picture, but rather to suggest that simplistic answers or the spending of more money may not be the most effective response to the need to improve the well-being of adolescents, both black and white. In conclusion it may be more creative to review briefly what might be productive approaches.

What Might Work?

Perhaps the simplest, but also a highly controversial response to the growing number of teenage mothers has been to make birth control counseling and contraceptives available to high school students. At least sixty high schools actually provided contraceptives to students in 1986 and the preliminary evidence revealed (a) the pragmatists pointed to a sharp reduction in the number of pregnancies among teenage girls in those schools and (b) the moralists protested over the value system being taught by a tax-supported public school offering such a program. Do the churches (a) side with the pragmatists, (b) support the moralists and agree that a value system is being taught by such programs, (c) wait for more evidence before taking sides, or (d) offer another approach?

From a long-term perspective the most promising approach, and one that should be attractive and acceptable to the value system of most churches, is that parenting skills can be taught. The research also suggests this may be an effective means of reducing crime, breaking the cycle of "babies having babies," and cutting down on child abuse.[16]

Among the biggest barriers to this approach are the resistance of parents to offered help and the reluctance of many church leaders to move into what could be criticized as a paternalistic (or maternalistic) role.

The churches, however, could pioneer the teaching of parenting skills to high school students who are not yet parents as well as to those who are parents.

This interventionist role is compatible with the social action stance of many of the churches at both the liberal and conservative ends of the theological spectrum.[17] All congregations housing either preschool programs or weekday child care facilities would be well advised to consider the merits of comprehensive and coordinated services that include classes on parenting.[18] The deeper the concern of that congregation for the plight of the teenage mother, the more likely this could be a productive road to explore.

From a social action perspective the most controversial road to follow also appears to be the most promising, but it raises a highly divisive policy question. The evidence suggests that a reduction in the number of twenty-nine-year-old grandmothers may require expecting the poor to live with the consequences of their actions. For example, in New York state those Work Incentive Programs (WIN) offices most successful in helping AFDC recipients find employment were the offices in which the staff was convinced that people have a social obligation to work.[19]

To place the issue in a larger perspective, the research shows very clearly that public assistance programs such as Aid to Families with Dependent Children (AFDC) have been effective as a "safety net." The value question is, Should those programs simply be made available without any expectations being placed on the recipients in terms of social obligations or should the parents be expected to learn the skills of parenting, to seek to move out of the poverty cycle, and to prepare themselves for entrance into the labor force? This is a value question in public policy which the churches should address.

This debate has been influenced by the growing use of the term "entitlement" to describe what once was called "public assistance." Do the recipients of tax-supported entitlements also assume obligations or do entitlements come without any obligations? This debate covers a variety of tax-supported programs ranging from access to a public school to free air (with the emergence of tax-supported programs to clean the air, industrial factories lost the "right" to use the air without obligations) to Social Security to unemployment compensation to AFDC.

Finally, in a political world of large annual federal deficits, a world in which mature adults vote but children do not have the franchise and a world in which most of the mainline denominations have become increasingly oriented toward servicing the elderly rather than children, it may be necessary for the churches to make the hard either-or choice of coming out on the side of children of nonmembers or on the side of older members. For those more concerned about tomorrow than today the choice must be to alleviate the increasing alienation of the young.[20]

Only rarely, back in the 1950s, was it necessary to choose between the needs of children and the priorities of adults. Frequently they coincided. Today on many matters of both public and church policy that is now an either-or choice. The reluctance of many to believe that an either-or choice represents reality makes it more difficult to be a leader today.[21]

NOTES

1. The text of Moynihan's report as well as a review of the criticisms directed at it can be found in Lee Rainwater and William L. Yancy, *The Moynihan Report and the Politics of Controversy* (Cambridge, Mass.: The MIT Press, 1967). For an earlier analysis of the link between race and poverty in Cleveland, Ohio, see Lyle E. Schaller and Charles W. Rawlings, *Race and Poverty* (Cleveland: Regional Church Planning Office, 1964).

2. Daniel Patrick Moynihan, *Family and Nation* (San Diego: Harcourt Brace Jovanovich, 1986), p. 36.

3. *Time*, December 9, 1985, p. 82.

4. "Debating Plight of the Urban Poor," *U.S. News & World Report*, March 3, 1986, p. 22.

5. See Ann Hulbert, "Children as Parents," *The New Republic*, September 10, 1984, pp. 15-23.

6. An excellent journalistic account of this new generation of social dropouts can be found in Ken Auletta, *The Underclass* (New York: Random House, 1982).

7. Charles Murray, "White Welfare Families, White Trash," *National Review*, March 28, 1986, pp. 30-34.

8. Edward C. Banfield, *The Unheavenly City* (Boston: Little, Brown, & Co., 1968) and *The Unheavenly City Revisited* (Boston: Little, Brown & Co., 1974).

9. Rainwater and Yancey, *The Moynihan Report*, p. 130.

10. Charles Murray, *Losing Ground* (New York: Basic Books, 1984).

11. Lawrence W. Mead, *Beyond Entitlement: The Social Obligations of Citizenship* (New York: The Free Press, 1985).

12. Moynihan, *Family and Nation*.

13. Wayne A. Meeks, *The First Urban Christians* (New Haven: Yale University Press, 1982), pp. 73, 190-92.

14. Many of these data are drawn from Peter Uhlenberg and David Eggebeen, "The Declining Well-Being of American Adolescents," *The Public Interest*, March, 1986, pp. 25-38.

15. A contrary view on the benefits of the large high school can be found in Barker and Gump, *Big School, Small School*; Harvey Passow, *Secondary Education Reform: Retrospect and Prospect* (New York: Teachers College Press, 1976); and Jonathan P. Sheer, ed., *Education in Rural America* (Boulder, Colo.: Westview Press, 1977).

16. For an introduction to this concept see James Q. Wilson, "Raising Kids," *The Atlantic Monthly*, October, 1983, pp. 45-56, or Travis Hirschi, "Crime and the

Family," in *Crime and Public Policy*, ed. James Q. Wilson (San Francisco: Institute for Contemporary Studies, 1983), pp. 53-68.

17. While a productive means of accomplishing this has yet to be identified, many concerned leaders, both black and white, and both conservative and liberal, are suggesting the critical point of intervention may be to broaden the avenue for bringing young black males into the mainstream of American society. See Charles C. Moskos, "Success Story: Blacks in the Military," *The Atlantic Monthly*, May, 1986, pp. 64-72; Nicholas Leman, "The Origins of the Underclass," *The Atlantic Monthly*, June, 1986, pp. 31-55, and July, 1986, pp. 54-68; Mickey Kraus, "The Work Ethic State," *The New Republic*, July 7, 1986, pp. 23-33, and Steven Kelman, "Gaining Ground," *The New Republic*, July 28, 1986, pp. 40-41.

18. For a plea for leadership to utilize forty years of research see Anne C. Lewis, "Another Generation Lost?" *Phi Delta Kappan*, March, 1986, pp. 483-84.

19. Mead, *Beyond Entitlement*. See also the argument by two Ohio economists "that subsidization of an activity will create more of it" and that the children of today are the real casualties of the war on poverty. Richard Vedder and Lowell Galloway, "AFDC and the Laffer Principle," *Wall Street Journal*, March 26, 1986. For another perspective see Ruth Sidel, *Women and Children Lost* (New York: Viking Press, 1986).

20. For a challenging statement on this divisive question see Urie Bronfenbrenner, "Alienation and the Four Worlds of Childhood," *Phi Delta Kappan*, February, 1986, pp. 430-36.

21. For a self-help proposal by a black scholar see Glenn C. Lowry, *It's OK to Win: A Development Agenda for Black Progress* (Washington, D.C.: National Center for Neighborhood Enterprise, 1986).

From Vocation to Profession?

For centuries the parish ministry, the practice of medicine, classroom teaching, and the practice of law were widely understood to be appropriate vocations for Christians. The Christian universities that emerged in the twelfth and thirteenth centuries were devoted largely to the study of theology, medicine, and law. Kenneth Scott Latourette noted that Christianity stimulated "fearless intellectual activity."[1] This may be one of the reasons that by 1500 canon law was studied more widely than theology. Or it may have been as Latourette suggests, "It was a better road to preferment."[2]

It is worth noting, since it is relevant to the contemporary scene, that relatively few parish priests were university graduates. "University men tended to go into the higher ranks of the clergy or into teaching, or to be absorbed in the central administrative structures of the diocese or the Papacy."[3] Those who today complain that too much education can ruin a person for the pastoral ministry are echoing a five-hundred-year-old cry.

The study and practice of law never received the same support as a Christian vocation in the United States as it had earned in medieval Europe and increasingly became perceived by outsiders as a means of making money, rather than as a channel for expressing one's commitment to the faith.

Until recently, however, the practice of medicine, teaching, and the parish ministry were widely perceived as Christian vocations. Parents usually were delighted and proud when a child decided to become a minister, a nurse, a physician, or a teacher. In each case it was presumed that while that choice would not produce a high income, it was an appropriate vocation for a Christian and the presumption also was that this would be a lifetime vocation. Today, of course, all four of those vocations often turn out to be the entrance into the labor force. After a few years or a couple of decades many of the practitioners switch to a secular job that provides greater opportunities for making money.

In a delightful autobiography Lewis Thomas, a physician, a scientist, and the son of a physician describes the transformation of medicine from an art to a science and from a moderately compensated vocation into a highly paid profession.[4] Before the introduction of sulfanilamide, penicillin, and other antibiotics in the late 1930s and early 1940s, the physician was limited largely to the art of diagnosis, the handing out of placebos, and a heavy emphasis on reassurance based on being able to predict how long it would take the illness to run its course. In less than a quarter century modern science provided physicians not only with better diagnostic tools, but also with the means to treat and cure a huge range of diseases. The personal care of the physician who made house calls was replaced by visits to doctors who appeared to many of their patients to be impersonal scientists with a miraculous power to prescribe the proper miracle drug. Today more than half of the physicians in the United States receive a major portion of their income in a salary from an employer.

The next vocation to be transformed into a profession was teaching, but that process is far from complete as of this writing and a great many teachers are vigorously opposing the change while others want that vocation to become a profession. *199* ∎

As recently as the 1930s a large number of elementary school teachers had had one or two years in a nearby normal school as their only formal academic preparation for that vocation. Teaching a class of children was seen as an art, not as a profession. Natural gifts and dedication to that vocation were seen as far more valuable credentials than a college degree.

Within three or four decades the combination of state laws requiring certification by a public agency, the consolidation of public schools into large districts with big bureaucratic structures, the emergence of teachers' unions, the pressures of university schools of education, and the adoption of salary schedules that have placed a financial premium on graduate training have increased the number of teachers with a college degree. Today approximately one-half of all high school teachers and nearly one-half of all elementary school teachers have at least one degree beyond the bachelor's degree. As recently as 1973 fewer than a fourth of all elementary school teachers held the master's degree.

There is no evidence, however, that increasing the level of formal education of public school teachers or increasing per pupil expenditures has raised the SAT scores of graduating seniors, improved the level of the reading or writing skills of the pupils, or encouraged a larger proportion of students to follow their teachers into that profession. In 1972 more than 300,000 college graduates chose the vocation of teaching. In 1980 that number had dropped to 140,000. In 1970 a poll revealed that 19 percent of all college students would consider a career in teaching. By 1982 that proportion had dropped to 5 percent.

Adults in vocations are far more likely than adults in professions to serve as role models for a younger generation when the younger generation makes career plans.

The Emergence of the Paraprofessional

One of the highly visible changes in the practice of medicine has been the emergence of tens of thousands of paraprofessionals who now do what physicians did in the 1950s. These include
• *200* Nurse-Practitioners, physician's assistants, nurse anesthetists,

and others. At least 60,000 of these paraprofessionals are now employed in hospitals, clinics, or physicians' offices or in private practice. Ophthalmic technicians alone numbered over 10,000 in 1985, and there are nearly 3,000 nurse-midwives.

An increasing number of nurses are returning to the pre-1940 concept of being in private practice rather than serving on the staff of a hospital or working in a physician's office. Perhaps the most widely discussed facet of this trend is the nurse-midwife. Another is the Nurse-Practitioner who establishes a private practice in a small town in the Great Plains with the nearest physician sixty miles away.

A parallel trend in the practice of law is the growing number of paralegals. In 1984 the Bureau of Labor Statistics counted 53,000 legal assistants, up from 31,500 in 1982. The Bureau expects that number to increase to 104,000 by 1995.

One counterpart to that in the Roman Catholic Church is the nun who serves as the "resident pastor" for the small rural parish which is unable to secure the services of an ordained priest.

On the Protestant scene the general trend in large multiple-staff congregations has been to reduce the number of ordained male clergy, many of whom were generalists, and to replace them with lay program specialists.

This change can be illustrated by looking at who attended a staff meeting in 1966 and at who attended the meeting of the program staff of that same congregation twenty years later.

In 1966 seven people came to this weekly gathering and four (the senior pastor, the associate minister, the youth director, and the part-time semi-retired minister of visitation) were male and all four were seminary trained and ordained. The three women in the room were the church secretary, the director of Christian education, and the part-time choir director.

Twenty years later, in that same congregation the weekly meeting of the program staff brought together fourteen people:

- The senior minister (male)
- The associate minister (female)

201 ▪

- The program director (female)
- The minister of music (male)
- The director of ministries with families that include
    young children (female)
  The director of youth ministries (female)
  The church business administrator (male)
  The parish visitor (female)
  The director of ministries with mature adults
    (female)
  The church nurse (female)
- The administrative assistant to the pastor (female)
    (When hired, the title was church secretary)
  The director of church growth (female)
  The director of congregational care (female)
  (Includes new member enlistment and
    assimilation)
  The director of the weekday early childhood
    center (female)

Six work on a full-time stipend and eight are employed on a part-time basis. Three out of the fourteen are male, but in many churches today the church business administrator is a laywoman. Only two, as compared to five in the 1966 staff meeting, have a seminary degree.

One of the big changes since 1966 in that particular congregation has been to drop Christian education as a major focal point and to look at program in terms of people and their needs, rather than beginning with what the church can offer. One result has been the replacement of the seminary-trained specialist in Christian education with a mature woman who has the full-time oversight of the entire program. A second has been to replace the children's division as a program component of the Sunday school with a more comprehensive package of ministries programs that includes Sunday school, Mother's Day Out, the weekday early childhood development center, classes on parenting, and a dozen other programs designed for families with

- These six positions are full-time.

young children. A forty-two-year-old divorced mother of two is the full-time director of that group of programs.

As the congregation now includes more members who have passed their sixty-fifth birthday, a part-time layperson has been added to the staff to direct ministries for that group and a church nurse (or minister of health) on a one-third-time basis has been added to lift up the importance of nutrition, health, and wellness. The focus on visitation, carried out two decades ago by a semi-retired pastor, has been replaced by the current focus on program and the active involvement of mature adults.

A second change has been the sharp increase in the emphasis on music. In 1966 this church had one adult choir, a youth choir, and two children's choirs. Twenty years later the music program had grown to fourteen organized and continuing groups including two adult vocal choirs, six handbell choirs, a children's choir, a flute choir, a youth vocal choir, a music encounter program as part of the weekday program for preschool children, an orchestra, and a drama group. The part-time person who concentrated on organizing and directing four choirs has been replaced by a full-time person, with four part-time assistants (who rarely attend staff meetings) who concentrate on a far larger and more diversified music program.

A third change can be traced directly to the impact of the church growth movement. This church had been on a gradually declining curve in both membership and worship attendance for twenty years when in 1977 the new senior minister insisted on adding a part-time person to the staff to be responsible for the enlistment and assimilation of new members. While she is paid on a half-time basis, everyone agrees she deserves much of the credit for the 15 percent increase in membership and the 40 percent increase in worship attendance that has been experienced since she joined the staff.

A New Approach to Staffing the Churches

The big change, however, and the one that represents a transformation in the staffing of churches, is far more complex and consists of at least a dozen strands.

One strand parallels the changes in the nature of medical schools. Up until perhaps three or four decades ago the focus in medical school was to train practitioners. Today a far greater emphasis is placed on producing researchers, scientists, specialists, teachers, and administrators.

The parallel in theological seminaries is represented by the change in self-identity from professional school to graduate school. The professional school trained practitioners. The graduate school directs more resources to programs for the student who already holds the Master of Divinity degree. One result is to produce candidates for graduate school, specialists, teachers, and graduates who seek a non-parish position—somewhat similar to what the study of canon law produced five hundred years ago.

The results of this trend can be seen in the parish where (a) an increasing proportion of associate ministers hold the Doctor of Ministry degree or an academic doctorate and (b) in larger congregations that are eliminating one or more positions for associate ministers and replacing them with paraprofessionals. A third aspect of that same basic trend is the increasing number of large congregations, averaging 1,500 or more at Sunday morning worship, that do not turn to the graduate schools of theology for new staff members. Instead many of these large churches recruit their program staff from among their own membership and provide training for them in the context of the parish ministry.

Because a seminary degree has become for an increasing number of people (a) preparation for entrance into graduate school or (b) preparation for a non-parish expression of the Christian ministry such as counseling, the chaplaincy, or consulting or (c) preparation for entrance into the secular labor market, a growing number of churches are turning to other sources for staffing.

A second strand also parallels the legal, educational, and medical professions. This is the rapid increase in the number of paraprofessionals as the professionals reduce their direct contacts with the clients. Graduate schools are far more likely than professional schools to attract introverted persons who prefer reading, research, and writing to firsthand contact with people. One result is a growing number of paraprofessionals in the practice of medicine who work directly with the elderly, the pregnant, and the moderately ill. A second is the rapid increase in the number of legal assistants in the practice of law. A third is the growing number of paraprofessionals in the nation's classrooms. A fourth is the growing number of paraprofessionals being employed by the churches. That trend was illustrated by the expansion of the program staff in the congregation described earlier.

A third strand is the rising discontent with credentialism. In a variety of vocations, with services ranging from training military officers to the delivery of babies to the protection of persons and property to teaching to dispensing medications to selecting new employees, American society has placed an ever greater emphasis on credentials. One example is the Durham-Humphrey amendment to the United States Food, Drug and Cosmetic Act of 1952 which prohibited pharmacists from dispensing certain medications without a physician's prescription. A second was the decision in most Methodist annual conferences in the 1950s to require a seminary degree for full ordination. A third is the requirement for certain courses before one can be certified to teach in the public schools or to take a job as a principal or superintendent.[5] A fourth is the requirement of a college degree to be commissioned as an officer in the military services (except in wartime when performance becomes more important than credentials).

Many of the proposals to reform the public schools, to improve the quality of teaching in the universities, to enhance the profitability of American business, to improve the quality and delivery of health care, to reduce the cost of having a will prepared, or to expand the program of a local church are accompanied by questions about the increasing weight given to credentials.[6] Increasingly the cry is "People skills are more significant than technical skills."[7] Once again performance is being recognized as more important than credentials in hiring people.

In several professions legal or institutional barriers still limit the role of the paraprofessional. These include classroom teaching, the practice of law, the practice of medicine, and, in several denominations, the practice of parish ministry. Despite these legal and institutional barriers the demand for the paraprofessional is growing and can be expected to grow. It is a different world than it was thirty years ago when the respect for paper credentials was far greater than it is today.

A fourth strand in this change in the staffing of churches can be described very simply, but it is not limited to the staffing of churches. It is economics.

"There is absolutely no doubt that any private enterprise could come into the city of New York at this moment and police it better, for hundreds of millions of dollars less," declared Anthony Bouza, a former Bronx Borough Commander in the New York City Police Department after he had become the police chief for Minneapolis. [8] The same article went on to point out it costs New York City nearly three times as much in salary and benefits to add a professional police officer to the payroll as it does a private security agency. In many states private security guards outnumber public police officers by a two-to-one margin. In Texas that ratio is five-to-one. Increasingly employers are finding it costs less to hire the paraprofessional.

In 1986 it cost the typical mainline Protestant congregation between $22,000 and $35,000 (salary, housing, pensions, insurance, and other benefits) to add a full-time seminary trained minister to the staff. The cost of adding three part-time paraprofessional specialists might range between $14,000 and $20,000, and their combined productivity often exceeded that of the full-time associate minister.

A fifth strand also can be summarized in one word, supervision. Many senior pastors have found it easier to oversee three part-time lay specialists than one full-time ordained generalist.

A sixth strand reflects the labor market. Nearly all the competent and skilled men and women who seek a full-time job are now employed in the labor force. The only large supply of gifted, enthusiastic, hard-working, and dedicated adults who do not have full-time jobs are mothers who do not want, and often do not need, full-time employment. It often is easier to find a woman for a part-time paraprofessional position than to find a part-time professional. (The ministry of music may be the big exception to that generalization in some communities.)

A seventh strand reflects the central theme of this chapter. Since many congregations realize that a full-time associate minister really is a professional with obvious concerns about the next step on the career ladder, it is easy for the leaders to conclude that "what we really want is a staff person who feels a sense of being called to this particular ministry in this place and who perceives this to be a Christian vocation, not simply a job on a career ladder." The greater the emphasis on the parish ministry as a profession, the greater are the chances that the people will seek a person who conveys a sense of being called to a vocation.

(This is another reason why it is harder to be a pastor today than it was thirty years ago. In the 1950s nearly everyone agreed the parish ministry was a vocation. Today one group contends it is a profession while most of the church members still believe it to be a Christian vocation.)

An eighth strand in this transformation in the staffing of the churches also can be described in one word, termination. Literally thousands of congregations have experienced divisive, frustrating, and disruptive problems when terminating the employment of an ordained minister. By comparison it usually is relatively easy to terminate the employment of a part-time professional, especially if that employee is not a member of the congregation.

A ninth strand parallels the experiences of those responsible for selecting high school principals, judges, accountants, physicians, engineers, and many other professionals. In the legal profession it is referred to as "judicial temperament." Two generations ago in the practice of medicine it was called "the bedside manner." In public education and the business world it is called "leadership."

It is relatively easy to teach academic subjects, to test for acquired information, and to measure skills in test making. It is *207* •

far more difficult to test for initiative, leadership, creativity, people skills, wisdom or inituitive skills. More and more churches are seeking these gifts, skills, and talents as they build a staff. The chances of finding these in the fifty-six-year-old mother who joins the program staff as a paraprofessional are at least as great, if not greater, than in finding these gifts, skills, and talents in the twenty-eight-year-old seminary graduate.

An eleventh strand is the rapid proliferation of training experiences for both paid and volunteer workers in the churches. Thirty years ago the theological seminaries had something approaching a monopoly on training people for Christian vocations. Today most of these experiences and programs are offered by other organizations and institutions. The opportunities for non-degree educational and training experiences for the paraprofessional have multiplied at least tenfold in thirty-five years.

Finally, and this may be the most influential strand of all, American society has undergone remarkable changes since the end of World War II. The women's liberation movement, the current devaluation of credentials, the widespread acceptance of paraprofessionals in law, medicine, and education, the increasing proportion of upper- and middle-class mothers employed outside the home, the impact of the Civil Rights Movement, the tremendous expansion of weekday programming in the churches, the shift toward a more egalitarian society, the contemporary emphasis on physical fitness, nutrition and wellness, the emergence and continued growth of the Charismatic Renewal Movement, the shift from the increasingly liberal religious climate of the decade following the end of World War II to a more conservative theological view, the decrease in the size of families, the remarkable increases in the life expectancy of the average forty-year-old person, the increasing number of men who retire well before age sixty-five, the increase in the rate of divorce among mature couples, the emergence of that huge array of parachurch organizations, the growing acceptance of the church growth movement among the mainline Protestant churches, and the power of television to raise people's expectations are but a few of the changes in the national culture that have produced a more favorable and supportive climate for the paraprofessionals in the churches.

What Does It Mean?

While it obviously is far too early to be able to identify all of the consequences and implications of these changes, several already have emerged that merit the attention of church leaders.

Perhaps the most obvious is that persons in professions do not receive the respect or the deference that traditionally has been accorded persons perceived to be called to a Christian vocation. The increase in the number of malpractice suits filed against family doctors is a measurable manifestation of this change. The decrease in the number of young white males enrolling in mainline Protestant and Catholic seminaries is another. The decrease in the number of high school seniors who want to become public school teachers is a third. The increase in the number of lawyers and judges who have been sentenced to jail is a fourth measurable expression of this change.

A second consequence, as has been pointed out repeatedly, is that more and more churches are turning to a lay paraprofessional, rather than to a seminary-trained ordained minister when the time comes to expand the staff.

A third is the feminization of what thirty years ago was a male-dominated field of religious employment.

A fourth, while far less visible, is the growing number of ordained clergy who sense a call to a specialized vocation within the parish ministry and go where that call takes them. One measurable evidence of this pattern is the growing number of clergy who hold their ordination credentials in one denomination but are serving on the staff of a congregation affiliated with a different denomination. (A variation of this is the United Methodist minister who is a member of one annual conference and who has been appointed by the bishop of that episcopal area to serve on the staff of a congregation in a different episcopal area.)

As the seminaries, like the medical schools, graduate an increasing number of specialized professionals, the proportion of ordained clergy in good standing who are not serving in parish ministries begins to approach or exceed the number of parish pastors in that regional judicatory. This raises an interesting question on the "one minister, one vote" tradition at the annual meeting of that regional judicatory. Who should have the right to vote on issues that may have a major impact on the role of parish pastors?

From the perspective of denominational leaders and policy-makers it may be worth looking at three trends followed by a question. The first trend is that as the practice of medicine has been transformed from an art into a science and from a moderately paid vocation into a relatively high paid profession, people have been less confident about the competence of practitioners. Some health insurance plans now require a second medical opinion before an operation. In addition, many people are raising questions about the reasons behind and the implications of a surplus of practitioners in some counties and a shortage in others with paraprofessionals filling the void.

The second trend is that as teaching has been evolving from a vocation into a profession, demands for higher compensation for teachers have been a predictable and natural consequence of that evolution. At the same time, however, an increasing number of studies are raising questions about the primary product (graduates) of that profession. No one has been able to demonstrate that higher salaries produce better teachers.[9]

The third trend is that as these studies and reports reveal that too many of the graduates of the public schools have enormous difficulty with communication and mathematical skills, questions are being raised about what has been happening in the institutions that trained those teachers.

The question is this, Do these three trends say anything to your denomination or raise questions that church members want answered?

For all church leaders the greatest implication may be in the area of values. Vocations rest on a strong value base and normally seek to reinforce and transmit those values.

As the practice of medicine has changed from a vocation to a profession, the scientific approach has not provided universally acceptable answers to such value-laden questions: (a) does a pregnant woman have the right to abortion on demand? (b) what should be done about the newborn baby who is so seriously developmentally impaired it may never be a conscious person? (c) what response is made to a terminally ill patient who requests, "Please give me a pill that will put me to sleep and I will not awaken"? and (d) should a ceiling be placed on the dollar costs of prolonging the life of a seriously ill but alert patient?

As teaching evolves from a vocation into a profession, people are asking profound questions about what values should be taught in the public schools. This was not a serious issue of public debate two hundred years ago. It is today and many contend it is the key issue in the growth of the new private school movement. (See the section on Christian day schools in chapter 4.)

What is the role of the churches in speaking to these and many other value questions? Is that role being affected by the gradual change from vocation to profession in the ministry?[10]

Finally, the forces described here have priced thousands of congregations "out of the preacher market." The increase in the educational requirements of ordination, the professionalization of what once was clearly perceived as a vocation, and the rising level of expectations of both members and ministers mean that thousands of congregations that have averaged fewer than 75 or 80 people at worship for decades no longer are able to afford their own full-time resident pastor who does not have any other source of income.

NOTES

1. Kenneth Scott Latourette, A History of Christianity (New York: Harper & Brothers, 1953), p. 552.

2. Ibid., p. 526.

3. Ibid.

4. Lewis Thomas, The Youngest Science: Notes of a Medicine Watcher (New York: Viking Press, 1983). See also Edward Shorter, Bedside Manner: The Troubled History

of Doctors and Patients (New York: Simon & Schuster, 1985). For a comprehensive review of the large influx of women into the practice of medicine in the nineteenth century, the surge in the number of women's medical schools, and the subsequent masculinization of the profession see Regina Markell Morantz-Sanchez, *Sympathy and Science* (New York: Oxford University Press, 1985). For a pessimistic view of the future of the physician-researcher and the impact of economic incentives see Gordon N. Gill, "The End of the Physician-Scientist?" *The American Scholar*, Summer, 1984, pp. 353-68. One of Gill's points is that the young doctor of today can make more money in the practice of medicine than in research. Today medical research is the vocation or "calling" and the practice of medicine is a profession just as the teaching of law is a vocation and the practice of law is the highly paid profession. The other side of the economic picture for physicians is described in "Hippocrates Meets Adam Smith," *Forbes*, February 10, 1986, pp. 63-66, which discusses the impact of the oversupply of physicians.

5. One of the leading scholars in the field of educational reform has written, "It is also common knowledge that the usual means by which principals are selected, trained and certified . . . are grossly ill-suited to the production of savvy, risk-taking, entrepreneurial education leaders . . . we should jettison 'paper credentials' as the means of determining whether an individual is qualified to lead a school." Chester E. Finn, Jr., "Better Principals, Not Just Teachers," *Wall Street Journal*, February 18, 1986.

6. For a lucid and persuasive analysis of this issue see James Fallows, "The Case Against Credentialism," *The Atlantic Monthly*, December, 1985, pp. 49-67.

7. For an influential argument in favor of people skills and leadership see Thomas H. Peters and Robert H. Waterman, Jr., *In Search of Excellence* (New York: Harper & Row, 1982) or Warren Bennis and Burt Nanus, *Leaders: The Strategy for Taking Charge* (New York: Harper & Row, 1985). A provocative review essay that questions some of these contemporary assumptions is Benjamin DeMott, "Threats and Whimpers: The New Business Heroes," *The New York Times Book Review*, October 26, 1986, pp. 1, 49-51.

8. Quoted in *New York Times*, November 29, 1985.

9. In 1985, for example, New Hampshire ranked among the lowest ten of all states in teachers' salaries but was first in students' scores on the Scholastic Aptitude Test (SAT). Iowa ranked thirty-first on average teachers' salaries and tied for first place in students' scores on the American College Test (ACT).

10. One of many statements that a pastor should be seen as a professional is James D. Glasse, *Profession: Minister* (Nashville: Abingdon Press, 1968). Another perspective is Lyle E. Schaller, *Looking in the Mirror* (Nashville: Abingdon Press, 1984), pp. 38-58.

From Doorbell to Mailbox

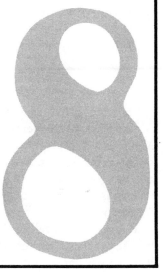

"Our system for ministers organizing new congregations includes an expectation that you will make two hundred calls every week on people who might be prospective new members," explained the denominational executive responsible for new church development to a minister being interviewed for a position as a mission developer.

"Where do I get a list of the people I should be calling on?" asked the candidate.

"That's your responsibility," came the quick reply. "Probably the best way to begin is by going door-to-door."

■   ■   ■

"If we expect to reverse the numerical decline this congregation has been experiencing for the past twenty years, the first thing we're going to have to do is to organize and train a group of our members who will call door-to-door in this community," declared the recently arrived minister at Westlawn

Church. "As near as I can tell from the records, fewer than 15 percent of today's members live within a mile of our building. If we're going to reverse this decline, we're going to have to reestablish ourselves as a neighborhood church and the best way to do that is by a visitation evangelism program."

． ． ．

For more than two centuries every person who has sought to be admitted into full membership in the ranks of the ordained Methodist ministry has been asked a series of questions that originated with John Wesley. The bishop, or the chief pastor, asks the questions. The first is, "Have you faith in Christ?" The second is, "Are you going on to perfection?" the fifteenth is, "Will you visit from house to house?"

This concept of calling door-to-door has long been part of the ministry and evangelistic outreach for American Protestantism. For many congregations it is still the central core of an effective church growth strategy. It is still a useful tactic for the person who has accepted a call to organize a new congregation. Pastoral calling still ranks second only to excellent preaching as the most effective means of increasing the frequency of worship attendance.

For many householders the mention of door-to-door calling brings to mind, not the ordained minister, but rather the college student selling encyclopedias or Bibles or the Fuller Brush salesman or the Avon lady.

A variation of that theme was the neighborhood Tupperware dealer who recruited hostesses to invite their friends and neighbors over for an evening of games and for the dealer's sales pitch. The system worked. During the 1970s sales increased by 20 percent per year and in 1980 nearly a billion dollars worth of Tupperware was sold throughout the world. During the 1980s, however, sales slipped, and Tupperware parties no longer are the effective delivery system they once were for those products with the air-tight seals.[1]

Similar declines in sales and profits have been reported by

Avon Products, Inc., Encyclopedia Britannica, and a dozen other firms that depended on door-to-door salespersons to sell their products. Both Avon and Fuller Brush have begun to mail out catalogs to supplement the efforts of their sales representatives.

What Happened?

Among the many factors that have been identified to explain why door-to-door salespersons are experiencing difficulties, a dozen, which are also relevant to local church leaders, stand out.

The number-one factor, of course, is the growing number of married women with full-time employment outside the home. They are not at home during the daytime. (See chapter 5.)

A second has been the unprecedented increase in recent years in the number of one-person households, from 4.7 million in 1950 to 10.9 million in 1970 to 21 million in 1985. In three and one-half decades the number of households consisting of three or more persons increased by less than half, from 26.2 million in 1950 to 38 million in 1985 while the number of one-person households more than quadrupled. The person knocking on the door of a one-person household is far less likely to find anyone at home than is the salesperson or caller ringing the bell at the three- or four- or five-person household.

A third factor is television. People are less receptive to a call from an itinerant salesperson when that visit interrupts their favorite program.

A fourth factor is the tremendous increase in the number of firms retailing merchandise by direct mail. The number of catalog firms grew from 3,000 in 1982 to an estimated 6,500 in 1985.

A fifth and more subtle change is a product of the increase in the number of women in the labor force. These women display less susceptibility to the peer pressure that both one-on-one and party selling depend on for much of the sales.

A sixth factor is the increasing number of people with two or three jobs or who work shifts. Either they are not at home or they are asleep when the doorbell rings. Overlapping this is the increase in the length of the workweek. According to Louis Harris and Associates, the average American with a job worked 47.3 hours weekly in 1985 compared to 40.6 hours a week in 1973.

A seventh factor is the change from shopping as a chore to shopping as a form of recreation. A great many people, especially those born after 1945, apparently enjoy a trip to the shopping mall.

An eighth factor is the increasing sophistication of a better educated population. Today's adult is far more likely to be better informed on prices than that person's grandparent was. The discount stores and the off-price retail outlets have made it difficult for the door-to-door salesperson to compete.

The desire for privacy has created literally millions of dwelling units that simply are not open to the itinerant salesperson. Many high-rise apartment towers guarantee privacy as a part of the protection from the elements.

An increasing number of Americans would place fear as the number-one factor, not as the ninth on this list. The fear of strangers, the fear of becoming victims of crime, and the fear of the unknown have made life more difficult for door-to-door retailers.

A tenth barrier to door-to-door sales is the municipal ordinance which prohibits it without prior approval. While often ignored, an increasing number of communities are enforcing these prohibitions.

An eleventh factor is economic. Time is money. As more time is required to complete a hundred calls, costs go up and those in charge of the profit-and-loss statement become more receptive to other approaches.

Finally, and perhaps more significant from the perspective of local church leaders is the results orientation of many policy-makers in the business world. If a new approach yields better results than the old approach, business leaders are tempted

to try the new approach. The 10 to 20 percent annual increase in catalog sales during the 1976–85 decade tempted many retailers to switch from the doorbell to the mailbox as their basic channel for the sale of their product.

By contrast the churches are far more likely to stick to the traditional approaches. It was not until the 1960s that the Roman Catholic Church switched from Latin to English for the Mass. It was not until the 1970s that many Protestants began to give up on the geographical parish as the basic definition of a congregation's constituency. It was not until the 1980s that the concept of offering members a choice in the format, music, and style of the Sunday morning worship experience became widespread.

Therefore it should not be surprising that the churches have been relatively slow to make the switch from the doorbell to the mailbox in identifying prospective new church members. [2]

Three Other Factors

Before moving on to look at a few of the implications of this new trend, a word should be said about why it may be difficult for many church leaders to consider this approach to new member enlistment.

First, and most obvious, it is difficult to give up on a system that has worked for generations and that was successfully used two or three decades ago by many of today's denominational leaders. The tendency in American Protestantism to draw the official leadership from among persons who have passed their fiftieth birthday is a predictable means of retaining old ideas and systems and of advocating their use to a new generation. It is difficult to replace a system that worked very effectively for an earlier generation if that generation is in control today.

Second, from the pastor's perspective this means learning a new skill. The theme of this book is: it is more difficult to be a pastor today than it was thirty years ago. To make the switch from the doorbell to the mailbox as the primary approach for enlisting new members means the pastor must (*a*) learn a new skill, (*b*) utilize a procedure rarely taught in seminary and often not endorsed by denominational leaders, (*c*) be comfortable *217* ▪

responding to those who allege that direct mail is "too commercial and really not Christian," (d) learn, practice, and teach persistence and patience, for these are two keys to effective direct-mail evangelism, (e) engage in creative foot-dragging procedures to delay those who insist the whole concept should be evaluated three months after it is inaugurated and abandoned if it is not producing impressive results, and (f) be prepared to respond creatively to unanticipated consequences if the new system does work.

From the perspective of the lay leadership, proposed expenditures (postage, printing, envelopes) for direct-mail evangelism offer a tempting alternative for reducing the size of the proposed budget to match anticipated receipts. Since these are new items in the budget, they are especially vulnerable to proposed cuts. (The operational rule is, "It is hard to get a new item into any budget. It is even harder to get a long-established item out of the budget.")

Ideally the congregation, and the finance committee, will make a two-year commitment to direct-mail evangelism before attempting to evaluate the results. A useful rule of thumb for the congregation seriously interested in direct-mail evangelism is that *at least* 5 percent of the budget will be allocated for the costs of that program *plus* the amount allocated for other forms of advertising.

What Are the Implications?

While rarely discussed, the most influential implication of this change for the pastor interested in reaching more people is a loss of control. In the 1950s the minister who wanted to emphasize evangelism could unilaterally decide to allocate more time each week to calling. Instead of spending an hour or two every week calling on potential new members, the pastor could increase that to eight or ten or twenty hours a week. While the minister might decide to announce this change in priorities to those present at the monthly board meeting, that often was not thought necessary. How the minister spends his or her time, as long as the essentials of parish life were cared for adequately, was seen as the minister's prerogative.

Today, if the pastor wants to inaugurate an effective advertising program, often he or she has to secure the involvement of a church growth committee, gain the approval of the finance committee to spend that much money, and help the proposal survive the priority-setting process that finally determines what will be funded for next year.

This raises the second implication. The decision-making process that involved only a few minutes as the minister walked home after a meeting at the church could be implemented unilaterally by the minister the following week, or perhaps even the next day.

The congregation that decides to undertake an attractive, systematic, and fully funded direct-mail evangelism program may use up several months between the time the idea is first proposed and the time the first mailing is dropped off at the post office. The time frame for planning and decision making is greatly expanded.

A third difference is that the pastor who decided to increase the time spent in visitation evangelism depended largely on his or her personality and perhaps a few skills learned in seminary or in a workshop to implement that decision.

The decision to turn to direct-mail evangelism requires a higher level of professional competence and depends on skills rarely taught in a theological seminary. The typical pastor will have to turn to an outsider to plan the program and to design the materials to be used. Frequently these resources are not available from within the congregation or from the regional office of the denomination.

A fourth consequence, which has caused some congregations to reject direct-mail evangelism, is the loss of the ability to screen out future members. When calling door-to-door, ministers and lay callers can decide whether or not they really want to persuade that person to come to their church. The most obvious expression of this form of control is in the decision on which homes will not be visited. A direct-mail appeal to everyone in one or two or three

219 ∙

zip code areas means a loss of that control to screen. Likewise, using advertising in newspapers, shopping "throw-aways," using television or the radio eliminates the possibility of screening.

For some members the most serious and upsetting consequence has been that direct mail does work. The clearest example of that fact of life is that in 1985 direct-mail retail sales totaled $45 billion. The number of catalogs mailed to consumers grew from 6 billion in 1982 to over 10 billion in 1985.

The effectiveness of direct-mail evangelism in new church development is illustrated by Discovery United Methodist Church, 2627 Pleasant Run Drive, Richmond, Virginia 23233. (The name refers to the self-image, "Where You Can Discover a New Beginning.") This new congregation was launched in the fall of 1983 under the leadership of Dr. James Lavender. Six months after the first worship service was held, the Sunday morning worship attendance averaged 140 and by the end of the second full year, the average attendance had doubled to 300.

Seven out of eight of the first 200 members to unite with this congregation were attracted to Discovery Church (which was meeting in a trailer) by direct mail. Two-thirds of the new adult members had no active church affiliation when they came to Discovery Church. Only 14 percent identified themselves as United Methodists, 4.5 percent were converts from Judaism, and 14 percent were ex-Roman Catholics.

In 1986 the congregation, which had become financially self-supporting within two years after its launching, was allocating 16 percent of its $110,000 operating budget to advertising with the primary emphasis on direct mail. During this third year of its existence this congregation also moved into the $400,000 first unit of its new building which is designed to seat 500 for worship.

One of the reasons Discovery Church is among the fastest growing new congregations in the nation is the emphasis on acceptance of previously unchurched people. A second is the warm and friendly reception accorded newcomers and a third is
direct mail. A fourth is a creative and venturesome pastor who

was willing to try a new approach to new church development. (One illustration of the Reverend Jim Lavender's venturesome spirit was his decision to use a live, full-grown tiger on Sunday morning to illustrate his children's sermon on the theme, "The Love of God Can Conquer Anything!")

An example of how direct-mail evangelism can be used to increase the membership and attendance in a congregation that had been on a plateau in size for several years is the Supplee Memorial Presbyterian Church (U.S.A.) in suburban Philadelphia.

Founded in 1958 this congregation had leveled off on a plateau with a worship attendance slightly over 100 when the new minister arrived in 1970. The new minister, the Reverend Walter Mueller, initiated a strategy of direct-mail evangelism. During the next 15 years the average attendance at worship tripled to an average of 325 in 1985 and the worship attendance-to-membership ratio is close to 60 percent, a remarkably high ratio for that size congregation. (Readers interested in securing a resource person for a workshop on direct-mail evangelism may want to contact the Reverend Walter Mueller, 855 Welsh Road, Maple Glen, Pa. 19002.) It is not irrelevant to this account to note that in May, 1986, ground was broken for a $1.2 million building program at Supplee Memorial Presbyterian Church in response to the growth resulting from direct-mail evangelism. Those interested in the power of direct-mail evangelism should consider the question, What if it works?

Four Cautions

Any congregation contemplating a switch from the doorbell to the mailbox as the primary channel for contacting potential new members would be well advised to reflect on four influential factors.

First, it is essential to have a program or ministry in which people can be invited to share at your church. In general the new ministry or program tends to be more attractive than the long-established program. (The basic operational rule is "new *221* ▪

groups for new people.") Frequently, new programs or ministries offered in the evening or during the week will be more attractive than the Sunday morning schedule. (There are many exceptions to that generalization such as "the New Sunday School Class for Newlyweds.")

Second, the invitation must be authentic. Do not promise what the stranger will not find on arrival! Truth in advertising applies to direct-mail evangelism!

Third, it may be necessary to finance the first efforts through designated second-mile giving rather than waiting for approval in the normal once-a-year budget preparation process. Rather than turn to a decision-making process designed to reduce expenditures, it may be wiser to count only the votes (second-mile giving) of those who favor the idea.

Finally, it is essential that all first-time visitors who come in response to a direct-mail appeal receive a warm, friendly, and sincere greeting that includes learning, remembering, and using the newcomer's name in conversation and also receive a follow-up visit as soon as possible.

NOTES

1. Marj Charlier, "Tupperware Parties Just Aren't Selling as They Once Did, Causing Lower Profit," *Wall Street Journal*, January 2, 1985, p. 14.

2. For an operational introduction to direct-mail evangelism see Lyle E. Schaller, "Deliver Unto Them," *The Lutheran*, June 3, 1981, pp. 12-14.

A World Filled with Choices

9

"**W**hen I was younger I used to offer to come early to meetings and make the coffee," recalled the seventy-seven-year-old Alma Miller, "but I'm too old for that now. In fact, I don't go anymore to as many meetings as I once did. It really isn't safe to go out at night."

"I remember when you did that," agreed the fifty-nine-year-old Myrtle Evans. "My husband and I came here in 1960 and I thought that was something I could do. When you announced you weren't going to come early to make the coffee, I offered to do it. About six years ago I told the pastor I couldn't do it anymore. It simply had gotten too complicated. Twenty years ago all that was involved was coming early and getting a pot of coffee started. Now some want decaffeinated, others want regular coffee, a few insist on tea, some want a soft drink, others ask for fruit juice, and there always will be some who want hot chocolate. I say let them make their own or go without."

When it comes to beverages for the monthly board meeting,

the world has changed since Alma and Myrtle made the coffee. According to the International Coffee Organization the daily consumption of coffee in the United States has dropped from 3.12 cups per person in 1962 to 2.26 cups in 1974 to 1.83 cups per person in 1985. Today people expect a choice of beverages.

For aficionados of chocolate chip cookies the most amazing trend of the 1970s began when Wally Amos opened his first Famous Amos cookie store on Sunset Boulevard in Hollywood. The year was 1975. By 1985 it seemed as if nearly every large shopping mall included at least one cookie store. The number of franchise stores has grown from that one in 1975 to over a thousand in early 1986 plus scores of independent cookie retailers. The devotee of chocolate chip cookies has scores of choices today including a variety of choices in most supermarkets.

Once upon a time matters such as birth, death, the premature termination of a pregnancy, attendance at family reunions, marriage ending only with the death of your spouse, and the place where you will live were givens. Today each has become a matter of individual choice.

This increased range of choices can be illustrated by looking briefly at the beginning and end of life. The number of legal abortions in the United States in 1972 was estimated at 586,000 according to the Alan Guttmacher Institute. By 1980 that number had nearly tripled to 1,553,900. In addition, an estimated million conceptions did not occur in 1980 because of the pill and other birth control devices not available in 1955.

At the other end of the age spectrum approximately 80,000 patients now receive kidney dialysis in any given year. According to a study conducted at the Hennepin County Medical Center in Minneapolis from 1966 to 1984, 9 percent of the patient deaths followed a decision by the patient to discontinue treatment. Those patients could choose, within a space of a couple of days, when they would die.[1]

At least 2.5 million Americans are alive today who would be dead if medical practitioners were limited to the techniques and procedures available in 1970. Thanks to the remarkable progress
in medical science people now recover from the accident or

illness that would have been fatal as recently as 1970. Most of these, of course, are either mature adults or newborn infants.

To state it another way, thanks to the choices now available to people through birth control procedures and legalized abortion, at least 20 million (and perhaps as many as 50 million) Americans who today would be under age thirty do not exist. They were not conceived, or if they were conceived, they were not born. At the other end of the life span a couple of million mature adults are now alive who otherwise would be dead and an unknown number are active who would be incapacitated today without the medical advances of recent years.

The availability of these choices on life and death help explain why the American population is older and smaller in numbers than the demographers of 1955 forecasted.

The availability of these choices on life and death also help explain why the counseling burden on pastors is heavier than it was in 1955.

This extraordinary increase in the range of choices available to people has had a profound impact on congregational life; it will not be completely understood until the people who grew up in that pre-1950 era of limited choices are replaced by those who grew up in a world filled with this wonderful array of choices. The initial impact of this new world can be illustrated by looking in more detail at seven areas of congregational life.

Where Do You Belong?

The first, and perhaps the clearest, is the impact on youth ministries. Before World War II, back when 30 percent of the American people lived on farms and back before the consolidation of small high schools into very large schools, it was relatively simple to organize a youth group of teenagers at the church. For many of the youth the choice was between staying home and helping with the chores or going to church to meet with friends and acquaintances. The big competition for time was the movies, the monthly meeting of the 4-H Club, or the radio.

In today's world, as the motion picture, *The Breakfast Club*, depicted so clearly, very few teenagers see that huge high school   *225* ▪

as a primary social group. They belong to one of the many "tribes" into which the student population is divided. The names of the tribes vary from school to school but include the jocks, the punkers, the kickers, the intellectuals, the socialites, the straights, the swimmers, the druggies, the greasers, the alcoholics, the freaks, the mods, the students, the preppies, the rockers, the norms, the breakers, and countless other designations.

Rarely is any one high school youth group able to include members from more than two or three of those tribes that constitute the high school subculture. The picture is further complicated by the much larger proportion than was true in 1955 of high school juniors and seniors who hold jobs during the school year,[2] by the wide range of extracurricular activities offered after school and on weekends by most of the large high schools, by the increased availability of automobiles, by the affluence of many parents, and by the attractiveness of television.

The competition is far greater than it was in 1955. For example, an overnight trip in 1955 had far more appeal to the fifteen-year-old who had never been out of the state than it does to the fifteen-year-old of today who has visited a dozen or more states plus perhaps Europe or Japan or Mexico.

As a result the congregation that is interested in a ministry with youth can go down one of two roads. The road that is familiar to the mature members includes weekly meetings of a youth group led by the pastor or youth director, a high school Sunday school class, a week at summer camp, and perhaps two or three rallies or retreats during the year. In the smaller congregations that approach may attract close to half of the high school students from that congregation. In the larger churches that model might attract as many as a fourth of the eligible teenagers, but the proportion is more likely to be closer to 10 or 15 percent.

The second road is far more complicated and is filled with choices that may include a Sunday evening in-depth study of the Scriptures for a couple of hours, a vocal choir, a Tuesday evening mutual support group, the choir trip every spring, eight or ten retreats and trips during the course of the year including a ski trip and a canoeing expedition, a handbell choir, an eight-day work camp experience, a half dozen money-raising activities every year, summer camp, a theater party, one Sunday school class that appeals to members of one or two tribes and another class with a different leader, perhaps at a different hour, that reaches members of a couple of other tribes, and several opportunities for juniors and seniors to participate with adults in what are primarily adult events such as a drama group, ushering, an orchestra, a discussion type adult Sunday school class, membership on the board and administrative committees, or teaching in the Sunday school.

Most of the high school age youth will boycott most of these programs and activities. Today's high school student has learned (a) the world is full of choices, (b) no one can participate in everything, and (c) no one can make you feel guilty for not participating.

The tremendous increase in the number of books, workshops, magazines, experts, youth directors and youth ministers, packets, programs, rallies, and parachurch groups concerned with youth is clear evidence that no one has a simple answer to what has become a very complex question. One reason for the complexity is the explosive increase in the range of choices available to today's teenagers.

The Complexity of the Weekly Schedule

"I grew up on a dairy farm," reflected the sixty-nine-year-old member at First Church, "and I can remember only one occasion when my father took what could be called a vacation. In 1934 he and Mother took the train to go to the Chicago World's Fair. They were gone for four days and my brother, the hired man, and I took care of the farm and did all the milking. My Mother said Dad worried all the time that something might come up that we couldn't handle."

"I remember your dad very clearly," commented an eighty-six-year-old who was the minister-emeritus at First Church as this group of four mature men waited for the rest of the people to appear for the annual meeting at First Church. "Right 227 ▪

after I graduated from seminary I spent four years as the pastor of that church where your family were members for three or four generations. The church council met on the second Monday of every month at 7:30 and your dad was always telling about how he had to milk early in order to make it, but he was always there when we were ready to begin. In the four years I served that congregation I don't believe your dad ever missed a church council meeting."

"Couldn't do that today," grunted a third member of this group of longtime friends as they watched the first arrivals for that night's meeting. "Now Monday night's either football or baseball or some movie everyone wants to see. Television has wiped out Monday night as a time for church meetings."

The loss of Monday night to television is only one of the factors that has made it far more difficult to devise a weekly church schedule that is acceptable to everyone. Today far more people work night shifts than was true in the 1950s, many supermarkets are open until midnight or later, retail stores are now open on Sunday, the journey to work is longer and more time-consuming, over one-half of all wives are employed outside the home, more and more people have a cabin at the lake or a trailer in the woods, more people hold two jobs, more members live beyond walking distance of the church, the time available for vacations has increased, three-day weekends now roll around several times a year, people have more discretionary income and time is required to spend it, and more people eat out than ever before.

As the choices open to people on how they can spend their time expand, it becomes increasingly difficult to schedule programs and meetings that do not conflict with the schedules of many members. It was easier to draw up an acceptable schedule back in 1950 when people had more time and less money.

"That Sermon Didn't Speak to Me"

"You know, Honey," commented Jim Rizzo to his wife as they drove to the restaurant following the eleven o'clock service at
Wesley Lutheran Church, "I believe that may have been the best

sermon our minister has preached in the eight years we've been members here."

"I'm surprised to hear you say that," replied Mrs. Rizzo. "I had great difficulty following what he was trying to say, and I don't think I heard even half of it. That sermon certainly didn't speak to me!"

While the topic is a very subjective one and historical evidence is lacking, this writer's observations of the religious scene suggest it has become increasingly difficult for any church to plan one worship experience or for any minister to preach a sermon that will be meaningful to everyone.

The increasing availability of televised worship services, the growing number of church members who visit two or three or four other churches every year while on vacation, the higher level of educational attainment of the adult population, the growing number of members who were not reared in the same denominational family as the church they now attend, the phenomenal increase in the number of northerners who spend two or three or four months during the winter in the Sunbelt, the decrease in the proportion of attenders who are in mainline Protestant congregations on Sunday morning, and the doubling in the number of interfaith marriages since 1952 are among the reasons that could be offered for this change. The more choices people have, the less likely everyone will agree on one course of action.

One early response to this phenomenon was the decision to offer two worship services on Sunday morning with one that would be more "informal" than the other.

Subsequently, many congregations decided to offer people a choice between a "contemporary" or "folk" service experience and a traditional worship experience.

A variation of that was the decision in many churches, which formerly scheduled Holy Communion once a quarter or once a month, to offer one service centered around the Lord's Supper and one around the preaching of the Word on every Sunday morning except Easter.

A more recent response can be found in several very large *229* ▪

congregations that now schedule two preachers for thirty-five to forty Sundays a year. Typically the associate minister preaches at either the first or third hour and teaches an adult class at another hour. The senior pastor preaches at the other hour or perhaps at the other two services. The usual pattern is the associate minister will preach at all services perhaps six Sundays a year. For thirty-five to forty Sundays a year, however, the members have a choice. Perhaps the most interesting consequence has been that a number of husbands regularly go at one hour and their wives go to hear the other preacher.

The most common complaint is that this requires two sermon preparations nearly every week. The most common objection from the clergy is it requires the preparation and printing of two bulletins thirty-five or forty weeks a year. Both usually agree, however, that the increase in attendance is worth the additional effort.

From Missions to Study and Choices

While far from widespread, another interesting sequence of changes can be observed in the evolution of the women's organization. In many churches during the first five or six decades of this century the women's auxiliary in the local church really resembled a movement organized around a cause. The cause was world missions and that was an attractive, unifying, and cohesive force. In literally thousands of congregations the power of that cause resulted in the women's organization emerging as the best organized group with the largest number of loyal, dedicated, and enthusiastic members of any organization in that church.

Gradually, however, the central organizing principle began to shift from missions to study and fellowship and the participants slowly began to grow old together.

In a minority of these churches the leaders recognized that study and/or fellowship tend to be exclusionary when they become the central organizing principle for bringing a collection
■ *230* of individuals together on a regular basis. Rather than watch the

numbers grow smaller and the membership grow older, these leaders accepted the role of being initiating leaders.

The old system, which called for all the women to study the same lesson, really offered only two choices. Do you want to be in a morning, afternoon, or evening study group? Do you want to be in a study group that meets in the homes of members or one that meets at the church?

The new system expanded the range of choices as new circles were created. One circle was a book review group, another made items to be sold at the bazaar, a third visited people who were in the local nursing home, a fourth picked a particular mission project and supported it, a fifth took over the obligations of the altar guild when it dissolved, a sixth was the Mothers' Club for new mothers who had worked for several years before leaving the labor market to begin a family, a seventh consisted of newcomers who had moved to the community in the past year (that circle had to be recreated every year), an eighth was strictly arts and crafts, a ninth was a liturgical dance group, a tenth was a traditional mission study group, an eleventh was the "C-section" circle "for new mothers who qualified," the twelfth was composed of a group of women who had decided to read through the Bible together in three years, a thirteenth was the equivalent of a local Women Aglow chapter, a fourteenth was a drama group that produced two plays a year, the fifteenth was composed of a group that met every Wednesday from 10:00 A.M. to 3:00 P.M. to help with office work, the sixteenth was a mutual support group for women who had experienced a painful divorce, and the seventeenth was organized to support a particular missionary.

It was easier to explain to a curious new member the nature of the women's organization back in the days when every circle studied the same chapter from the lesson book every month. It also was easier for the new pastor to become acquainted with everyone in the women's organization back in those days because it was smaller and everyone was a member of that congregation! In scores of churches today at least one-third of the members of the women's organization do not belong to that congregation. *231* ▪

What Happend to Our Singles Group?

One of the new ministries that swept the continent in the 1960s and the 1970s was the concept of a special group for single adults. While the typical large singles program required a substantial investment of staff time and energy, by most criteria these were remarkably successful ventures. Many deep and long unmet needs were met through these ministries. Here and there the staff deliberately dissolved a group when the proportion of healthy personalities who could help carry the burdens of others slipped to a lower than desirable number, but many of these singles groups continued to exist for years and a few for more than a decade.

By the mid-1980s, however, the world had changed and a new generation of young never-married adults began to arrive on the scene. As was pointed out in chapter 5, this new generation represents a return to the "good old days" of 1890 to 1910 when a relatively small proportion of people had married before their twenty-fifth bithday and many never married. Not only did most of the women born in the 1930s marry (96 percent will marry at least once), most married early. Marriage was the name of the game. For the never-married person born in 1938 a singles group in 1965 was a good place to look for a spouse.

Today the emphasis has shifted from marriage to careers. The babies born back in the late 1950s and early 1960s not only are less interested in marrying, or in marrying early, many object strenuously to any system that categorizes people by marital status. For a fair number of young never-married adults, "single" is somewhere between an obsolete term and a dirty word.

This change confronts the churches with at least four choices. The one chosen most widely continues to be to ignore the fact that singles constitute an increasing proportion of the adult population and continue to concentrate all efforts in ministry on husband-wife couples, their children, and single adults, especially widows and older formerly married persons who are comfortable with this approach.

A second alternative is to continue the 1970s approach to

singles and watch as the clientele ages and is increasingly drawn from among people who formerly were married and are now single.

A third approach is to recast the old approach into a more intentional and carefully planned effort to focus on ministries with the formerly married.

A fourth response is to expand the range of ministries designed in response to the needs of the formerly married and to create a new set of ministries, programs, and activities for the younger never-married adults who want to replace the old question, What's your marital status? with what they see as a better question, What will we do?

How Do You Organize the Sunday School?

A parallel change can be seen in the ministry of Christian education. For generations the three dominant organizing principles in classifying people for the Sunday school were gender, age, and marital status. With the exception of the high demand congregations that are highly directive in telling the members what to believe and what to do, that system no longer works as well as it once did.

Today people seek choices. These choices include size, pedagogical style, content, duration, commitment, and a dozen other variables. Some are organized around that magnetic personality who is an exciting teacher and attracts people without regard to age, gender, or marital status. Others are primarily social groups organized around the principle of growing old together. A few are organized against the enemy (frequently the current pastor), and age, gender, or marital status are not factors in deciding who belongs. An increasing number of classes for teenagers and/or adults are organized around events and experiences. In other classes the stage of one's religious development, rather than gender, age, or marital status is the central factor in organizing new classes. In many other adult classes the distinctive factor is a particular approach to Bible study.

It was easier to oversee a Sunday school when age, gender, and   *233* •

marital status were the critical factors in dividing people into classes.

What Happened to the Unified Budget?

One of the biggest ecclesiastical casualties of the inflationary wave of 1967–85, which was the longest inflationary era in American history, was the unified budget. The idea of combining all the financial needs into one budget can be traced back to the early years of the twentieth century. It received a big boost in the first quarter of this century when several agencies of one denomination combined their appeals to congregations into one campaign. Earlier each denominational agency went out and unilaterally raised its own funds.

The concept of one budget that included all needs got another big boost after World War II as people recognized the merits of one major annual appeal with the promise, "If you pledge or contribute to this budget, we won't ask you for any money for another year."

The church building boom of the 1950s reinforced the idea. Twice a year a financial appeal was made to the members, once for the unified budget that usually included all benevolences as well as all the local expenditures and a second for the building fund. The budget preparation committee, with an overall view of all needs, could set the priorities and allocate the resources accordingly.

In thousands of congregations this became the goal and it was achieved. With the exception of the women's organization, the youth fellowship, one or two adult Sunday school classes, and perhaps three or four special financial appeals at Easter, Christmas, Thanksgiving, and other occasions, all of the giving of the members was channeled through that central treasury and reported as a part of the unified budget.

Gradually, however, various forces began to erode the concept of a unified budget. The first big one was the building-fund drive. Everyone in the congregation agreed that if we were going to be able to construct the proposed new building, we could not

finance it out of the unified budget. There would have to be a special financial campaign. Several years later, after perhaps the second or third building-fund drive, the remaining years of mortgage payments were consolidated into the unified budget. This produced a modest squeeze in other items in the budget, particularly benevolences and salaries, but the goal of a unified budget prevailed.

A more modest erosion of the concept can be traced back to the beginnings when it was agreed that all expenditures would be included in that unified budget, "except, of course, the special offerings at Christmas, Easter, and Thanksgiving." Gradually the list of approved, or at least acceptable, special offerings grew from three to four to five to six to perhaps eight or ten.

In several denominational families the most obvious departure from the concept came when the decision was made to launch a major denominational financial drive for missions or ministerial pensions or a church-related college or an expansion of the camping facilities or a home for the elderly or a theological seminary or for black colleges. These multi-million dollar campaigns usually (a) were conducted outside the unified budget of both the regional judicatory and the congregations, (b) met or exceeded the goal, and (c) caused at least some leaders to reconsider the merits of special appeals.

One of the most significant factors was the emergence of what one research project terms "The New Audiences."[3] This study pointed out that the new generation of church members was less motivated in their giving than previous generations by such factors as guilt, fear of God, social pressure, or habit. This new generation seeks a voice in the decision on the allocation of resources. Designated or second-mile giving is one way the laity feel they have a voice in the allocation of resources.

Further erosion of the concept came with the inflationary wave that began in the mid-1960s. Following a fifteen-year period during which the increase in the consumer price index was approximately 2 percent per year, these increases averaged nearly 8 percent during the 1970–81 period. What did that do to the unified budget based on a once-a-year financial appeal?

In an inflationary era most people seriously underestimate *235* •

their own income. As a whole, Americans report a higher family income figure to the Internal Revenue Service than they do to the Census Bureau. Most people calculate their total income only once a year and that is early in the calendar year when they prepare to file an income tax return. The typical Protestant congregation asks members in the fall to make a financial commitment for the coming calendar year. That meant that back at the peak of the inflationary wave in 1978–81 a request for a pledge for 1982 made in the fall of 1981, often was based on the member's perception of his or her income, and the last time that had been calculated was the previous winter in reviewing that contributor's 1980 income. In the 1950s that two-year lag amounted to only 4 or 5 percentage points. In the 1979–81 era that lag ranged between 17 and 26 percentage points. A second product of the inflationary wave was that the items that the churches buy (energy, paper, printing, people's time) increased at a faster pace than did the rest of the items in the Consumer Price Index.

Overlapping that is the increase in the pessimism about the future. Today's adults are less optimistic about the future than were their counterparts of twenty-five years ago when the idea of a unified budget flourished.[4]

The erosion of denominational loyalties and the weakening of congregational ties in the churches with a high turnover rate (and most growing churches have an above average rate of turnover in the membership) encouraged the idea of special appeals.

Finally, the increase in the level of the economic well-being of the vast majority of the people has undermined the concept of asking people to make a financial commitment out of anticipated future income toward a unified budget. Millions of people give out of current income to the operating budget of the congregation to which they belong, and if asked, they will give out of accumulated savings to a capital funds drive, whether it be congregational or denominational. This pattern is an increasingly common phenomenon. It can be seen most clearly in those congregations that have experienced a severe squeeze in their operating budget, but a special appeal for missions or to repair the roof or to support ministerial pensions or to install a new organ or to fund a scholarship program quickly is oversubscribed. It appears that many church members give out of that right-hand pocket of current income to the congregation's annual budget. When asked, they dig into that left-hand pocket of accumulated savings to respond to a major mission appeal or for some other attractive cause. Since 1980 at least seventy congregations have raised over a million dollars in cash in one day.

The result of all this is an increase in the number of congregations that schedule from fifteen to seventy-five special designated appeals for second-mile giving every year. This is most common among (a) black congregations, (b) rapidly growing churches, (c) congregations seeking to sharply increase the proportion of total receipts that are allocated to missions and similar causes, or (d) churches in which the members do not display a high degree of loyalty to the denomination with which that congregation is affiliated.

This expansion of the range of choices that people demand is an outstanding characteristic of the contemporary American world. It has been cited repeatedly as a significant factor in explaining the higher cost of American-made automobiles when compared to the cost of cars in Japan or Korea. It also is a characteristic of many of the rapidly growing Sunday schools, and the costs include a more complicated schedule and a larger cadre of volunteer teachers. It is a common characteristic of those larger congregations that reach a large proportion of the generation born after 1955.

The Cost of Choices

Everything in this life, except grace, has a price tag. Expanding the ranges of choices carries a price tag. One example is the reduction in the number of producers of vaccines to reduce the incidence of polio, whooping cough, and other diseases. One in every 4 million persons vaccinated with the OPV vaccine can be expected to be permanently crippled and may die. By contrast the IPV vaccine does not carry that risk, but with that vaccine *237* ▪

perhaps 2,500 out of every 4 million persons vaccinated will contract polio while the OPV vaccine provides complete protection to everyone. Which vaccine should be chosen? Which has the lower price tag?

The rapid increase in product liability suits in the mid-1980s caused many municipal parks to remove equipment. These suits caused American Motors to discontinue the "CJ" Jeep and caused hundreds of physicians and midwives to stop delivering babies. The cost of litigation reduced the range of choices available to people.

On the ecclesiastical scene the consequences of choices can be seen by referring back to the numerical decline of the mainline Protestant denominations described in chapter 3. Among these decisions that reflected the cost of choices were (1) the decision to reduce the number of new churches organized each year with the consequence that in the 1960–84 era a majority of new congregations were started as independent churches or by other denominations, (2) the decision to ask members to give to a budget rather than a cause with the result that many members gave to organizations promoting a cause, (3) the decision to select as denominational leaders persons who were more liberal on political, economic, theological, and social issues than were a majority of the members, (4) the decision not to embrace the Charismatic Renewal Movement when it emerged in the 1960s, (5) the decision to allow parachurch groups to pioneer new approaches to youth ministries rather than to do that through denominational agencies, (6) the decision in several denominations to cut back on the number of foreign missionaries and allow parachurch organizations to use missions as a rallying point for enlisting supporters, (7) the decision by several denominations to concentrate denominational resources in support of smaller congregations when the generation born after World War II was choosing to go to large churches, and (8) the decision in at least eight denominations to make control over the decision-making processes, and/or to place a denominational merger at the top of the agenda, rather than to rally people around mission or

• *238* missions was a choice between division and unity.

In each of these examples a deliberate choice over priorities in making choices had consequences which probably contributed to the numerical decline of that denomination. There is no free lunch, and every choice has a price tag.

This increase in the range of available choices has made the task of being a leader in the church more complex and more difficult than it was in the 1950s. Being able to recognize that every choice has a price tag, encouraging people to understand the matter of trade-offs, and being able to identify those trade-offs makes the responsibility of serving as a leader in the church today far more difficult than it was in 1955.

NOTES

1. The complexity of the debate over who will live and who will die is discussed in Earl E. Shelp, *Born to Die?* (New York: The Free Press, 1985) and Joseph A. Califano, Jr., *America's Health Care Revolution: Who Lives? Who Dies? Who Pays?* (New York: Random House, 1986).

2. Those who are concerned about the increased number of high school students with part-time jobs can find documentation for their alarm in Ellen Greenberger and Laurence Steinberg, *When Teenagers Work* (New York: Basic Books, 1986).

3. Douglas W. Johnson, *North American Interchurch Study* (New York: National Council of Churches, 1971), pp. 176-77.

4. Joseph Veroff, et al., *The Inner American* (New York: Basic Books, 1981).